FINDING HOME AGAIN

FINDING HOME AGAIN

Our Quest to Belong

RICHA SHARMA

NU VOICE
PRESS

First published by NU VOICE PRESS 2025
An imprint of Hubhawks Pvt. Ltd
www.nuvoicepress.com

ISBN: 978-81-984189-4-4

Typeset by Saanvi Graphics, Noida
Printed at
Published by Nu Voice Press

To Mummy,

For every ounce of strength that every character holds is from you …

I stand amid the roar
Of a surf-tormented shore,
And I hold within my hand
Grains of the golden sand—
How few! yet how they creep
Through my fingers to the deep,
While I weep—while I weep!
O God! Can I not grasp
Them with a tighter clasp?
O God! can I not save
One from the pitiless wave?
Is all that we see or seem
But a dream within a dream?

–"A Dream Within a Dream"
Edgar Allan Poe

A search began and ended too. Within a few hours.

Kranti had found Mridula at the relief camp, where she was also waiting. Her search wasn't over. Yet, the pleasure of ending, a preferable one, gave Kranti the satisfaction of success, even though incomplete.

Leaving the inquiry desk, they now walked away from the camp, turning whines into whispers, merging the blue of the tents with that of the sky.

They now stood under a tree's shade. A temporary shield from June's heat, when it was the rain that had brought them here. Planting themselves firmly on the ground, they got ready to speak again.

A Nahor tree stood silent, listening. It extended its arms and pushed the trembling leaves outward, like kids ousted from the elders' conversation. On one of its branches, a crow perched. It wobbled its head and fluttered its feathers, while its claws held on a branch whose existence it seemed to mistrust. It was also waiting, unsure of the reality it was perched on.

'Why did you come like this?'

'Like what?'

'*Arey* ... you know *na* what I mean,' Kranti softened his line of inquiry.

Brushing off his curls and restoring the glint on his forehead, much fairer this time, which Mridula had noticed, he waited for his cousin to answer. Placing his hand on her shoulders, Kranti looked down at her—a habitual look—not only for her, but for everything in general. His height gave him that luxury.

Mridula stood silent, rubbing off the mud blotches on one shoe with the other. Shoes—not hers, but Priyom's. Well kept, now soiled. In front of her, Kranti squinted, looking visibly troubled when her knee-length white tunic ruffled with the wind. He was not ready to face the blinding whiteness yet.

White, the colour of the shroud, the colour smeared with red, of blots and wounds, shrouding a body, in the shape of its shape, a little swollen and a lot broken. White, the colour of legs left too long in water, muddied in brown, with dirt and burial ground. Distracting himself, he focused on Mridula again and asked, '*Achcha*, are you sure he was travelling? I mean, you're sure he messaged you?'

Mridula replied with a slight nod. Her shocked, wide eyes stared past him. Blank eyes on a freckled face; an overdose of beauty spots on an otherwise smooth skin. Her lips, the colour of dried rose, were pursed so tightly as if opening them would have brought another calamity.

So, after a while, Kranti signalled for an auto rickshaw. He had to go and get a room for himself at the hotel she was staying in.

The knobby road to their hotel reminded them of their auto rides with money stolen from home, and how they invented new games while his sisters and her brother stayed back and complained. As the memories voiced themselves within, they too broke the silence.

'Remember that time you bruised your knee?'

'*Hmm*. That road was way more pathetic,' she said, pointing to the patch of muddy road they were on.

'You had cried so much.'

'*Dada* (brother), I was a kid!'

'Really?' He smiled, looking at her.

'You scolded me for falling down as if it was in my control!'

Kranti laughed at the recollection, while Mridula brooded over the slap she had received at home for her ripped frock. Although they shared the memory and remembered it together, the feeling it ignited differed.

'Why can't this state develop like the others? In Delhi we have better roads at least,' he grumbled, distancing himself from the present—in the state he was born in.

Suddenly peeved, he took out a cigarette from a steel case, a compass engraved on its oxidized silver lid. A dent on the edge hinted at its authenticity. It was a vintage piece he had asked Anchal to gift him on their last anniversary. Mridula agreed, thankful for the change of subject. Memories, after all, were both—difficult to recall and impossible to block once the vault opened. Memories—free and eternal, forever shifting shapes. Memories would hijack her thoughts and leave her in the void. Thoughts which Mridula held very close. Occasionally, they would slip away into the narrow lanes of spoken words. Thoughts—uncivilized, unaware of the etiquettes she ought to follow and the requisites set by the society she lived in. Her thoughts were like wild dogs that couldn't be home-trained to fit our whims. The best kinds, after all.

Today, that wasn't the case. Today, Mridula wanted to control her thoughts like an overbearing parent. She would let them roam freely, but only within the boundaries of her mind. She would guide their flow, oversee their growth, and often escort them to stagnation. She would allow honesty only to an extent where the conscious projection of herself wasn't affected. With memories, she would instigate them into a path chosen by her, cajoling them to give her a story—a well-crafted one. She would force them, too. Like a desperate romantic, love often tightened with anger. Sometimes her memories yielded in, but mostly they yielded back.

'You know, sometimes I feel like going back to our childhood.'

Meeting her had made Kranti nostalgic. He wished to go back in time and live. To live better this time, of course.

'But we won't be the same,' she said, aware that their dreams would be curbed by their experiences, dented by reality as they were now. Their experiences would put a halt to every desire they had.

'*Haan*, it won't be the same,' he agreed, dismissing the conversation he had started himself.

SECTION I
THE NEWS

1

'Reading the news gives me chills.'

Maya often told others about the restlessness she felt. She had been avoiding the news, especially the 'sad kind', for many years now. That is, until this morning.

She was in her mother's room now. Tomorrow, she would travel to Maajorghat to bring Ma back, and probably her father too, for the first time. It was a resolve she wouldn't let falter despite Kevin's detailed account of the accident and its severity. Knowing that she wouldn't have watched the news, he had walked up to her cubicle to inform her.

'I don't need more reasons to feel depressed,' she had told Kevin once when they were on their post-lunch walk to the tea stall.

She didn't tell him that watching the news made her feel helpless—sometimes even selfish that she wasn't putting in enough effort. Maya often silenced her inner turmoil by donating money, an act she hid even from Ma. It was her faint attempt to feel useful as she would sit cross-legged on her sofa, bound by a subjective and often limited view. A touch of helping hands amid the comfort of ignorance. Charity gave her a hint of authority, and the privilege of access cured her guilt to some extent.

But tonight, no money could salvage her from the guilt she was experiencing. Maya needed someone. She missed her mother, craved her presence and assurances—and a bit of her courage too. Her warmth, the occasional hugs, her calloused fingers running over Maya's head, and the soft thumping of a head massage doused under the list of instructions on how to be and not to be. Maya wished to hear Ma's stories of childhood and womanhood, pleasures and sufferings, of a bird set free from a cage it was raised in; a domesticated bird whose wings flapped against the wind—who, when let out, wasn't left with any more zeal to fly.

Over an hour had passed since she sat on the plastic armchair in Ma's room that her mother, in spite of Maya's objection, had bought from the supermarket. Its ordinary features challenged the elegance of a custom-made bed. Looking at it, she found it hideous. *Ma, too, is stubborn for things dear to her,* she thought and smiled.

She and I form a good team, Maya thought as her eyes hovered around the room. They seemed to be looking for a key to the mystery of her mother's whereabouts. The bed lay empty. At its head were two flattened pillows, because puffed ones gave Ma neck pain. There was a huge puffy cushion for her feet to rest on. A pouch of blue glass melon beads still rested near the pillow. An integral and revered part of Tani tribes for centuries, these beads were sent to her mother by Margam Panor as a token of their twenty years of friendship. 'These are special beads, traditional and real. I will get a necklace made for you,' Ma had told Maya. Her friend, like every other woman in the Adi community, had worn the turquoise blue necklace on her wedding, which Ma had admired then. To Maya, these heirloom beads now appeared as an essence of Ma's life too. Still holding them in her hands, she looked up.

Above the bed was an exposed window, its horizontal black grills coated in fine dust, the curtains still at the dry cleaner. The window had not been opened for two months now; the window that her mother would never close, even insisting on using the air conditioner with the curtains drawn. 'Windows should be left open. Let fresh air in,' she would say.

She ran her hand over the Jaipuri patchwork on the bedspread, an orange floral pattern over a navy blue sheet. 'Bright colours to brighten the room,' Ma would often say to persuade her into buying ethnic sets for both the rooms.

Maya then got up, planning about things to do, especially shopping, once Ma was back. She walked out of the room, carefully closing the door behind her, as if not to disturb Ma from her deep sleep, to keep the idea of her intact.

With an enforced faith to meet Ma the next day, she went to her room upstairs, phone in hand. She was sure it would ring soon and sever this suspension between hopes and fears.

She was going to the land she had once decided to never return to. Home—a feeling so tangible that it remained in her thoughts forever. Yet, a home so far away that even the idea of going near it felt unreal now. Tomorrow she would touch Assam, this time not as a pit stop for Arunachal, but as a destination in itself. Pit stops and destinations were constantly changing in her life. Change—a reason for her pain *and* peace.

But tonight, she wasn't thinking of the changes, or her childhood town that she wouldn't be visiting this time as well. Sigo Dolung. A forever piece of home and alienation. It was Maajorghat that she was trying to focus on, where she was sure of meeting her mother.

In a few hours, she was to embark on a journey she wasn't sure of; yet, she was waiting. She was waiting for the announcement of their arrival. She checked emails. She even called the ever-busy helplines and everyone in their limited circle. She glared at the computer screen while her fingers held the phone tight. She had been waiting unabated, convincing herself to stick around for a moment longer.

But the wait stirred an old urge, the urge to run away, the compulsion to do something, just to elicit a response, to gather a hint, a clue, anything about Ma. She constantly tapped her phone to refresh. She scrolled through different apps on her phone, photo albums, bundled memories, a checklist of things to do, and a file of things to undo. She scrolled through the news stories on her apps, watching clippings of accidents, political rallies, analyses of newly launched policies, and a new India ready to shine. She busied herself in watching videos of prime-time debates done essentially wrong and zoomed in on images of celebrities with their new-borns. After a while, she put the phone down, but her fingers raced for more things to fiddle with—a tiny pebble or a pen; switching off the light only to switch it back on. She needed to hold something tangible, something to divert her mind—anything and everything to settle her agitated self.

Her mind had never been at peace, but tonight it was uncontrollable. The weather mimicked her restlessness too. Winds, blowing with impatience, were shaking not only the leaves but also entire trees with furore. Nature seemed to imitate her in its understanding of her turmoil. Her struggles unsettled the clouds and earth alike. The cosmos surfaced to take on her inner fight as its own, trying to communicate her message to those who were unreachable through worldly means.

After a while, Maya went out to see lightning. It often fascinated her to see them or miss them in a blink. Half a second of brightening up an ash grey sky. She hoped to clear her dull day through those few bright seconds.

As she stood in the balcony, she pushed her face outward a little, letting a few drops fall on her face. She closed her eyes, listening to the thundering clouds being hulled from one corner to another. Their sound implied their heaviness. In between the resounding thunder, she heard the faint chanting of *mantras* from the temple a few metres away. Soon, heavy techno-beats reached her from a hostel nearby, from a room where youngsters still believed their lives were in their control. She could hear vehicles passing by too, their engines blaring, horns loud and low. The music, chants, and honks were merging into a perpetual cacophony of construction. As she heard it all, she assured herself that her parents were fine. *Ma is fine. I will find them.*

And with that, Maya tried to block any memories related to them, memories that could hamper her search. It was a tactic she had learnt early in life, especially when she was subjected to events she couldn't really grasp. It was a solution she'd found to impending doom—an escape from possible beating, something her father was proficient at. Also, to protect herself from her Ma's pain—a pain palpable enough for Maya to feel. The sorrow her mother would hide, the memories of which still pierced her skin and throbbed in her veins, making her life a result of its flow.

Despite the efforts to keep her mind shut, the weather reminded her of the endless days of monsoon in Sigo Dolung. Those windswept days and nights, dimmed lights of flickering kerosene lamps, and damp candles. Days spent in anticipation of a flood so close that she could still hear it approaching.

It reminded her of Ma and the neighbours going out in stormy rains to check the level of water—of being on alert. The metal trunk, stuffed with important documents, her mother's jewellery, and extra clothes, was often kept within reach. Discussions oscillated between the fear of impending destruction and blaming the neighbouring country for opening its dam to notifying each other of the arrival of *jawans* with the rising level of the Siang River. It reminded her of brownish muddy water, of an otherwise clear river slowly engulfing the playground in front and submerging her school's gate by almost half. Back then, it excited and scared her simultaneously. Although those days were filled with a longing for the rain to stop, the air to dry, and the normalcy of life to be restored, she would find a calming consistency in the rain. The way the raindrops persistently pattered on her umbrella, and dampness of her clothes that would stick to her like a wet hug.

This was the reason she still felt conflicted about it. The drops she wanted to feel but not see. She still wasn't sure of how to receive this rain or the news.

She repeated to herself, aloud this time, 'I will find Ma.' She wondered if the message would reach where it was intended. Maya would often find it difficult to express herself entirely. But tonight, she felt that the universe had manifested to rescue her. This hope of rain relaxed her.

She knew that Ma would come to her eventually. She too wouldn't be able to stay away.

She knew Ma well, at least to this extent, if not completely. What she didn't know was what exactly had happened in that town of Assam where the flood wouldn't cease and neither the tossing of lives, where a few clueless coaches succumbed to the indulgence a train and a bridge decided to go ahead with.

2

The plane had touched down but was still pacing fast. At equal speed, a mist traced the contours of Kranti's face on the windowpane. A sheet of silver over his curls; his nose blurred into a wet smudge. His tapered chin cut through the clouds he breathed on through the windowpane. Outside, the air was moistened by monsoon, filled with warnings of overflowing rivers, lands sliding away, and shifting homes. Not his, of course. It was a welcome difference from where he was coming from—Delhi, a city where every June burnt relentlessly. Kranti heaved a salutation, regardless of the June that drowned everything here. After all, how was it to affect him? He, who had arrived undeterred by these incessant rains. Incessant floods that he grew up seeing now increasing with the incessant changes done to the climate.

As the plane landed, his phone vibrated, indicating a stream of messages. Text messages welcomed him to Assam, offering free roaming plans to recharge his phone with, while others validated his arrival and inquired about his health. Seven missed calls from Anchal. One from Ma. None from *Deuta* (father).

Seven times, he sighed. He called Ma. Ma—his mother, a woman like every other, her uniqueness cloaked in similarity. Cotton-clad, wrinkled eyes, a touch of sandalwood paste above the red *phot* (a decorative dot-bindi) on her forehead, with faith above husband—often, not always.

'Kranti, you reached?' His mother spoke in Assamese before he could utter the usual 'hello.'

'Still in plane, Ma. So, what are you doing? Has Mridu reached?'

'We are waiting for you, *baba* (son; an endearing term for child).'

Kranti had come for his annual visit. At Ma's insistence. Two months later than she would have preferred, though. Rongali Bihu, that is, his birthday month, was when she had wished for him to come. But she never asked. His visits were the rope of routine he wouldn't snap. She didn't know. He did. A slight acceptance of reality. Not Kranti's forte.

Ma disconnected the call, leaving his questions unanswered. Sliding the phone back into his pocket, an unsuspecting Kranti looked around. Many passengers were pulling out their cabin bags, and a few stood and stretched impatiently in the aisle. Distancing himself from the crowd, Kranti berated them for their perennial hurry to achieve, to snatch, and to get ahead.

But ahead of what? he thought as he climbed up the pedestal of awareness, a well-paying job, and a lifestyle encompassing foreign tours and opulent localities. A life fabricated around ease. He enjoyed the sight of their excitement, almost bordering on impatience. By reproaching them, he amused himself.

After collecting his luggage, when everyone else was walking towards the exit, Kranti meandered. He was reluctant to leave for home immediately, a resentment at the prospect of meeting his father lingering until he whisked it aside. He still wished to change his childhood, although it was unclear what he wanted to redo. Like an agnostic's faith in God and Her omnipresence. Faith swung with situations.

Kranti was becoming restive, a typical emotion whenever he was at or about to be home. It was as though he was stuck in a kilometre-long traffic jam, irritation mounting with each passing minute, hands clenching the steering wheel, and the mind wishing to drive past everyone. Kranti needed to calm himself down. So, he decided to spend some more time at the airport.

At this airport, like every other that Kranti had visited, people sat within a distance of a few inches, but many galaxies apart. Faces hidden amid the folds of a book, earphones plugged in, thoughts sealed, legs criss-crossed or spread out, backs stooping, heads bowing down to phone screens. A rare few taking quick naps or simply staring into nothingness. Although bustling with regular activities, there was a morose undertone to everything. Like a bird's quivering song for a free flight.

Having nothing in particular to do, he went to a bookshop and flipped through a few magazines that suggested ways to glamorize his home and diet, provided tips to varnish his body, and warned about the effects of smoking and drinking—selling hopes and fabricating dreams while shredding them on the side. He then glanced through books, recent releases and classics alike, read introductory passages of many, from cries of lost love to homecomings, from travel tales to mythical stories. He had to buy one when he caught the shopkeeper eyeing his movements. It was the way he looked at him, weighing Kranti down with his judgement, sending waves of discomfiture, spearing his spine, rupturing his self-confidence. A gaze just like his father's. But this time Kranti retaliated. He answered the querying gaze. Carrying *The Metamorphosis*, he walked into a café. In his hand, the story of captivity and freedom was a story to belong and alienate.

Even at the cafe, there was discomfort, like the eerie silence of a graveyard, its peacefulness wounding you. A gloom enveloped faces—chins cupped, fingers tracing foreheads, rubbing eyes, or pinching noses, the solidity of features ensuring their existence.

Picking up his decaf cappuccino from the counter, Kranti went and sat next to a couple. They were in the middle of an animated discussion, refuting each other's claim and asserting their own with the proof of news. Both were engrossed in sharing their findings in between their search. They were preparing themselves with the latest updates to participate and flaunt authority in soon-to-come discussions on this accident, one of the biggest in decades. Kranti took out his phone. He too wanted to know, even if it was a mayhem.

As he swapped open the News app, headlines popped on his screen. Few among them were legitimately informative, the rest were clickbait.

RAINS BRING MISERY IN ASSAM

1 DEAD 21 HURT IN INDIA'S BIGGEST TRAIN ACCIDENT

MAAJORGHAT-GUWAHATI EXPRESS DERAILED

The flood, a yearly occurrence that had been unable to garner much national interest until now, was all over the headlines. A national news channel was running a news story on the rail accident in Maajorghat. Kranti took a closer look at the screen.

Footage of coaches off the track, pictures of an aslant train, a wrecked bridge, a few people walking on its remnants and a few around the coaches, the Railway Protection Force personnel asking some to step away; a team from the National Disaster Response Force standing and evaluating. Passengers narrating their experiences—they wanted to run away but didn't know from where. Some had found the gate above and climbed out; some pushed themselves out of broken windows.

Eyes intent on the screen, his fingers flipped from one channel to another, searching not the repeated telecast but fresh images from the site. Soon, Kranti came across a local channel broadcasting it live. Blames were being flung about, and so were the demands for inquiry. Press conferences were being held. The opposition was speaking and so was the government. Responsibilities were being tossed from one to another.

A scapegoat has to be found, at the earliest, he thought. He watched the news and assumed the series of events that would follow the derailment. An inquiry committee would be set up and everyone would wait for its findings. By the time the reports would arrive, the public's goldfish memory would've moved on to some other 'Breaking News'. Till then, the news would play on.

He thought about how people around the country would now be busy in online searches of Assam, the best time to visit, the distance from Delhi or Bangalore, ways to reach Maajorghat, and the worst train accidents in India. Kranti couldn't control his habitual critiquing.

The news channel airing the footage continuously zoomed in on the signs of impact. Blood dripping from a child's scarred forehead; a man sitting with a slashed limb; scarlet stretchers; a woman clutching the body of her dead son; dried tears and long wails of disbelief; bodies curled up in mud; a young girl identifying herself and asking relatives to take her away; dishevelled men in muddied pants and blood-soaked shirts pulling bodies out of mutilated coaches that were thrown down in a fraction of a second. As though lost in time, blue coaches with rusty heads lay covered in the muck, and a once-sturdy bridge now stood alone, split in half.

These pictures shook Kranti more than he would have preferred. He couldn't look at the news objectively. It was the same route—his childhood was carved along the same railway lines. Images pierced him, taking him back to the times when he, too, travelled on this train. Every year, twice. His memories were being derailed, diminishing a major share of fond memories from his limited collection.

Those days of travel, from the small hamlet of Dhemaji to the city of Guwahati, the city of tall buildings and concrete roads. City of hotels and velvety sofas, where glass doors thumped on their way in and out, and fancy restaurants revelled in their circulated air—the pride of air conditioning, where taxis and big cars would swoop by, leaving a musty scent of petrol in their wake. It was nothing much but the city of his dreams—back then. It was from Maajorghat that they used to board the train to Guwahati.

Maajorghat, once a connecting junction for him, had gradually intensified into a relish he shared with friends. But that memory of childhood, a link to holidays, had now metamorphosed into an agony—an eyesore that pricked with each blink.

Dream city, he thought cynically. *Not anymore,* he told himself while sliding deep into his chair, his eyes still on the phone.

Deuta didn't believe in holiday destinations. To him, holidays meant going home to *his* mother. So instead, they went to Silchar, to their grandparents' house, every year without fail, till the reasons ceased to exist and took leave forever. Then, his parents decided to stay permanently in Guwahati. It was then that those journeys too ceased. The memories remained, though.

They would make preparations for the train journey many days in advance. Suitcases would be brought down to be dried and dusted in the sun. An Usha sewing machine would emerge from its wooden dome, and identical frocks with different collars would be stitched. A new pair of shorts and a T-shirt would be bought, and *mekhela sador* (traditional dress of Assam; a two-piece attire) would be starched. A gold chain would be worn, gold earrings would dangle with red stones, and bangles too would be replaced, always with glass. Kranti could still hear the pulsating sound of the sewing machine and the crackle of puffed rice larrus and til pitha; he could still taste mohura. Those journeys with his father's colleagues and their families used to be an unspoken competition over children's ranks at school, wives' dedication, family's appearance, and the class of food brought from home.

Looking at the screen, Kranti was sure that those people in the pictures also relished snacks from the food stalls at the station, ran to the taps to fill their water coolers, and waved to the passengers on other trains. *How could they not?* He remembered how Deuta would get down at stations and bring paper-thin white chapatis wrapped in a newspaper, gooey potato curry in a bowl of dried leaves, and green chillies and onion on the side.

But soon a picture of a ten-year-old boy popped up. He was clinging to his mother's tunic. Looking sideways, he was facing the derailed coach. Scared, with tears on the verge of slipping out, his lips sealed in fright, an understanding of pain and the maturity of it seeping through his face.

Kranti, all of a sudden, reminded himself that not every journey was about eating and looking out of the window. It wasn't always fun, not even easy. He slowly drifted towards the memories that were not so pleasant.

It was easy to see things changing when they weren't close to your heart. It wouldn't matter then if the bridge didn't exist anymore, or if the train was lost in a sea of filth. Dreadful memories were not to be stored; they would unnecessarily take up space. Kranti's mind was like a camera roll from which unsmiling faces were deleted to make space for happy memories where one would smile when the camera-person said cheese.

Only the befitting ones were to be kept, printed, and hung on the walls. A staged display of happiness. Kranti was now thinking of the times they had to run and catch the train. Those moments of fear of missing the train, of holding his sisters' hands and hopping inside the coach, of worrying about Ma, who would be loaded with bags and water, and whether she would make it in time or not. Those moments of invariable fights for their rightful seats. *I used to dread those fights,* he thought, still looking at the boy in the picture.

One particular journey popped out of his memory vault. The journey in which after the customary settling down, of chaining suitcases under the lower berth, keeping the water cooler between the seats and the overstuffed food bag on top, safety pins holding its zip together, Deuta had asked men on their upper seats to get down. Hours passed, but they didn't. So a squabble started, initially with smiles, later with denial, and eventually with threats. When Deuta started pulling their belongings down, his finger got caught in the fan. With each drop of blood, his anger mounted, and those around were alerted in attention. A few arrived from the other coaches too. A mass-approved fight started, cornering the men on the upper berth. When Deuta's pride was being resurrected, Kranti had sat behind his mother, whose sador, smeared in sweat, had shrunk into a slippery rope. Beads of sweat mushroomed on his face too. He wouldn't wipe; he wouldn't move. He had stayed behind, peeping once in a while.

Thanking that he was past such journeys and that life, he subtly started erasing those episodes from the past that were haunting his present, threatening to ruin his day.

While accepting that nature played a game of death and they all were trying to survive, Kranti comforted himself with the assurance that he too was trying to fight in his own way. Closing the news telecast, he went up to pay his bill and walked out.

'Hey Anchal.' He was speaking to his wife, to his reminder of good times, times that he could control and change.

'Hey! How was the flight? When did you land?'

'A while back. Going home now.'

'Hmm, why didn't you call earlier?'

'*Yaar!* I was busy.'

'Doing what?'

'Doing nothing.' Frustration took over his tone.

'Is the weather good?' Anchal spoke after a few seconds.

'Haan, nice only. Achcha, you want anything from here?' he asked, calming himself.

'Hmm, not sure.'

'Mekhela sador?'

He went ahead, his right hand in the pocket of grey linen, hefty shoulders fighting their way out of a slim-fit blue T-shirt, and left hand dragging his black leather bag. Not reminiscent of the past, with no memories of the accident. Life for Kranti was once again as it was supposed to be—unaltered and opulent.

PAST

Past, it comes out of nowhere; an unexpected phone-call out of a deathbed
to dismay, to control; command its presence.
It muddles thoughts; the broken remembrance of a loved song.
It demands attention; an overbearing guardian.
It stays hovering; a mosquito over your ear.

3

His mother saw him approaching. Kranti was at the far end of a narrow street. An ageing house stood at the other end, ruminating its once dazzling past.

It was such a constricted alleyway that the driver refused to even enter. 'Can't enter, *Saar*. See, the road is so bad, my *gari* will get stuck.'

The insult was explicit in his tone.

After all, it wasn't the Zoo or the GS Road or the envy-inspiring Spanish Gardens. It was Malegaon, reeking of the past and a humble present, a point which the driver didn't miss raising. The point became all the more apparent during monsoon.

As the taxi rushed away, Kranti looked at the house. The glamorous aura of the pillars seemed to have withered, yet the veranda still presented a strong front. The placement of the house and its view had led to its selection. 'Feels as if this road is just for us,' his father had said. And indeed it was, leading a path not just to their home but to their inquiries, too. Questions defined Kranti's growing years and influenced his later ones. Questions that started as innocent concerns but tightened their grip each time Kranti tried to free himself. 'Where is your umbrella?', 'Why were you not in class?', 'What did you throw in the bushes?', 'Why do you hide inside your room?' Intrusive concerns that persisted till he left home for good, for his studies and career.

Agitated, he hopped out. A pleasant breeze blew at a comfortable pace like the soft touch of silk, but Kranti wasn't impressed anymore. The gravel road coated in thick sludge didn't make it any better. It was the rainy season. Weeds had wildly encroached on whatever remained of the road, and a wet stench confirmed it.

A bag in hand, he walked towards the house like a dog to his kennel, an invisible leash pulling him inwards. To Kranti, the house appeared defiled despite its white-washed walls. Each decade had left a crusty mark on its old structure. Much like Kranti's past—a similarity he was well aware of. The burden of an unceasing ugliness, to be borne by him as he tried to navigate his life around it, more often through it.

Through the half-sheer curtain, his mother saw Kranti walking towards them. She searched for the vestiges of the past in him, of that hesitant young boy who would hide behind her. Her only son, who wouldn't come and talk but would get her fresh tamul paan (areca nuts and betel leaves) every evening, would sulk but still pluck flowers for her prayers. She looked at his assured walk, his fashionable clothes, one hand in the pocket and another holding an equally modish bag. She noticed the change in her son. The scorn with which he looked at the houses confirmed it further. *For the better*, she reassured herself.

'Kranti *aahi aase* (Kranti is coming),' she called out to her husband in Assamese. In a cotton sador mekhela, she stood with a slight hunch. Seeing him inch closer, she swiftly covered the oil stain on her blouse with the sador's loose end, its blue embroidery replicating the intricate Kingkhap motifs, a style from the times when the Ahom Dynasty lived a life of royalty. Motifs of the past, of lions, of the king of the jungle, shouldered by her.

Her husband, on the other hand, in a loose white *genji* (vest) and lint-ridden tracks, waited inside. He wasn't keen on presenting a sun-drenched picture. He knew his son sufficiently well to even delude himself with any consoling thoughts. Yet, he didn't confront his wife. He, too, continued to abide by the rule of pretence. Together, son and father created a mirage over the rugged relations they all stood upon; a delicate illusion of proximity; an imagined sheen of happiness. One that could shatter with a mere touch.

Manufactured hopes to bolster reality.

Acting on his wife's happiness, he too came and sat by the window, curtains drawn to a close, and shuffled as he adjusted himself on the sofa, opposite to the television set. His reflection on the dark grey screen was apparent, its protruding surface making him look rounder than he was, his face slightly distorted.

Kranti waved to his mother, who, by now, was on the veranda, waiting eagerly. Father wasn't there. A relief to both.

Kranti glanced at her. He found her looking much older now, but instead said, 'Ma, you look good,' as he reached for the door latch. Avoiding any touch with the damp gate, he pulled out the metal hook. She smiled, her paan-stained teeth radiating happiness galore. Kranti found it painful to see her wrinkled face, blaming his father and the city for her premature ageing.

Kranti's Ma was an image of drooping shoulders, holding on to prayer beads that moved faster if a dog howled at night or a cat mewled; beads that didn't leave her hands when her son travelled (the times she knew of). Her son, with olive green eyes, her favourite colour, an incomparable prodigy of his breed, her favourite child. Her son of weekly calls and yearly visits, of stolen jewellery, sold and used on shoes and perfumes. Her Kranti, who would rain gifts and designer sarees on her from online stores. Sarees that she never wore—Banarasi, Ikat, Kanjeevaram. Even pure chiffon ones that she once spread on the bed and slept over, their smoothness reminding her of the words her son would speak.

They hugged quickly before walking inside. Reluctance slowed Kranti's steps, the ties of blood overpowering decades of practiced detachment.

Entering the room, he looked around. It was the same as it had been the year before and the year before the previous one. Time did halt under the tight fist of this house. Not everybody could slip away. The rancid air amplified stagnation, and the house appeared to be in an unaltered state.

Kranti noticed that fresh additions had been made, but on their side, obsolete years had piled up. A stainless-steel cooker; a set of bone china showcased through the glass door of a wooden crockery cabinet; new cushions; a plastic cabinet mounted in the balcony to accommodate growing needs; plastic sheets tied to the window grill as a permanent solution for the insidious rain; velvety saffron curtains this time. To Kranti, the house felt even smaller; it appeared to shrink each year.

Clothes drying under the swirling fan on the rope tied across the hall didn't add to the aesthetic Kranti was looking for. It added to the portrayal of everyday life in a middle-class Indian family in a rain-prone state that the son of the soil had forgotten to notice.

'How are you?' Deuta interrupted Kranti's scrutiny. Right leg on his left, hand massaging his knee, he was sitting in the hall—drawing room, as his parents called it. A three-seater cane sofa slumped deeper under his weight while a glass-top cane table witnessing the assault stood firm on the ground. Two cane stools stood mutely on the side, covering the rest of the space.

'*Oi* Kranti, wash your feet first,' Ma instructed as she stood behind him. She spoke as though she were a younger Kranti who would have walked inside in his muddied slippers after an evening of strolling with Mridula.

The bathroom stood next to the only bedroom of the house where his sisters and mother used to sleep. Kranti later got a separate room in the backyard with an isolated entry, while his father slept in the hall. On some days, his mother would lock his sisters in and sleep in the hall. They all avoided eating together on those days, keeping their glances at everything but each other.

Walking closer to the bedroom, Kranti peeped inside. A wooden cot, which once was considered too small to accommodate them all, now filled the room with its hefty self. The side table pushed to the corner displayed an assortment of his father's medicines and mother's massage oils. A shallow red plastic basket held them all in. Near the window, a small mirror still hung with its faded pink plastic rim. Two calendars adorned the wall opposite the bed—one with the painting of a hill station with clouds intersecting mountains, and another with a sketch of Goddess Kali, smiling. On the right corner was a small balcony covered by a black iron grill—a prison gate, as Kranti and his sisters used to call it. It was partially covered by blue fibre sheets now.

At the back, standing aloof, he could see the other room. Painted walls with a dash of blue, the colour of a happy sky, were chipping off. Slow disintegration in swollen moist flakes—a predictable occurrence during monsoon. Water droplets dripping occasionally from the tin roofs made it obvious. With drapes drawn to a close, he couldn't see the insides.

'What happened?' Deuta called out.

'Nothing.' Kranti rushed to the bathroom.

He looks the same. Only Ma has aged. He seems to be growing younger, Kranti thought as he came and sat opposite his father.

'Journey was fine?' Deuta asked in Assamese, the way he always did, now more so because Kranti had shifted to Delhi and married a 'Hindi Girl', as he would often snigger at the mention of Anchal.

'Ya, fine only,' Kranti replied in English, a neutral language, to distance himself from all that his father was and had.

'Lunch?'

'Not now. Will eat later.'

'When? It is almost lunchtime. I got fresh fish. Do you know how difficult it is to get fresh ones in this season? Ask your mother.'

'Kranti, you saw roses outside? Deuta planted them this season. Already blooming,' his mother intervened from the kitchen.

After a mellow reply to his mother in Assamese followed by a smile, the way he had been doing since childhood, Kranti stepped out. He slid his hands into his pockets, fondling the cigarette box and the cool of its engraved compass.

Smoking, his secret weapon to de-stress. The more smoke he inhaled, the more stress he exhaled. But it wasn't the tension that brought cigarettes to his lips; it was just his curiosity to inhale and hold it between his fingers. As a young boy of fifteen years, he was awestruck when he first formed smoke spirals. The reason was as simple as that. That's how it had been for Kranti. A simple reason, but an apt explanation for his every action. He would often tell others that it was not a cigarette but his cue to ease that he carried in his pockets. And the more he believed in its power, the easier it became to smoke and lie about it. Sometimes, like today, his parents became the reason to smoke. In Delhi, Anchal, his boss, petty office politics, and sometimes people in general, instigated him towards his constants—chai and *sutta*.

He walked a little further from the veranda with the sponsor of his calmness, especially when in Guwahati. Glancing inside to ensure that none of them were looking from the window, he took a cigarette out, lit it, and blew the smoke downwards in the direction of the wind. A practised smoker, he could blow smoke as he wished. It was a habit that he had kept hidden till now, even from Ma.

Kranti's Ma. Servility ingrained—towards parents who married her off to a man she hadn't seen before. Towards a husband who didn't send her to meet her parents even when they were on their deathbeds. Children's yearly tests took precedence. Kranti's Ma would maintain a dedicated humility even for relatives and friends—his, not hers; many of them controlled a large part of her life even without uttering a word. And these people, all combined, blinded her with the requisite glamour of marital bliss and motherhood. She, too, believed that her existence depended on it. It was her bowl of existentialism. Thrust upon her. A fast rusting, depleting bowl. Its presence eliminating hers. His Ma. One, like many, who wouldn't leave her husband even to go and visit her son.

After a few quick puffs, Kranti cleared the smoke around him, rubbed roll-on deodorant on his neck and wrists, and finally popped a peppermint gum. By the time he walked inside, Deuta was gearing up for a game of chess. It was his way of straightening things out with his son. With a chessboard on the cane table, pieces neatly placed, they sat facing each other.

Kranti had black pieces, while his father kept white on his side, like always. Deuta made his first move, but Kranti felt an unease. He fiddled with his pawn and wondered if this game could fix anything between them.

Could a crushed sheet ever be straightened out with a mere caress? It needed water and the burning heat of an iron box to ease the wrinkles out. If not, they would show up again. Creases of the belt, red on skin, were too harsh, even if the child was found cheating in an exam, his nails buried in a fist. Pangs of hunger—his penalty for a broken radio, showed the carefully pleated parenthood. Seen on a fragile neck, reminiscent of a rope; of tears for denied chocolates. Although aware of the marks that even a lifelong game of chess wouldn't be enough to justify, they both tried.

'Ma, what are you doing? Come here,' Kranti called out to his mother, who had gone to the kitchen.

The kitchen still had the crochet door hanging on it, Kranti noticed. That small space inside belonged to his mother, where she cleaned for herself but cooked for her husband.

'Making tea. She also prepared pitha for you.'

They had only started playing, with a few pawns lost on both sides, Kranti's Queen under the gaze of Deuta's Knight, when Ma arrived with tea and a plate full of kordoi and til pitha.

The smell of home-cooked food brought back memories of his childhood. How he would sit near his mother, watching her prepare kordoi and eating it the moment she took them out, slightly golden, red-hot! Yet, he would grab and eat, hardly leaving any for his sisters and father. She would smile, content with her son's happiness. Kranti reached for one.

'Take more, finish it,' Deuta said, as he would have told a young Kranti.

'Come more often, baba. Whatever you want, I will cook,' said Ma, her tone a wishful plea.

'I will.' Kranti made the promise so quickly, so openly, with utmost sincerity of keeping. But time had always been a challenger to his promises.

Amid those brief moments of happiness, Kranti felt comforted to be with his parents. Yet, somehow, those moments of tender talks always brought out the past, overpowering the fragrance of the present, like decaying wood in the rain.

'How are Kuki and Tapani? Haven't spoken to them in months.'

'They are fine,' Deuta replied. 'They feel bad. You don't call them.'

'*Wah!* Why can't they call me?'

'They want their brother to show some affection.'

Kranti kept quiet and focused on the greeting cards on the wall behind Deuta. Cards stapled together to form a rhombus; a Victorian-style flower vase followed by a young girl with a flowering plant stapled to a litter of pups in a basket that looked down at the candles around a Christmas tree which stuck to a huge clay lamp with a platter of sweets beside it. An anomaly of wishes—Happy Diwali, Merry Christmas, Happy New Year. To Kranti, they were nothing but forced emotions clubbed together, hoping for a happier year.

'But baba, their area was flooded last year. Even then you didn't call. That's why they are feeling bad.'

'So what? They don't stay in slums. Is their house in a low-lying area? Why do I need to call them? There is a flood every year. Have we lost anyone? It's all those people who get affected. Not us.'

No one spoke for a while. Few origins were still capable of bringing silence. His mother's efforts to remove every trace of her class had finally seemed to succeed when her son also forgot her origin. Her wishful exclusion from his ingrained contempt.

Ma's side never behaved like one. Ma is practically us, he reasoned to himself. Seeing their faces, Kranti realized his mistake, but he quickly brushed the thought aside and spoke again. 'Every year so many people die! This government should do something. What they are doing is wrong. They need to plant more trees. I read a report last year on the flood and its recurrence.'

'They build embankments and repair it every year. Everyone is trying.'

'No, not at all. That's not the right step either. You should read the report, Deuta. I will show you. The state suffers. They should take better steps,' Kranti said, plunging into his habitual analysis.

'Rivers are such. What can we do? So powerful, and we have so many. We are at their mercy.'

'They should enlarge the floodplains. Planting more trees in upstream areas is also important. But who is doing that? No one. Every year so many people become homeless, and it takes months for them to settle again. Every year I hear similar stories. But who is taking charge of it?'

Kranti had forgotten that he too was unseeing the plight for many years now. His nonchalance was not unusual. His contempt for those who didn't belong to the status he liked to associate with was obvious since childhood. He would often refuse to visit his mother's maternal home. *It's so poor*, he would say, and stay back at Mridula's house. Even to this day, Anchal had no idea where her mother-in-law had grown up. Daily wage labourers were not the lineage Kranti liked to associate himself with. He, rather, made peace with his father's humble yet respectable background. His mother was aware of it, but accepting the invisibility wasn't always easy for her.

'How difficult is it to call for two minutes? Your wife can call them too. She doesn't even call us,' Deuta remarked, shifting the focus.

'My wife has a name.'

Cutting the looming argument short, Kranti inquired about Mridula, who should have been home by now, as he pointed out.

'Mridu came yesterday only. She and Rimi both.'

'But this morning she left,' Deuta added.

'Maajorghat,' Deuta said in a low voice, fearing his volume would increase the gravity of the matter. They were whispering, their voices slightly louder than the crunch of kordoi Kranti was biting on.

When he asked more, all they could give was a vague explanation, not of why Mridula left but of how she had been. *Was someone in the accident? The reason for her going? And the time of her return?* They couldn't hold up to Kranti's line of questioning, ambiguous as they often were.

'She didn't tell us anything.'

After a while, Ma spoke. 'She seemed happy. She brought gifts for us, like always. Was asking about you as well. She was waiting to meet you. You both would have met after such a long time, na.'

'She went alone? But why? Why in such urgency? Was there someone on the train? To help? To search? But who is she searching for?' Kranti asked a barrage of questions, his mind racing.

'Yes,' Deuta uttered an answer, vague and unconvincing.

'She was in a hurry. There was no time even to talk. We dropped Rimi to Mridu's house,' Ma added.

Since then, Mridula's number had been switched off. They hadn't been able to contact her after that. But Ma hadn't told him this.

'Didn't want to stress you needlessly,' she said in a placating tone when he accused them of hiding it from him.

'Really!' Kranti spoke louder than he'd intended.

Kranti got up, his hair brushing against the wooden shelf. The unpainted shelf nailed to the wall displayed an assortment of ceramic dolls and a small brass *xorai* offered to Deuta for his contribution to the colony. Its larger version was gifted to

Anchal during their initial years of courtship, not as a traditional symbol of respect but more to keep up the exoticism she used to find in him. A red glass vase by the side of the xorai was still empty. Kranti looked at the shelf built by him and Deuta. How excited he'd been to bring nails from the shop nearby and hand the hammer and pieces of wood to Deuta whenever he asked! How proud he'd felt of this addition to the house! How enthusiastically he'd arranged those statues with Ma!

Wrenching his head away, he felt repulsed by the thoughts of those days, when even his dreams were limited.

4

'Ma,' Mridula called, trying to peep in through the sheer curtain. The sun sat behind her and the light bulb at the door flickered in pride as its turn to shine arrived. Dusting soil off her tunic and leggings, she waited for her aunt to open the door. On her forehead a small black bindi stayed put, which she had started wearing upon Priyom's insistence. *You look surreal in Indian dresses*, he would say. So, each day she marked her forehead with a dot of changing colours, mostly red then, now black.

'*Aei* Mridu!' Her aunt was pleasantly surprised to see her arrive sooner than expected. Smoothing the creases on her cotton mekhela sador, turmeric yellow embellished with white floral patterns, she smiled. Her fingers spread flat on her chador and moved up and down, a rhythmic occurrence when excited, or nervous.

'We went to the zoo today.'

'*Oi swahili* (girl or daughter), come here.' She gestured to Rimi who was standing beside her mother and licking the ice cream off her cone that dribbled down her frock's collar.

'Today?'

'*Noe noe* (no), we just came. She doesn't remember anything,' Mridula replied as she bent forward and ran her hand over Rimi's head, tightening her ponytail and fastening the red hair bobble. Its shape, similar to a wrinkled piece of paper, resembled a paper rose, depending on the way one chose to see it.

'*Aaha, Boha* (Come, sit),' she said in Assamese as she pulled them inside and inquired about routes, roads, and the increasing water level in Dibrugarh.

'Where is *Khura* (Uncle)?' Mridula asked as she sat, running her hands on the round handles of the cane chair. Above them, a tube light flickered like a star, arresting Rimi's attention and irritating Mridula.

'This tube light is acting up again. Oh, your uncle went to market, *Majoni* (daughter), to get fish for tomorrow!' Her voice beamed brighter than the tube light.

Mridula couldn't help but smile at the thought of meeting Kranti. A reluctant smile. She wasn't sure how he would take the news; but she wouldn't be able to hide anything from him, even after years of distance. There were times when Mridula blamed Kranti for the silence between them. But it didn't matter anymore.

'How have you been?' her aunt asked as she stood at the door, while Mridula unpacked her bag, taking out for the gifts she had bought for her favourite aunt—tea leaves from the gardens of Dibrugarh, 250 grams of second flush, a kilogram of last year's monsoon produce, and a woven shawl she'd picked up on her recent visit to the market.

'Fine, *Xoru* Ma,' she said, still rummaging through her bag.

'How is he? Does he meet Rimi?' Her aunt finally asked what she had been meaning to. Of course, only after confirming that her niece was doing fine—as she had expected. Priorities set right.

'Who?'

'He... who else Majoni?' she said, as though uttering his name would bring him back to the family. A bad omen to be kept at bay. 'He is also here. Not sure, but Kuki told me,' she said and left to make tea even before Mridula could offer any reply.

He was indeed in Guwahati. Mridula knew this, and also about his departure.

He, the one Mridula was made to choose. She, who would roar the loudest, who would stand firm even when others trembled, who took pride in her severe reviewing, had accepted Priyom with sheer calm, as if challenging herself. Once into the marriage, she had given him the benefit of being different from her, his mentality an outcome of his upbringing, his actions a result of peer pressure. So, on some occasions when she felt the urge, she blamed not Priyom but his childhood, friendships, surroundings, patriarchy, education—and the lack of it. She blamed the women's presence in his life and their collective strength, their absence too, and their exposure and varied impacts for making him the way he was. She placed him on a pedestal, which eventually grew to a height even Mridula couldn't reach. To deal with it, Mridula distanced herself in a corner, creating a home only she could see. Whenever she found herself slipping into dejection, she would let a part of herself crawl into that home of hers, quietly, secretively. The rest of her would stay upfront, taking charge and strengthening the pedestal, until came the time when even that crumbled down.

It was past eight in the evening. Rimi sat at the dining table and toyed with the plastic tea coasters. Mridula set up the plates meticulously while her aunt brought out the dishes from the kitchen and placed them carefully at the crochet coasters. Her uncle also walked in and settled himself opposite Rimi.

Mridula's aunt served dinner, first to her husband, then Rimi and Mridula, and finally to herself.

'She is not eating anything,' her uncle said to no one in particular, as though offering a sermon to his subjects.

'Rimi, eat *payokh*. This is better than your pizza and toffees. Your *Aaita* (grandmother) made,' he spoke to Rimi now, who was fiddling with the rice pudding while wishing for it to turn into something more satiable—maybe a chocolate cake with an extra portion of cream and a small pink flower on it. Dreams could be elaborate and specific even for a five-year-old.

Mridula sat and looked at her daughter. She knew Rimi wouldn't eat the rice pudding, not even a spoon, especially now that she had been asked to. A faint smile surfaced on her lips, carrying a fleeting hint of pride. It was sufficient to mark her contentment but subtle enough to go unnoticed. Rebellion was something Mridula always prided herself on. To act on it or not was something she didn't often think about.

However, before she could realize, her uncle's attention shifted to her 'Mridu, you don't come nowadays.'

'She stopped coming after that day.'

That day. Yes, the day marking eight months, recalled Mridula. An emotional text message that was sent hurriedly tried to make its comeback too, but she brushed the memory aside.

'Not her fault. He was drunk that day. What could she do?' her aunt said, reflecting on the day Mridula had visited them last. Not with Rimi, but alone, to discuss a few legal proceedings with her uncle. Her divorce was due in a few days. They had just sat down for dinner to a simple meal of bhaat and masor tenga maas with her aunt's special alu pitika that Mridula was looking forward to eating, when Priyom had barged in, accusing Mridula of ruining his life. He had threatened to ruin her life in return, as if it was possible for him to go any further. His act, although in a drunken state, seemed intentional now, whenever Mridula reflected back on it; a staged display of anger to support his false integrity. Memory of that event—not his words, but the feelings it incited in her—a sensory memory—made it easier for her to look at the event now.

'I know. I am only asking her.'

'Aei Mridu, it's okay! Already a year na?'

'No. Eight months, Xoru Ma.'

'It is good that you came today.'

'He was not good. But she didn't know, na.'

They discussed her while her daughter sat quietly, trying to keenly understand the discussion being held. Rimi could grasp that it was about her father, who had stopped living with them for a year now. They had met recently, but no one seemed to like him anymore. But she couldn't understand the event; no one had informed her, but everyone whispered about it.

They kept talking, disregarding the fact that not only was the topic of their discussion sitting right in front of them, but also the person who shouldn't be listening at all. But then, discretion had never been their forte. Her Xoru Ma and Khura meant well, Mridula knew.

How could she know? Her aunt's words rang in her ears repeatedly. It was true; there was no way that Mridula could know. Yet somewhere, she did. In that corner of her heart, where his words hovered above the solitude of comfort—it was there that she knew. Too many apologies, too often. Too many bruises, no time to heal. Absences too often, reasons too many. Too many demands, too little money. A silhouette of a child unborn. Too crumpled a relationship, no space for dreams. Yet she had plunged into it.

Shouldn't and wouldn't had never been separate in Mridula's life.

5

Mridula was now back in the room that once used to be Kranti's and now belonged to a tenant who had been asked to shift to his friend's room for a few weeks. An unusual request by the owners, but he had obliged. Free dinners and homely comfort at a price lesser than the market rate had convinced him for the bargain.

While trying to put Rimi to sleep, Mridula tried to reiterate what she had taught her on the way to her aunt's home. Rimi had her own queries to quell. 'Why did *Koka* (grandfather) say *Pita* (father) is bad?', 'Why doesn't he like pizza?', 'Can I get one tomorrow?', 'When will I see Pita again?' and 'Who is coming tomorrow?'

But Mridula's mind was preoccupied with things of the past, and a few that might occur soon.

'Rimi, promise me again majoni.' She kept her palm open in her daughter's lap. 'We will not tell anyone about today. It is our secret. We are like friends, right *moromor* (my dear)? We only share with each other.' Mridula was trying to make her five-year-old daughter do something she might not be capable of. She was trying to make her understand the complexity of relationships and involving her in matters beyond her reach. Rimi had increasingly been unable to handle any promises or secrets. *A genetic fault*, Mridula wondered sometimes. A child's trait she had often ignored.

'Tomorrow Kranti Khura is coming,' she said to cheer up the child. This was the first time Rimi would meet her uncle. She had been told about Kranti many times, but spoken to him only occasionally.

While Mridula continued her monologue, Rimi fell asleep. Sleeping sideways in a foetal position, her nostrils flared with every few breaths. Her heart-shaped nose was just like her father's. She had more of her father's features than hers. The same cat eyes and soft hair. *Exactly like her father*. Mridula often wondered about how Rimi took most from Priyom and scarcely from her. Under the overwhelming cloud of confusion, a pang of guilt ran through her. These similarities made it hard for Mridula to trust even her child. They were the painful reminders of her dubious married life; although there were times when she loved these uncanny similarities.

This wrestle of emotions was a common occurrence within her.

That night, Mridula dreamt of being pushed inside a well by a hand wearing a gold watch—a strikingly heavy watch. It was the same hand that later pulled her out, with the help of a rope tied to her waist. The hand didn't free her, though. It held her by the shoulder, deciding her fate.

She dreamt of her home, of many years before her mother's affair was caught and father had regained his supremacy. She dreamt of soft hands caressing her, same hands closing the door, outside which two sets of hands hit each other; two men in a brawl. Multiple dreams, each shifting shape, till nothing remained concrete for the next morning.

That night she also dreamt of Zue, the only friend she had in school, the one even Kranti had approved of. Two girls, giggling and devouring the ice cream procured from Zue's brand new fridge. Laughing out and wide, more humility and less pretence.

Two girls playing on the wooden flooring of a big house while the house servant served them milk and biscuits. Two girls sneaking in and watching movies on a VCR. Two girls trying out the face cream in a small glass bottle with a purple cap kept on a white dressing table. Two girls—one plump with cheeks that everyone would come and pull, another with oiled hair and protruding teeth whom no one would admire. Two girls, one in frilled frocks with roses and pearls attached and matching footwear; another in hand-me-down clothes and a black sandal to go with everything. She dreamt of two girls. Especially about the one who couldn't be like the other. One who was almost the same age as her daughter. One she was still trying to know.

6

Mridula woke up, reached for the curtains, and pulled them aside. She lay on a queen size bed which had been pushed underneath the window. Morning light filtered through the iron mesh. Outside the window, the trees stood soaking in sunlight while the leaves brushed water droplets off them. The wind still had the wetness of last night's rain.

The room, almost bare, had a lone cupboard standing in one corner, a bed in the centre, and a small desk and chair filling up the remaining space. The walls were unadorned, except for a wall clock enclosed in a brown rim. The present austerity of the room was in total contrast with the overabundance of Kranti's acquisitions.

The pleasure of ownership had hit Kranti early. A list of gifts and purchases, his collection of books, cassettes, pens, and keychains, empty boxes of watches and shoes atop cupboards, walls filled with posters. This used to be his cavern of hoarding—the ideal place for him to be in. An iota of himself piled and stacked in categories, segmented mounds, a slow dive in the hole that refused to fill up. In its present state, the room looked barren, its essence snatched away.

Although the room was in the backyard, at a slight distance from the rest of the house, Mridula could hear the rattling in the kitchen, the whistle of the cooker, and the clinking of cups on the slab. Her aunt was up and active, preparing for the day.

It was seven in the morning. As her sleep weakened under the flicker of morning sun, Mridula idled on bed for a while, moving from one side to another and burying her face in the pillow. Finally, she mustered enough determination to get out of bed. As she got up with a fuzzy feeling, she blamed her dreams, even though she hardly remembered them. Her dreams had been nightmares for many years now. Sleep mangled with images from a stifled past and fears of a lonely future often left Mridula more tired than refreshed.

Rimi was wrapped under the quilt, except for one hand that had escaped out, taking her share of both the worlds. One was never enough, just like her father. It pleased and frustrated Mridula.

Her aunt was in the kitchen, preparing the morning tea. It was a small room with a granite slab covering three corners, a gas stove on one side, and a washbasin on the opposite end. Above her, on the wall, shelves were stacked with steel containers of the same size, each labelled clearly—rice flour, salt, sugar, tea, lentils, and so on. She was pouring tea in three cups, one chipped, two comparatively new, hers and theirs.

'*Oi* Mridu, did you sleep well?'

'As usual, *Khuri* (aunt),' Mridula replied, taking two cups of tea and walking out.

'Khura, what are you watching?' she asked her uncle who was sitting in the hall, waiting for his tea.

Unlike others, with her uncle she shared an understanding she was quite fond of. A morning discussion on the latest news over an aromatic breakfast of *paani* pitha or Mridula's favourite poita bhaat with alu pitika, and a game of chess in the evening was inevitable whenever she visited them. Even when her uncle would tease her and the 'female species' in general, Mridula would smile and sit next to him, asking his opinions on topics she already knew. 'It is better than the TV serials you women like,' he would say, despite knowing that Mridula had similar tastes in TV, and hardly, if not never, watched any series or movies. Until a few years ago, Mridula used to put up a vehement protest against his sexist generalizations. However, with time, and especially after her marriage, she started to ignore his comments as thoughtless and candid, as something said with good intentions but poor choice of words. She would consider them as innocent slips of tongue, although the slip happened every time. There was a time when she would quote Freud and catch many off-guard.

With Khuri, her talks were mostly about the dishes Mridula would want to eat. Mridula would ask her to prepare and she would eagerly cook; cooking was something she identified her aunt with. She knew her aunt loved it and did it with plain honesty. Her simple means for validation. A purpose for her aging years—her delicacies that everyone loved and remembered her for. She would often make a list of dishes she would cook if a guest were to arrive. If they didn't stay for long or hadn't eaten to her satisfaction, she would pack a considerable amount of each dish and coax them to take and eat later.

Handing over the tea, Mridula stood near her uncle who was watching the morning news telecast.

'There is an accident?'

'In Maajorghat. Train fell off the bridge. Looks bad.'

'Put on some other channel Xoru Khura, let's see in detail,' she said, sitting next to him, unmindful of the tea she'd spilled on the sofa. Her body was losing control, the cup too heavy for her fingers and torso too heavy for her legs. She landed on the sofa, as if she had been dropped on it. She peered into the TV screen to search for a known face, for a gold-rimmed spectacle that never left his eyes, not even on bed, until she would ask him to remove it. Amid the fingers pointed at each other, she searched for one with a gold ring, a round yellow sapphire mounted on it, the one that didn't save their marriage. She watched with such stillness that the sofa seemed to merge into her. Chaos enveloped her, pain pinning her down and fear rising in her heart, burying the resolve. Anger at her fate started burning Mridula, yet again.

For a second her mind went blank. She could see on the screen the horrifying images of the accident, but no, she wasn't able to register it. A moment later, she was back to her senses, her muscles straightened as if getting ready for a fight. A fight with whom? *Maybe it was not a fight but a need to scuttle around.* She wasn't sure. She wanted to be outside, out of the time frame when she got this news, to run backwards and stop him from boarding the train.

Yet, she sat with her uncle and watched everything the news channel was telecasting—a man getting injected, a woman being pulled out of the submerged coach, a huge cutter being carried to the site. Seeing an RPF personnel trying to divert the kid's attention from the rubble that had entombed half of his body, Mridula thought of Rimi. She was glad that her daughter was sleeping in the safety of her aunt's house. But very soon, guilt overpowered her for feeling relieved, and in reflex she thought of Priyom and felt dutifully scared.

The news channel was continuously zooming in on the signs of impact—on rainy eyes and frosty faces. Seeing it all, Mridula wasn't sure whether to think of him among those being taken on stretchers, bleeding as they went, or to imagine his face among those hidden under sheets and tied with ropes, their hair not flowy anymore. She prayed to find him among those resting somewhere, his coach unscathed too. Only two or three coaches had suffered major damage, according to the reporter.

But she didn't know which was his. The once imperishable bridge on which she had travelled all her childhood was now breaking her resilience. She felt the need to save herself from getting strangled too.

Mridula got up and left for her room. His number was switched off. The toll-free numbers and helplines were busy. She looked at her daughter; she was still sleeping. She went up to Rimi but decided against waking her. She turned to the left, sat on the floor, and opened her suitcase. The clock above her rested on nine for a moment before starting to tick again.

She opened her suitcase and took out things of immediate use. She emptied Rimi's multi-coloured backpack, which her daughter had insisted on carrying. She then transferred a few kurtas and jeans, a cotton stole, her all-essential travel kit, lingerie, emergency medicines, and an umbrella in the backpack. Her daughter's small backpack was already full, so she decided to not carry anything else.

Now, dressed in black jeans and a collared tunic the colour of a weeping bottlebrush, a bag on her shoulders, and an irked Rimi in her arms, Mridula walked out to the hall. She sat Rimi on the dining table, who was sulking from being woken up and rubbing her eyes. Dried saliva ran down from her lips to her right cheek and hair fell on her face aimlessly. Her mother hadn't pinned them behind her ears today.

Behind Mridula stood a wooden cupboard, proudly displaying her aunt's possessions. These included colourful crockery sets which were used only when important guests visited, and three pickle jars arranged according to their size.

'I am going to Maajorghat, Xoru Ma.'

Mridula said nothing else, while her hands pulled Rimi's hair back into a ponytail. She was leaving for the eleven o'clock train, rejecting her favourite aunt's request of meeting Kranti before leaving or having breakfast. She wouldn't even tell her about the work she was leaving so abruptly for.

'Moromor, you stay with Aaita today.' Mridula looked at Rimi intently, who was insisting on tagging along.

'Go shopping with Aaita,' she suggested, seeing her grumpy face. 'When I am back, we will go to the zoo. *Ma Kosam* (mother's promise),' she added.

Leaving Rimi, whose long face and closed lips showed unacceptance of this sudden departure, Mridula turned to her aunt and said, 'Xoru Ma, if you are not free, leave her at Kuki's. She can play with the kids.' She then kissed Rimi, bid a quick adieu to her uncle and aunt, and ran outside.

'Paltan bazaar station,' she told the driver as she climbed in the auto rickshaw, hoping for its movement to halt the commotion within.

7

'All lines you are trying are busy at this moment. Please wait or try again later,' the automated voice on the other side repeated itself for the fifth time as Kranti dialled Mridula's number. Letting the phone slip back into his pocket, he walked inside.

Deuta was already at the dining table, which was pushed to the wall next to the kitchen door. Four wooden chairs were arranged around the remaining three sides. Diners faced the wall as they ate, not each other, unless accompanied by two more people.

A few inches away the chess board lay still, King and Queen patiently awaiting their fate like the remaining pawns. Next to them was the half-eaten til pitha, black sesame seeds and jaggery sneaking out from it in their combined effort to escape.

Kranti pulled the chair and sat opposite to his father, while his mother occupied one of the two chairs in the middle, serving equal amounts of food on both the plates. Her plate lay empty, to be served last.

'Your shirt looks nice. New?' his father said, smiling.

Kranti ignored his father's comment. It felt pointless to notice the newness of clothes when they met once a year.

'Guwahati has better markets. Cheaper clothes too.'

It frustrated Kranti to see him gloating over his mediocrity and passing it off as desirable. To him, his father's words reeked of superficiality.

'I like these kinds,' he replied briefly.

'Money should be spent judiciously,' his father said as he dipped his fingers in a bowl of lau khar, pouring some on his heap of rice.

'Should be spent, at least.'

'Ha! Getting trained.'

Kranti stopped eating, rice from the spoon spilling back on the plate, a piece of mutton still stuck to the fork. Words like rocks were hurled at each other, while his mother quaked under its burden. Accusations—of marrying against their will, of bringing home a daughter-in-law who must've tricked their innocent son, of a being a neglectful father, of creating boundaries in and around. Both branding each other, with the best of their anger and the worst of their feelings, as inconsiderate, selfish, greedy, and miserly.

'Take larru, baba,' Ma intervened. 'Do you get good *Narikol* (coconut) larru there?'

'She won't know any Assamese dishes.' Deuta was not to be talked down to. His words were supposed to be final, as they always had been.

'She doesn't need to know.'

'*Kyo?* Her husband is Assamese.'

'What does she cook, then?' Ma spoke under her breath.

'She doesn't. Our Cook does.'

'Your Ma still cooks all my favourite dishes.'

Kranti had been expecting this turn of conversations even before he entered. It was a familiar pattern now. When in Delhi, their telephonic conversations would often end with him refusing to indulge Deuta further and asking for Ma. He had once overheard Anchal on a call with a relative too. He'd felt a moment of togetherness in that moment. Although he had only heard one side of the conversation from her responses, he could feel her share of suffering. 'Yes, *Taiji* (aunt), I know they eat pigeons. He can eat whatever he likes. Haan, our cook prepares meat for him. No, his mother cannot speak Hindi. Why should she learn? *Bas karo* (stop it) Taiji, I am not turning into an Assamese.'

'Hey! Just got free, honey.'

'Me too. Came for a movie.'

'Oh nice, how was the movie? Any dinner plans?'

'We are thinking where to go.'

'*Oho*, enjoy, enjoy.'

'*Uff*, Kranti. Don't start again.'

'Chill, it's just a joke, *yaar*.'

'Anyway, how is everyone there?'

'Same. Everyone is fine.'

'Why didn't you call the entire day?'

'Didn't get time, *jaan*.'

'Of course. They will have issues even if you take two minutes to call me.'

'Anchal, I have told you earlier too. They don't say anything about you.'

'And you want me to believe that?'

'Why are we talking about them?'

'Because you get defensive. Accept that they are rude!'

'Not rude, yaar. Just conservative.'

'Oh? So all they did to me was just being conservative?'

'I don't want to talk about it. Bye.'

Disconnecting the call, Kranti came inside the hall and lay on the plastic mat. He could hear his father snoring. He fetched his earphones and plugged them in.

Anchal or he never spoke about bringing a balance of culture. Acceptance of each other's and sticking to none was their middle ground. Mother tongue and food habits were not the things they'd discussed before getting married. There were no discussions, as a matter of fact. Six months in separate cities after several years in the same. Weekly travels, deteriorating health, impending office work, and unfamiliar surroundings brought out the adequate realization. Longing got termed as love, a dinner became a proposal, diamonds reflected the chandelier above, its eager acceptance flattered the proposer, two cities merged, and a home was formed.

Eventually, a few rules were set. Discussions, like the one that'd happened just now, were avoided, and a peaceful stay was maintained. Disagreements were burnt down to non-existence. The skeletons did show up once in a while, though. Once, Kranti had complained about Delhi's ordinariness and unhealthy air, and how he missed Guwahati. They had taken a trip to Shimla that weekend.

Once, at a friend's party, he had praised the Kamakhya temple, the temple where even menstruation was celebrated. He spoke at length about its structure, cutting a piece of sky with its hemispherical dome, its ancientness, and the rare peace he had always felt. He thought of happy memories, but the bitter ones crept in slowly. Later that night on their way back, he had told Anchal about frauds and conmen in the guise of devotees, endless queue of beggars who wouldn't budge without cash, shops on the road, sheets spread with stacks ranging from idols to bangles and bracelets, and stalls of plastic toys and snacks as a joke on the very concept of worship.

'Only Gods and their devotees should be allowed in and around the temples,' he had concluded.

What he wished to tell Anchal was how his Deuta would drag him into the massive flux that the temple often witnessed, holding Kranti by his wrist as he would make their way in the crowd, how his hands ached afterwards, and how his shirt would be smeared with vermillion. He wanted to tell her how he looked expectantly at his mother to remember and buy him the toy gun she had promised, how his sisters and he would come up with stories, mostly of horror, on seeing the stream of blood.

Things that Anchal too came to experience on her first visit to Guwahati post-marriage. The visit where she was watched, measured, told, and refuted; the visit where she was expected to slide willingly into their bottle of expectations. And so, it became the visit where she shopped as if she wasn't going to return soon. A prophecy depicted through action. Cane jewellery bought for gifting and several sets of mekhela sador from Government Emporium. She even wanted a set of cane sofas couriered, the sight of which appalled Kranti.

The past was threatening to fill up his present. He slowly retreated and they came to a solution. For three years now, it was only Kranti who came to Guwahati, meeting and shopping for both.

8

Maajorghat-Guwahati Express Derailed, Twenty Dead

Maajorghat: Nine coaches of the 011188 Maajorghat-Guwahati Express train derailed on Sunday near Maajorghat station in Assam. Six sleeper coaches - S1, S2, S3, S4, S5, S6 and three AC coaches - B1, B2, B3 derailed at 5.30 a.m. IST.

20 passengers have been reported dead and 150 passengers have reported injuries. Passengers with serious injuries have been taken to the city hospital. Passengers with minor injuries are being treated on-site. The search for passengers is still going on.

Maajorghat's Divisional Railway Manager and a medical team are on the derailment site. Helpline numbers have been issued. RPF have arrived at the derailment site. Accident relief trains with cranes have also reached the site. NDRF has set up a camp for the estranged passengers.

No reason has been given for the accident. 'The cause of derailment will be ascertained after a thorough inquiry,' the officials said. However, it is speculated that the deteriorating condition of the bridge and excessive rainfall might be the reason behind derailment.

'Due to the train derailment this morning, train services between lower and upper Assam will be suspended for five days,' the Chief Public Relations Officer of Northeast Frontier Railway said. 'Some trains have been diverted to the Tinsukia-Namrup-Simaluguri mainline,' he added.

'Tracks and the bridge will be repaired during this time. Senior railway officials from the Maajorghat division have been assigned to monitor the work at the site,' the official said.

This is a developing story. More details are awaited.

SECTION 2

JOURNEY TO THE SITE

It was the wall that wronged you,
but
you blamed the window for an airless evening.
If you would have stepped out,
or
just unbolted the glass
and looked around,
you would have known
that the sky was gearing up for you.

1

An overstuffed bag hung over her hunched shoulders as Mridula stood facing the empty tracks, her head tilted sideways, a tight ponytail resting atop. Two platforms, separated by two rows of iron tracks, and between them a scatter of gravel and litter. A few metres away from where she was standing, a concrete path connected the two platforms. A few people hurriedly crossed sides on that path—something that had never been easy for her. Further out stood a small bridge. Seeing a lorry cross it, she imagined its tyres getting chafed by the dented concrete. She also felt for the bridge, which was shaken by just a fistful of trucks passing by.

Soon, a crowd thronged from every corner, nearing the platform edge. Mridula pushed her way to the front. Standing close to the platform gap, she saw the train approaching like a snake. She wondered which snake it looked like. *Anaconda*, she decided. She felt like it was coming to swallow her, and the thought scared her. The train slowly crawled towards her, its mouth as gigantic as she had seen in pictures, with bulging eyes and teeth ready to shatter. It curved and slithered ahead, a touch of leisure and grace, a sorcery of cruelty.

Mridula stood there inspecting till an eager traveller's elbowing brought her back to the train and its advent. In her worry about Priyom's whereabouts and the urgency to track him, she had forgotten to book a berth. She was hopeful that a few extra bucks and the ticket collector's mercy would fetch her a seat. So, following the crowd, she rushed towards the sleeper coach.

As she approached the door, Mridula deliberated her move—whether to step inside and let this train drag her back to the stagnation she came from, or to abandon this journey and move on to something unmarked by her past. She realized that she hadn't thought it through. She wasn't sure how she would deal with whatever the finding would be. But before she could act, she was inside the coach, jolted forward by the crowd, leaving her with no choice. At least that was what she believed.

The passengers were quickly settling in, some dangling their legs down, some sitting meditatively, cross-legged, some snuggling inside their shawls or sheets. A few looked outside, inspecting the station they were to leave soon, while a few busied themselves in taking note of every one who stepped in, vexed at their entrance. They were annoyed at any further infringement to their personal domain, in which they'd bought only a seat.

Squeezed between two passengers, Mridula sat hunched, her backpack on her knees. A blot of faded orange tunic, an indigo shirt on one side, and a deep red saree on the other—an incomplete rainbow. The other two, like her, were sitting transfixed too. Three pairs of eyes looking outside the window. The usual greetings or inquiries about each other's destinations seemed impossible.

The coach, even though filled to its capacity, carried a strange silence. The silence that lingered not from an absence of sound, but in spite of it. The kind which wouldn't break even by a scream; the kind inside a coffin when the ones surrounding it wailed. The quietness of pain, bearing separation, yet an understanding of its peace.

Immersed in this strange mix of relief and grief, slowly dwelling in silence, she looked up and saw a young girl settling on the opposite seat by the window side.

Outside the window, hawkers were getting ready too. Their cane baskets topped with snacks and mixes, containers of spices, and a stack of newspaper pieces. One came and pushed a clay cup towards her, urging her to buy a cup of tea, while simultaneously calling out to other customers with a melodious '*Chaiaa Chaiaa*'. Soon, someone from the pantry would come too for lunch orders, with choices limited—vegetable and chicken biryani, chapati with vegetable or egg curry, vegetarian or non-vegetarian meals served in metal trays that would be heaped over each other, accompanied by cartons of packaged water, one with each plate.

The train was now moving fast, in a bid to catch up for the slow start. With frequent jerks and rapid turns, it passed through meadows. At the far end, mountains were beaming with greenery, overloaded with trees that could be spotted if one really wished to see. The world outside echoed freshness, a happy gleam under the rare sun. Train went past a pond with oversized lotus leaves and two flower buds floating between them; cattle roamed freely and birds perched on them; the trees stood aloof or in groups. The world of segregation was made apparent. A patch of barren land; few freshly ploughed fields; a house with a tin roof; houses with two storeys; concrete roads with cars parked on one side; roads out of sight; cycles and carts halted.

India this and India that, segregated with land, water, or road. Trains crossed all, surpassing the boundaries, running on paths it had created anew. Not really. Rail lines, a souvenir of colonial times, a symbol of a futuristic dream, running deep within us, even now.

Mridula rubbed her fingers, as though dusting the mounds of dirt. Her index fingers started mapping her fingernails, seeking comfort in repetition. Above her, on the upper berth, a boy spread his home-brought sheet, tied his jacket to the metal chain that held the berth up, and then placed his bag as a pillow. He was soon asleep. She noticed that further inside the coach a passenger had decided to pull out the middle seat, forcing those on the lower berth to either sit hunched or lay down.

Mridula's focus shifted back to the girl in front, who had started to comb her hair with the elegance of a princess—the kind one saw in fairy tales. About the real ones, she wasn't clear.

After all, reality, like everything else, could be concocted too, especially for Mridula. Fabricated presentation of beauty, elegance, style, and happiness that made the royals all over the world alike. Despite her pulling out strands of hair from the comb and throwing it out of the window, Mridula was moved by the refinement in her movements. *Like a dancer's practised grace,* she thought. The girl was fastening her hair in a ponytail when her phone rang. An inverted arch spread across her face. A smile of love; a touch of shyness. The girl's undiluted happiness reminded Mridula of the times she had it too—this bewitching rawness that she too had embraced once.

Memories of those days returned, of the time when their courtship was new. Theirs was an arranged marriage, with a brief dating period to help them decide. Limited were the ways to understand each other, but they had concluded positively from whatever they could judge, mostly based on the guts and influence of over-zealous relatives.

Back then, the charm of the unknown still pottered through them, giving them hope—the perceived precursor to happiness. The bliss of ignorance was soon to be hampered by the woes of knowledge, but they didn't know it then. With passion running high, she felt beholden to him, while he panted over her. His phone calls would make her feel angelic—a power to change the world with just a whip of her wand.

Love was indeed fortifying in that sense. It often cemented one's own beliefs, even if it was based on a passing moment. In that fraction of a second, it took a feeling of permanence. The one in love felt powerful—powerful enough to love themselves too. And soon it transcended and took other forms.

Soon, all Mridula wanted was to get Priyom's attention. She would write long letters to him. Handwritten letters. Although she never heard about her letters unless asked, she believed for a long time that he did read and love them. Until one day, after marriage, she found them unopened in his keepsake box, still glued. He had saved them to read later, he had told her that same night. Believing him was the only way to keep her idea of love intact.

Back then, Priyom's love for her was as exaggerated as gigantic hoardings advertising houses with wide open balconies at locations impossible to find in a city, with the residents in the pictures ostensibly smiling and celebrating. She had believed in that hoarding; just by looking at it she had lived inside those walls of luxury. For her, even the idea was enough, a thought of luxury, a scent of love, an impression of companionship. An arranged-cum-love marriage, they had told everyone, which, in their case, was as delusional as the hoarding.

As the day passed, Mridula leaned back and closed her eyes, but sleep wouldn't come. Nothing new though—her relationship with sleep had always been a tumultuous one. A wretched wooer pursuing a heartless beloved. So, she sat there while her mind hopped from one thought to another. She tossed a passing glance and categorized everyone; the magical girl in love, the man sitting next to her; another with a white sack on his back; women sitting by the door; in front of her a pair of slippers aligned in perfect symmetry.

She looked out of the window and mulled over 'whys'—she casted a *why* on the colour of the sky and the clouds, about the happiness she felt whenever she looked at them, on the changes in their colours, and why those changes unsettled her. She then suddenly thought of the sea and wondered why the waves always swayed, as if they were drunk on their own water.

And then she thought of 'where'—*where* to stay, and places to search in Dibrugarh and other cities if she planned to shift base. But soon expanded it to some recent news. *Where did the MH370 go? Could she also vanish without a clue? Where is that place where you could vanish without a clue?*

And then she came upon 'how'—*how* could she get that address? The address of no trace?

Exhausting herself on topics so far, she shifted her focus on the train she was travelling in. Why were there no upper berths in general compartments, just a lower and slightly higher middle berth? As a kid, she used to love upper berths the most—the ideal place to distance herself from her family, away from the incessant cold war between her parents and her brother's bullying for the window seat, away from snooping passengers on the remaining four seats with endless questions. She would lie with her back towards them, peeping on the other side through the metal grill, imagining their relations, their life through their actions, and as per her whims. It used to be her way of connecting with both the worlds.

Today, however, Mridula didn't create a world out of the people surrounding her. Instead, she questioned the train. Why were the roofs of trains made the way they were? Even as a kid she would have to hunch and sit so as to avoid hitting her head against the roof. If they could make the coach high enough, why couldn't they make the roof a tad bit higher as well? Why did a train have to make us perennially bent?

It was the 'why' that was affecting her. *Why did he treat her the way he did? Why was she still travelling back to him? Why didn't she love herself enough?* And she concluded that like the coaches, life too had made her bend, bow, and coil, a flexibility she'd learnt in her marriage. The thought made her uneasy. So she thought of Rimi instead, of calling her up. She didn't.

A red heart pillow with love engraved all over it, a bouquet of red roses arranged in ascending order in a cane basket, and a cake was delivered a week after their marriage was fixed. They had met only twice before. Diganta, Mridula's brother, had received the parcel, and on seeing the sender's name had called his sister to the hall. Opening the cake box, he'd laughed out loud. Their parents, too, had come out to look.

The cake had Mridula's picture on it—the one they had sent for match-making. In the photo, she seemed to be leaning on the wall for support. She was squinting at the flash, with her hair falling over her shoulder, fringes covering her forehead, and lips stretching in an awkward smile. She was wearing a navy blue mekhela sador to enhance her skin's tone and her mother's gold chain for the picture. 'I love you' was written in italics below the picture in pink cream over white frosting, with pink roses circling it.

Mridula had flushed on seeing the cake. It was a love confessed too soon, in a manner too brash. Especially in a family where her father hadn't spoken to her and her brother had avoided seeing her during *Tuloni Biya,* the function to announce her puberty. In a house where she was married to a banana tree, where tender talks were hushed and fights were done audibly, where love was concealed, and mostly stolen. In such a house, reading a message of love from her soon-to-be husband was more embarrassing than emotional. So, they all stood around it, awkward and uncertain.

'You are so lucky. He is a nice man!' were her mother's words the night she was sneaking out like she would do every time her brother and father went for a walk. It was felt by Mridula too. A mere cake and pillow had shown efforts, his care, and her luck. She had called and thanked him, blushing when he asked her about it. She, too, had confessed her love. Although, the expectation of love was too soon, if given a thought. But they didn't think about it.

Mridula woke from a deep dreamless sleep, a sporadic experience. A hazy grey trail of smoke emerged out of chimneys and windows—the houses outside were getting ready for dinner. She was about to reach the station, from where she would take a taxi. A direct bus to Maajorghat would have been the easier choice, but Mridula chose to travel by train. It was her trial to relive her childhood. She needed a place to associate, a reminder of reality and its stability. She needed to remember those moments of excitement, of reaching their planned destination, the happiness of accomplishment. Rudimentary nature and populous stations provided a base to her memories. Train journeys were cathartic for her, wheels rubbing against the metal tracks, delicately balancing the train on the edgy tracks, the sound and feel of it all. Afterwards, her body would ache and a sound would whir in her ears, yet she loved the experience.

In trains, Mridula was at home, a drop of pain and peace mixed together.

The train halted. She had reached Makum Junction. Dusting thoughts off her tunic, fastening her ponytail once again, and checking her phone for messages that Priyom might have sent from a safe place, she got down at the station.

Mridula, with a hope of getting whom she wanted and reviving what she had lost, shone like the sun on a winter morning, until the sight at the station subdued her orange glow. It was late in the evening and the station looked like an old tree, its barks peeling off, roots buried beneath the layers of dead leaves—yellow, golden, and decaying brown. Everyone wore a morbid expression that spoke of frustration, waiting, and a hopeless decline of the day—of a disappointing today and a nervous tomorrow.

Mridula went out to look for a taxi to Maajorghat.

2

I am sorry, patni ji, Kranti typed the message while waiting at the bus stop. He thought of giving an explanation, but while typing, he got confused about what exactly he wanted to say. So, he decided against writing anything else apart from the prescribed sorry. For him, the timing and frequency of apologies was the key to maintaining his marriage. *Let's finalize Bali once I am back*, he sent another text after a while.

'Don't go to ISBT. You will get a bus at Paltan. Capital (Travels) isn't running. Take Ratnagiri.' Deuta gave Kranti a list of instructions before he headed for the bus stand. He went to Deep Travels. This small display of rebellion still mattered to him. With his father, even an implausible act of freedom felt like a victory to Kranti. That teenage boy who used to fight for his right to go to the movies with friends would surface again. That ten-year-old Kranti who was slapped repeatedly in front of their neighbours for losing his bicycle, who had then promised to avenge himself, would often feel the necessity to challenge his father.

Deep Travels, a private bus operator with a fancy building of extended glass canopies, was booked to its capacity. So, he went to another bus operator, Blue Hills. He had gone with the confidence of being a local and his willingness to pay extra, only to realize that he had forgotten his native ways. Reaching the Blue Hills' office, he had found the conductor selling pink paper tickets in between his rhythmic screaming of Maajorghat. The duration of stay seemed more relevant than the touch of ethnicity, although when in Delhi he preferred to believe otherwise. The failure to connect had become a common occurrence in his life.

Now leaning on a pillar at the bus stop, unaffected by the otherwise nauseating smell and shoulders that rubbed his, Kranti waited for the bus. It had rained heavily for the past few days, begetting temporary bogs everywhere. Next to him, a man loudly discussed the Maajorghat derailment and the flood while buying tea from a stall. It was a small cabinet of bamboo walls under a tin roof. Glass jars of biscuits and plates of deep-fried snacks were kept next to each other. A kettle was kept outside, drops of tea dripping from its nozzle.

On the opposite end of the road were a few shops, each with a colourful board with names written in English and Assamese. In front of them were electric poles and a tangled web of wires, a few wires attached to the boards as well. Seeing the intermingling, Kranti felt an urge to straighten them. To him, the entire area felt tiresome with the cemented steps and walls covered with a thick layer of mud, slimy and relentless, while a heavy air waited to be pushed down by rain.

A newly opened restaurant, 'Shyam Bhojnalaya', displayed in bold letters, caught Kranti's attention. His father would often bring them to similar kinds of restaurants while he demanded for a meal at the then famous Nandan hotel. The steep slope of stairs, still adorned with mango leaves and flowers, once tender, now brittle, bothered Kranti. It was the living nostalgia of celebration, of a new start, the story of every middle class household.

After waiting for half an hour, a bus arrived, and the driver honked to signal its start. Kranti, lacking the dexterity of other passengers, boarded last. Finding no other seat, he sat next to a man reeking heavily of betel and slipped his bag between his legs. Stiff with unease, he clenched the handle in front with one hand and his bag with another. The engine screeched loudly as the bus jerked to a start. Outside, he could see the red flag fluttering from the top of Nepali Mandir. Kranti prayed for Mridula.

The bus further crossed Fancy Bazaar, where an open market was bustling with makeshift stalls outside the closed concrete shops. Faux leather handbags hung on ropes; heaps of jackets were visible, and atop them was a placard stating their price—200 rupees, and pyjamas for fifty. The market was stretched up to the centre of the road. Buying and busy haggling for a price, the people didn't mind the encroachment for a day. *Ma would have said we don't need any of these,* he thought.

'*Bhoyanok* (terrifying) accident,' the person sitting next to Kranti said. He nodded and tried to focus on the road in front. The bus went upwards on a road that seemed to move no further—a free fall offered to everyone. As the bus reached the top end of the road and Kranti waited for the bus to fall, his phone rang and Anchal's photo blinked on the screen. Smiling, head inclined towards the right, a sharp bob cut accentuating her jaw line, and a tender smile—probably for the photographer. In the background were the snow-covered Alps. It was a picture from their Switzerland trip that they'd taken last year for their anniversary. Anchal wished to see the Himalayas, while Kranti fantasized about Egypt. So, they had gone to Europe. They had returned satisfied with the charm of the new. Kranti was especially pleased to strike out four countries from his bucket list in a single tour.

Kranti's list was an ever-growing one that accumulated memories of fulfilled desires—the desires that grew, the growth that never ended, the end he couldn't reach, and the destination he hadn't found yet.

Almost an hour past the phone call, Kranti still fiddled with his phone while the person on his side snored. The bus lulled everyone to sleep. Tiredness, fear, and anticipation about tomorrow cradled them all in their arms.

Much to Kranti's irritation, the conductor switched on the blue lights. Drawing up the curtains, he further curtailed the view of the road which Kranti was beginning to like. Yellow blobs of light tore through the thick layer of night, illuminating a small section of the road for a moment before moving ahead, the emptiness filled by the engine's thrumming as the bus sped into deep darkness.

The conductor then checked each passenger. Adding to Kranti's ire, he later took out a sheet from the top cabinet and spread it on the aisle next to Kranti's seat, a temporary bed for his night's sleep.

As the night subdued to complete silence and blue light filled the empty space, Kranti also fell asleep.

'Why don't you get out of my house?'

'It's my house too.'

'No, it's not.'

Deuta pushed Kranti out of the main door. His red stained teeth, betel leaves between them, were ready to tear him apart in case his son revolted.

Kranti found himself lying at the station, face down, knees bent. He felt like a toddler who was trying to crawl. The train was whistling now. It was to leave soon. 'I don't want to go, Ma. Why don't you stop me?' Kranti cried while his mother stood silent. Her face young, doe-eyed. She neither blinked nor spoke. A statue, still and stern. The train pulled Kranti inside, its flaccid hands cupping him inside their coach. It was sticky and slimy; Kranti wanted to puke, but couldn't. He wasn't allowed to. So, he gulped down his vomit, while those hands caressed him. He cried and struggled to get free. And then, all of a sudden, those gigantic metal hands threw him out on the platform. As the train started to leave the station, it closed its doors and slowly turned into a blurry red, its blue turning into a haze of smoke.

As he looked around, he saw Ma standing where he'd left her. Mridula was by her side now. They had aged. Ma, wrinkled, was still wide-eyed and unsmiling. To her left stood Mridula. She, too, had grown. This wasn't the Mridula Kranti knew; she had changed. She didn't have her high ponytail, not even the frill frock, and she was wearing the same mekhela sador as Ma. She wasn't smiling either. Kranti went to them, crawling, his shirt dripping slime, his shorts torn, but they wouldn't give him their hand. He couldn't get up; he needed to get up; he wanted to walk. He must walk; he had to.

'You had that dream again?'

'I am always alone in these dreams. You don't even help me. Why?' Kranti asked.

'If it was my dream, I would have,' Mridula replied, smiling. 'Do you also get scary dreams?'

'Always.'

Kranti and Mridula were sitting on the stairs leading to the veranda. Nearby, a small river gushed in urgency. They could hear the sound of water hitting the stones and the birds flocking in for their pick of small fish. During rainy days, they would often go and float their paper boats in it, sometimes even dumping the leftovers of Kranti's tiffin. *Food wasn't to be wasted,*

Deuta had warned them. And the river, like always, often came to his rescue.

The house was connected to a patch of grassy land via a thin bamboo bridge, which was essentially four whole bamboos tied together across an open ditch. They could see the game of seven stones being played there, with Kranti's sisters, Kuki and Tapani, defending a pile of flat stones on top of each other, their wobbly pillar of happiness. The opposite team, with Diganta in the lead, was getting ready to hit the pillar. Mridula and Kranti had boycotted the game, calling it unrefined.

Mridula often played *Kith-Kith*, though. It was a game she would win invariably. Leftover pieces of chalks from the classroom were often put to good use in making the eight boxes. Mridula would always carry her flattened stone for the game, landing it in the exact box she preferred. Holding her breath, she would chant 'kith-kith' and hop on a drawn box, or two boxes at the same time, and cover up the eight boxes faster than anyone at school. A kith-kith champion, she hid it from Kranti. Only if she knew that the game wasn't local but a global one, the one which supposedly originated in the streets of Rome, dating back to the seventeenth century. Only if she knew, she would have told Kranti about its other names—Hopscotch, Paandi, Kunte Bille, Tokkudu Billa, Khane, Ekhat-Dukhat. With even a single name different from theirs, she would have gotten his approval too.

3

Dreams and memories, alike or lookalike?

Do memories make dreams or dreams decide memory?

Recipe for tomorrow's thought, Mridula concluded as she lay exhausted from the journey.

Should a memory be only about a physical event, the kind that I could experience even outside my mind? But the memory determining the course of my life originated from a dream I had. Remembering dreams should be counted as a memory too, she thought as tried to curl up on a coarse mattress under an over-washed sheet in a hotel she had checked in a few hours ago.

But my favourite memory of him was not to dream about him, but the dream I had about him. Does having a physical, tangible past make a memory valid? Has a memory ever been bona fide? She questioned herself as she covered the bedsheet and two curiously puffed pillows under the blanket, her futile fight with the dampness and smell. A smell that was as incessant as the rain outside her window.

Memories delineated the life Mridula led; cluttered experiences stitched together. Experience, memory, and thoughts—maybe a hint of imagined reality. Not for her. She had been drunk on memories long enough to erase the doubt. When memories lurked around influencing actions, the line ought to be insubstantial. A handmade cloth ball rolling over a dented road.

Now laying on her bed, slowly internalising the room where she was to stay the night, Mridula hoped for a happier tomorrow. Tomorrow—a day that would soon be etched in her memory, like the smell of home food. Familiarity reigning over taste.

Half asleep, on the threshold of consciousness, in the waking capacity to have a dream of her choice, she chose memories to make a dream for tonight. A needed distraction from the reality that was crashing on her.

Her mind wavered to the green pastures; she marvelled at the curves of those hillocks. She always had. Flatness revolted her, land's, and hers. *Let it be tonight's dream*, she decided. *Today is the night of memories. Memories that bring smiles,* she told herself.

Eyelids heavy with the day's journey, hidden tears and hurried goodbyes waited for the lullaby of dreams. Mridula closed them to complete darkness, awaiting images of her choice.

Smiling, she looked at the turf, its blinding greenery, vast and barren with no flowers to bloom. Soon, a set of block heels marched ahead, crushing the clueless grass in a moment while setting them free the next. Toenails, painted in red, peeped out of the black leatherette straps. Hopping over a puddle, she pulled the man walking on her left. With her right thumb, she brushed aside a leech from her face. A thunderous pull, with gentle intention, of course. She took him everywhere, to every piece of land she had walked on as a child, not knowing then that one day she would bring him, the man of her life, to the same pastures, under the shed of the same Neem tree. The man, who now stood beside her, smiled, approving her excitement.

She showed him the tree, where once sat Puhor, her neighbour's two-year-old nuisance-cum-prodigy, musical to his parents, ear-splitting to everyone else. Fitting perfectly on its curved branch, he sat swinging his legs. The branch, with its dried rind, was flaking out in parts. The tree still stood strong with its sturdy trunk and coarse bark of faded brown. She gave a nostalgic smile. At the top were dense mazes of branches loaded with leaves, aged and young, faded and fresh green. The sight pleased her.

She used to often caress its rugged bark, sometimes pulling red ants out of its holes, letting their delicate body dance-walk over the curves of her palm, eventually leaving them at the main gate, a white wooden slab holding together a disintegrating bamboo fence. A stream of red ants was still encircling the hole, making time stand still.

She took him to the tree which bore jackfruits, flavourful as she was often told. It was overloaded with ovate leaves mostly matured to dark green, while a few showed goldish onsets of aging. That tree, because of which teenage boys, oozing their characteristic rogue, always raging, would climb up, devouring ripe fruits with their bare hands and dropping the remains onto her lawn, their legs dangling from the branches. The sight of them all but one nauseated her. These boys would not ask, but straight away enter her home, asserting their ownership on the tree, extending it on her. A careless comment or loud singing or just faces peeking behind the windowpane. A slap seen, birthing laughter at the tears. Fatty written on the wall, a wall she had to wash and leftover jackfruits she would be tasked to clean. She didn't like those boys, she never did, she reminded herself and took her mind off to the mango tree.

Tonight is the night of memories, memories that bring smiles, she told herself again. It was not for the memories that hurt, even now.

So, she dreamt of the mango tree.

The mango tree which was behind the kitchen pleased her with its swing and memories of laughter. To its left, a garden flourished. Happy green over a grumpy soil. An unkempt one, but with a lot of vegetables, where butterflies would hover and so would the bees. Occasionally snakes, too. She would think of snakes, but tonight was not the time. She left them there, in the garden, hidden amid the bushes, slithering to their burrow, hissing as they always did.

Appearance is a sly thing, Mridula thought.

From there they moved further, crossing the rest of the wall. They were again on the front lawn, behind her veranda, where the wooden railing rested, painted in blue. 'I would lean on these railings and watch people taking evening walks and children playing there,' she said, pointing to the open field in front of her house. She could never go and play with them. Why?

Tonight was not the time to discuss, she reminded her dozing self.

Shifting her gaze from the railing to the main door, she decided to take him in. But they were stopped from entering. A woman appeared at the door. Bare feet firm on the floor, slightly apart and facing outwards, arms crossed over the chest, and with a slightly nudged chin, she assessed their worth. When a swift wind hustled the chequered tunic that hung loosely over a protruding stomach, the grey shine of her unblinking eyes wrinkled with an abrupt smile. She was amused with the mirroring that the woman saw in front. A slice of past foretelling the future.

Avoiding all conflict, because tonight wasn't the one for any, Mridula turned around and showed him the place where there used to be a tree. Its shed was a remedy for her summer afternoons; she would pull cane chairs and sit under it, leaves shielding her from the bright sky as she gazed in admiration, her attention often shifting from its branches to passers-by to comics under her textbooks.

'But it fell one day. I had no place to sit since then, no shed,' she said.

Mridula woke up again to find herself under the shed she had created for herself. A temporary shield from what was soon to fall upon her. For a second, she searched for him in the flicker of the night bulb. A wardrobe with a loose door stood empty except for a multi-coloured bag; a blinking red light asserted the position of the TV. Next to it, a wooden coffee table held a pile of dirty dishes. The chair next to it looked naked in its neatness. Everything was exactly as it had been, but Priyom was not there. She couldn't bring him into her waking reality. His presence ceased with the end of her dreams.

'What's the time?' she said aloud, talking to none but herself.

The wall-clock showed 3 a.m. as the minute-hand took a slow walk from eleven to twelve, while the hour-hand stood fixed at three, resolute, sure of its position in the world of clocks. Yet, looking at the watch, Mridula trembled. She, who wasn't sure of her existence in his world. The second-hand, similar to her in a way, was faltering too, in a painstaking run, without any notice of the minute- and hour-hand. Their presence was irrelevant to its run of panic.

After a while, she got up and pushed the window open. Its creak silenced the clock for a moment. The road in front was deserted. The streetlights didn't work, but their silver poles glistened in the moonlight. She came back to her bed and fell asleep again, unaware that she was to leave soon.

4

On the *kutcha* road leading to the last stop, the bus, as if exasperated after an arduous task, stomped loudly before coming to a halt. Its audible vexation had woken Kranti long before his fellow passenger, who now puffed out a thick layer of putrid morning breath, followed by regular snores. Kranti pushed off his sleepy head that once again landed on his shoulder.

He was flabbergasted by the ten-hours journey in a bus as unsteady as the path ahead. Its seats of coarse foam and torn leatherette added to the reasons why Kranti couldn't get a sound sleep and a dream that he hadn't been able to stop. *Can dreams ever be stopped?* he often pondered. No one could, he believed.

What are dreams? Kranti wondered. He wanted to walk inside his dream and ask for clarifications. He wanted to change them, those haunted situations in which he was always a puppet in the hands of people who merged into each other. They often left him feeling helpless, a feeling he detested the most. But he knew it was impossible to be fully aware of his subconscious, so he stopped trying to understand them as well. He had been learning about ways to stay unaffected by his dreams. Anchal also insisted him to see the therapist again. He deemed this suggestion unnecessary.

Once out of the bus, the morning breeze relaxed him a bit. The view was not extraordinary for residents, but years of absence had made them alluring to Kranti's senses. The place had a fluent beauty at a time when cities were making efforts to make nature look conveniently natural.

The bushes, unkempt and unaltered, were just the way they would have been even if no one was admiring them. Tempting curves of road, the rustic lure of mud over it, the sound of wind and the rustle of leaves. Green mixed with brown, a happy blue sky covering them all.

On his left side, two more buses came and parked themselves. Behind him was a small bus stand, two feet tall cement walls on three sides, covered with a tin roof and a square opening in front. Unlike Guwahati, here the floor wasn't concrete, but a subdued turf with wild growth towards the back side. Yet, if looked at from afar, they would appear like a velvety carpet; a carpet of happy green, fresh and bright, not tired like the green he often saw, mostly on the sides of highways.

Behind the bus stop, he could also see mountains far away, seeming close. Below them were villages on the verge of getting submerged, seeming distant.

Kranti walked out, thinking of how to start his search. *Should I first go to a hotel, sleep for a few hours, and then start? Or should I go to the camp first and submit the details?* He decided to do the latter. Camp, he came to know, was not very far from where he stood. Only a maximum of half an hour of walking.

Priding in its past while trying to live with its uneventful present, Maajorghat was a seemingly satisfied town with its residents quite content with their life of seclusion, until now. Seclusion not from the world but from the advancement that appeared to hypnotise everyone but them. While cities were growing intimidatingly, imposing themselves like a demanding sibling, it cuddled in the arms of nature, snuggling between the high of the mountains, enticed by the curves of a river that flowed over its red turf where rice seedlings veered with the breeze, their grip on its watery ground still firm.

Maajorghat kept its residents warm. Houses with tin roofs and some with thatch marked human settlement, while the chipped walls of the railway station and bamboo benches at the bus stand received commuters. Nothing much ever happened in this peacefully hidden town, except for exchanging news of death and birth at the local market, meeting the ailing at the hospital, and greeting the Doctor Saar who would invariably grunt in reply, getting glued to their own or neighbour's television every evening as soon as the electricity came, for it hardly did. Occasional bouts of friction did happen between locals and travellers who would halt for a few hours before embarking on their journey. But this peace didn't stay for long. Now the town had witnessed an accident that would snatch the very peace it boasted of.

The accident of twisted tracks, suspended train, and many lives under them. The Maajorghat-Guwahati Express derailed, and coaches fell off the bridge. On a twisted track, a train lost its balance. As it lurched, some of the coaches tumbled down the once-sturdy bridge. They undulated on the beats of death for a second and then stopped deep in mud like a crushed cup thrown out of the train window.

Derailment was like a violent horror movie played in fast forward, every emotion laid out, every kind of bloodshed, screaming and pleading shown in just a few minutes. In a span of those few minutes, the once-smooth and robust coaches lay broken; within those minutes, many journeys ended and were never to be started again. With a thud and a groan, some lost their limbs, some their families, and some their lives.

He wasn't prepared to witness an accident of this gravity. Kranti, too, was becoming one with Maajorghat. He too was imbibing a transition he hadn't known until now.

5

It was a sunny morning with a slightly sultry breeze. A vast spotless blue with no trace of clouds. Looking at the innocent sky, it was hard to believe that just the previous day these clouds had poured heavily on a duteous bridge, shattering a mammoth train.

Maya took a taxi to Maajorghat, a long journey that would cost her ten times more than a bus ticket which she would have taken had she arrived at any other time. The car slowly plodded on the narrow road with vehicles parked on both sides. A check post on her left, a tea-seller hunching under an umbrella and a few stand-alone houses, their conical tin roofs reflecting back the sun were a few sights on her path to reclamation.

Settled, she looked out, the sun now subdued into a dull and faded ball by the tinted glass of her taxi's window. She loved travelling alone, sitting all by herself, and looking at the road ahead of her.

Travelling gave Maya a sense of constant movement, a reminder that nothing was stagnant. Nor could it be. Travel to mere distance of a few meters were enough. Even walking to neighbour's house used to be enough whenever she sensed tension at home. With a change of scene, she would hope for a change in the situation she was in. Later, travel took prominence. The Goa trip after her first break-up. The day she had received her boyfriend's message to end the relationship, she had planned a tour with her friends. It was her way to restart, and had been since then. Although travel for her had not always been physical. When she failed her entrance exam, she'd distanced herself from her dream college and decided to study in Bangalore.

Travel was her most acceptable way to recover from disappointments. Yet, she couldn't stay put even in places she ran away to, mountains and oceans alike. She, who liked the sea, also ran away from it. Because the ocean didn't end at the end she saw. She deserted the beach where she walked, talking loudly because there was no one to hear. She would speak her heart but wasn't sure if she wanted the sea to hear. So, she would walk back, leaving the sea and her sound behind, to the dancing lights and the music of distancing.

Journeys, for some time, offered a place in the near future where she could hide. But this day was different. Today, her thoughts twisted into a maze as she moved forward, getting hazier with each passing minute. Sitting straight, as though vigilant, she attentively gazed ahead, but her fingers fiddled with the strap of her bag. It was then that she saw an ambulance. She assumed it to be coming from Maajorghat. She thought of those who were affected, and about those two whom she knew.

Who got hurt the most in this accident? she thought again. *The poor, of course. It is they who suffer the most, in every situation*, she concluded. It's us, the poor and the omnipresent middle class, that travel by train.

Although it was not always 'we' for her. On any other day, Maya would not have thought of it with the same emotional intensity. Reading only the headlines in her phone to get updates of the world, she had often tried to feel the pain while keeping the barriers untouched, of comfort and ease. Now sitting in her car, Maya thought about those bleeding faces and amputated bodies, a crowd of walking corpses. Learning about the accident, she had shivered with the possibility of being among them. The inability to find out where her parents were terrified her.

The driver switched on the media player, which instead of easing the silence, amplified it, as though taking cues from her mind. 'My favourite song,' he told her. It was Lata Mangeshkar's *Aye mere watan ke logon*, an indispensable asset on Independence and Republic days. None of them were anytime soon, though. The song sent her mind to wander again. Maya thought of soldiers, of the fights in and out. She worried for the country, for it had, and would have to face so much. She felt sad for the dying soldiers, for everyone grieving. She felt sad for the river she was crossing then, its stagnation and its everlasting struggle to reach its home, for the ocean that waited for its arrival, for the old man she saw waiting on the footpath right after the river, probably fighting hunger, clear from his torn apron and tattered shoes. Maya felt miserable, but soon her focus shifted when she looked into the rear mirror.

She saw herself in her bright mauve lipstick and kohl-lined eyes. She looked into her own eyes, and she couldn't feel bad. She smiled.

Now, searching for her headphone, she felt the need to calm herself. 'I am calm and peaceful,' she muttered. *This place looks nice; it makes me want to smile. No, that's not right. But it's okay to smile even now.* She was trying to find reasons to lighten her mood while meandering through the perpetual guilt she often felt. Every thought of happiness was loaded with reasons to not be. Even as a child, she would often feel it wasn't appropriate for her to be happy when her parents weren't. She would feel awkward if she laughed too loudly. She wouldn't sing her favourite song, even in the privacy of her room, and wouldn't eat if she craved any dish. She couldn't dance freely, even at her farewells. It was difficult for her to let herself loose even when there was no responsibility in sight. A need to be careful and vigilant of upcoming issues persisted in her. Fulfilling even a simple desire felt like she was pampering herself. She would struggle, and so she would try further to make herself happy using affirmations and often, distractions.

There could be hopes too, even at a place like this, she reasoned further. This reminded her of the series on happiness index which was suggested to her by a colleague in her office. Of her Ma too, who used to believe in thinking positive, especially about others. Although, Maya wasn't sure if her mother included herself in those thoughts too. She had seen Ma being happy for others, but never heard her uttering a wish for herself. *Ma and I should watch it together*, she concluded.

'Hmm... hmmmm... *dehliz pe...*' She played a Bollywood song and started humming it, but soon went back to her internal soliloquy.

Sitting with her legs up, she looked at her shoes pushed under the front seat. *I should have bought the orange one, they looked better.* But they were uncomfortable, she remembered. She then shifted her focus on her walking style, always straight and in measured steps, never a hop in between. Kevin admired it, while she found his walks better aligned and more confident. Thinking of him, she felt a pang of loss. She had been finding him less interested in her for a few months now. She thought of his girlfriend or 'good-friend'. They would be spending more time together now that she was away. She hated her.

Why did I carry so many clothes? I could have brought a small suitcase or just a backpack. Her attention shifted when the luggage in the car's boot bumped forward. She then noticed the driver, who was looking at her through the rear-view mirror. She felt uncomfortable but ignored it.

'Uh oh … oh ah … oh ah … ya … so amazing how this world was mad…' she hummed again, this time a little loudly in an effort to display confidence. She loved this song, it made her feel strong. She often dreamt that Kevin would sing this song for her—one of her many unfulfilled expectations from him.

Ma is strong, way too strong even for her own good, Maya suddenly thought of her mother as she felt those words were written for her. 'She will protect you like a child, that woman…' She was trying to find a trace of hope in the song she was listening to.

'Don't underestimate … strength of a woman.' She hummed the songs more openly now. For a brief moment, Maya forgot the reason for her journey—the relationships she had come to search for.

Wilful amnesia—a habit she'd mastered over the years.

6

Kranti ordered tea at a kiosk positioned next to the bus stand. '*Dokan*,' he said out loud, pronouncing the Assamese word for 'shop' in an animated attempt at familiarity. On its white wall, ice cream's availability was written in bold letters, with colourful ice lollies drawn next to it. The bottom of the wall was covered in pamphlets, illegible unless one bent down to read. A boy in his early teens came out of the kiosk and handed Kranti the milk tea, his fingers away from the protruding rim of the hot conical glass, giving a point of hold to Kranti. Oversized clothes, a hand-me-down from his owner or someone similar, hung loosely on him. He dragged his feet as he walked back. The strap of one of his rubber slippers was held together with a safety pin, a quick fix to life's everyday problems.

Looking at the boy, Kranti associated himself. He too had lived in scarcity and won over it, he thought, not missing a chance to become a Mahatma of his own world, although his wasn't a dire condition.

Kranti still resented not getting the toy of his choice, or a ranger bicycle. Instead, he'd received the basic model of Hero cycle. His entire collection was filled with the ones his father bought. Those were the cheaper toys, inferior to what his friends had, something he knew even then. There were no new clothes, except on birthdays and a handful of festivals. Clothes were like a lineage, passed on from the eldest of the family to the youngest.

From father's family, from mother's side, the exchange went on. The exchange grew further, from clothes to books to bikes, till Kranti found a way to erase his disparity.

He perceived his upbringing to be so underprivileged that he hated it, often when sitting on the leather seats of his friends' cars or in Anchal's arms, his girlfriend back then. He saw traces of his deprived life in his sisters who could neither strike a meaningful conversation with his friends nor speak fluent English. He saw its signs in his father, whose reluctance to shell out money lent him an education loan of ten years, and in his mother, who had forcibly put a *tilak*, which left a red mark on his forehead after wiping it off—the one he couldn't hide under his mortarboard.

Putting his empty glass on top of the dirty dishes piled in a round plastic tub, Kranti started walking on the road that led straight to the camp. A narrow road covered in stone grit, almost dry, seemed to run straight into the blue mountains. Their hazy shapes were soon to turn green or to be blurred completely. Although the clouds above threatened to dampen the road sooner than later, a subdued sun was fighting its way out. On the ground, a patch of grass was priding in its dysfunctional growth around a shallow pit. Kranti admired its similarity to an exotic vase, the kind that Anchal would have liked to keep.

Within a few minutes of walking, a light drizzle started. Almost enjoying the soft sprinkle on the yellowish day, Kranti walked without an umbrella. With his bag on his shoulder and hands in his pockets, he glimpsed around when houses began to appear, a hamlet on the borders of the town. A faint smell of cooking, clear sounds of laughter. A community water tap surrounded by children, each with their buckets, with some busy splashing water while others foaming themselves for a bath by the tap. The sight disgusted Kranti, more so for its familiarity.

Memories flashed again—memories of filling water at the public tap in five litre oil cans while other children brought shiny, silvery buckets of aluminium. There was a bright blue one with a cover on it. On the first day, its owner had smiled throughout his time at the water tap amid the applause and sugary words of everyone around. Kranti hated that. That feeling of inferiority in front of their ironed clothes and new buckets. He had then wished for everyone's bucket to break. He had also protested against the chores given to him and tried to get it reassigned to his sisters. Still he was sent till they got a water connection, when a tap was built outside the house, after many years.

Frowning, Kranti crossed the hamlet and came across an open area. It had been more than thirty minutes of walking. He could see the camp now. A miniscule speck of blue in the midst of wild green. It was then that a strange smell flowed into him.

The odour of damp soil, its sweet musty smell replaced by one of slow decay. The smell felt sinister, as though just by inhaling it Kranti would transit into an obnoxious world. He felt an immediate urge to block its arrival, to stop it right away. His body tensed, as if getting ready to fight and prevent it from entering.

The intuition of its wrath was indisputable. But what could Kranti do? How could he fight that intangible something, with no time to prepare? A presence that wafted through the air, flew inside him, touching his every part, slipping inside the hidden corners of his mind, into his body, mixing with his blood. A presence that was nothing more than a smell, if he had to explain.

Kranti covered his nose, but the smell grew stronger as he walked ahead. It was coming from his right, from a vast open patch of land. He followed the smell, an unbearable pull. He could see freshly dug earth, heaps of soil laid out in the open, still damp. The black lumps of soil mounted with a gap of a few metres between each. Above him, the sun sought refuge behind the clouds, while its rays, once golden, were now losing themselves in the mounds of murkiness. Under the distressed sunlight, above the haggard earth, were the birds in haste, hovering around. Kranti took off his sunglasses and looked ahead.

He had come to find his sister, whom he could take back and talk to, about his life, and maybe about hers as well. But what he found instead was a line of wooden stretchers, with bodies wrapped in white cotton. The decay was apparent from the patches on them. A few men stood around, their bodies drooped, less with fatigue, more with the enormity of the task assigned to them. Kranti became rigid; his stomach churned, and his hands clenched in a fist. He craved for a smoke, to hold a cigarette in his hands. To replace this stench with the familiar smell of tobacco.

As he stood there, his mind went back to the picture of an old man he had seen many years ago. It was featured in a photography magazine. The man in the picture sat hunched, showing his long nails to the camera. Kranti couldn't not take his eyes off a particular finger with an extended, overgrown nail, long dead since its birth, now rotting in its present state, curving inward, yellow and thick, filled with grime, merging with the cracks of his skin. This was a sight as revolting as that.

Kranti was standing in front of the burial ground, dotted in white. Stupefied, he started walking towards the camp.

7

Probe into Maajorghat-Guwahati Express Derailment

Maajorghat: A railway committee has been set up to probe into the recent Maajorghat-Guwahati Express derailment. Sabotage is being suspected after a piece of iron was obtained from the bridge. The committee will probe sabotage as well as other angles. The five-member committee is headed by Mr B.S. Sarma, Senior Divisional Safety Manager. The panel comprises senior officers from various railway departments.

'We are waiting for the committee's final conclusion. Based on the outcome, appropriate action will be taken,' a senior railway officer said.

There are also reports on the negligence of the driver and the gang-man, hinting at their lack of training to act in emergency situations. They are also being questioned by the committee. 'Faulty track and the overused bridge can also be a reason,' a senior railway official said, who wished to remain anonymous.

Maajorghat-Guwahati Express (Train number 011188) derailed near the Maajorghat station in Assam at 5.30 a.m. IST. Six sleeper coaches and three AC coaches were derailed, killing fifty people and injuring 210 passengers. The train, carrying 890 passengers, was running at the speed of eighty-two kilometres per hour at the time of accident.

SECTION 3
THE SEARCH

1

Maya had come directly to the accident site. An overstuffed suitcase stood next to her.

It wasn't a planned trip. She didn't have the time to think about what to take and what not, to pack and unpack again, to find space and fill in an extra pair of socks, to take out those extra bottles of sanitizers and replace them with one, to rearrange the clothes—making rolls of t-shirts, double folding the pants and counting the pair of underwear, keeping two extra pairs in any case, to search online about on things she could buy on the trip and keep empty bags accordingly. She didn't do any of these.

Time was so limited that she'd simply taken the essentials and dumped them in her suitcase, unsure of how many days she was to search. She'd taken some more clothes and added them to her suitcase till it was full to its capacity. Her favourite suitcase, the one she wouldn't lend even to Ma. It was old now, her sky blue suitcase, the one she never cleaned, the one she bought for her first ever trip, which proudly displayed stamps of all her tours until now. Her faint attempt at adventure. Her constant trial to live a life other than her own. A leather sling bag, camel coloured, hung at her side.

Paying the bill, she looked at the taxi leaving. It sped on the dirt track ahead, splashing stagnant water on the passers-by, who were looking with contempt at the car and then at Maya, as though blaming her for the driver's recklessness.

She turned away, aware that their glances still followed her. The place looked like a calm paradise, barring the discomposure that a certain broken bridge added to it. The mountains were clear from where she stood. Hazy blue pyramids from a world afar. The sky too appeared clear, but the air felt heavy, like an aftermath of an insistent crying, tears dried, but breath still slow and uneven.

The bridge lay in front of her. *How could such a sturdy looking bridge give in so easily?* Maya had been thinking a lot about it. Somewhere in the midst of using its whole strength, it must have emptied itself into a complete void, its porosity giving away to its death, taking even the ones depending on it. Or, was it because of its dependence on the system? Was it the flash flood that couldn't be controlled, or a rusted bridge that was conveniently ignored?

A bridge, a system, or a family, everything and everyone dissipates eventually. So did floods, pain, and her search, she was soon to learn.

Below the bridge, she noticed those fateful coaches, sunk in a pool of water, vegetation scattered on their side. Unsettled sediments had turned the water to a dark grey mess. One coach had broken into two parts. One part on top of the other, windows submerged. Maya shuddered thinking of the passengers inside that coach. She noticed a few swollen bodies being taken out.

Death came ugly to them. For some, it came with dignity, in a peaceful sleep; for some with courage, a fight with chronic illness and pain; some with age, graceful. But for those inside that coach, death didn't allow any dignity, no decent farewell, no one to send them off.

Maya walked down to the ground where bodies were still being taken out on stretchers and carried away in ambulances. A group of men walked symmetrically, their clothes smeared with mud, their hands holding stretchers. They frequently emerged out of the green mass, and with the same promptness vanished into the same pit. Their faces gave away no emotion except the dread they carried, and might carry all their life.

The air was filled with a strong smell—decaying flesh, medicines mixed with a stream of rotten food, vomit, and blood. A mix of wail and anger. Wails like that of a yelping dog whose puppies were being snatched away, the kind that would penetrate ears, hitting one hard. Cries that would turn one deaf, not for its loudness but for the pain it carried, leaving one numb.

Maya saw a passenger without a hand—a large blob of blood on his shoulder, spilling more blood. She then saw one kid lying on the ground and gaping at the sky, head straightened, pupils rolled up, the blankness in them filling the white around. As she turned to see others, the kid's face was covered with the cloth her body was wrapped in. A few more bodies, mangled to an extent that they had to be covered and tied with rope, were laid on the ground. News reporters took pictures, relatives keenly looked, and reluctantly moved. Maya couldn't go nearer.

A man walked by. He had bruises on his swollen hand and kept asking people about his daughter and son. He came to Maya and asked her if she had seen a teenage boy wearing a blue t-shirt and beige pants and a girl in green frock. Before she could reply, he turned and asked another man about them. Delusional, he went on murmuring their names.

On the road, an ambulance stood. Helpers with high visibility jackets were taking those who needed immediate medical assistance. Around it were squashed shoes, a pair of slippers, a dropped bag, a muddied *dupatta*, and a torn shawl. The ground showed bloodied proof of death, an abduction not even God could reverse. So, they all departed to the world that no one owned.

As the rescue efforts continued, many people stood to watch it. Some came out of curiosity, while some came to search. A few just walked out of their houses to see, while others travelled for hours with a hope to return soon. Some faltered, devoid of any will, while some trembled and ran in a swivel-eyed anxiety. Maya, too, was one among them.

I must have a systematic approach to my search if I want to succeed, she thought, although unsure of where to begin. Turning back, she looked at the dirt track and the approaching crowd avoiding the clogged pits of water, the same road where a while back her taxi had driven away, splashing sludge on everyone around. A blatant show of apathy by a car that was washed every day on those whose clothes couldn't be.

'Don't just stand here!' an agitated voice startled her. 'Move aside, you are blocking the road,' said another and stomped off.

'*Didi*, come to this side,' a young man in his early twenties guided Maya to the side of the road. His left hand was covered in white bandages, a blood patch slowly widening on it like a drop of paint on plain paper. He was unmindful of it. His eyes, thoughtful, were searching, seeing past Maya as he spoke to her. His hair was tangled with dust and grease. He held a smile. He informed her that he was one of the travellers.

'Oh good! Then you can help me. Please,' Maya said, but soon added a sober tone, befitting the gravity of travelling in that train. She spoke with an urgency, holding on to her diminishing hopes, as if he could give out the key to the place of her parents' hiding.

The young man nodded while staring at the void ahead. He seemed to be in a vacuum, the one in which he was stable, even if uncomfortable. Maya looked around and saw people struggling to find their way. A man was trying to clear the way for an ambulance to move but failed every time someone advanced towards it, asking him to open the door to check who was inside. He, irritated, refused to open, his curly hair fluttering against the wind, his expensive looking clothes smothered with dirt and blood.

'Not everyone got hurt. Right? I am searching for my parents. Maybe you saw them?' Maya spoke after a minute.

'Yes, lots of people are fine. I was in S7. That coach didn't fall. It tilted, though. I am sorry,' he added, as though guilty to be alive.

As she asked him for more details, he cut her interrogation short and asked if she wanted to go anywhere. Without waiting for her reply, he informed her that she could go to camp, or even the station, and signalled for an auto rickshaw. Temporary camps were being set up on the outskirts of the town, Maya too knew this. The details were all over the news.

An auto rickshaw with a customized exterior stopped in front of them. Maya found it garish. There were blue floral patterns around the windshield, with multi-coloured block prints on each side. The fabric doors showcased a cat playing a guitar. Phrases like 'Horn Please' and 'Too Fast, Too Fures' were scrawled on the mud flaps. This error, 'fures' instead of 'furious', would've made her laugh under any other circumstance—but not today. It was much bigger than the three-seater auto rickshaws. It was a Vikram Auto—a name that often baffled Maya. *Why do we call a vehicle Vikram?! To signify its masculinity?* She drifted into her world of ruminations, their frequency usually increasing with the gravity of the situation around her. She found the auto rickshaw perfect for the mood she was in, a lurid ode to a hideous time.

As the auto started with a jarring sound of the engine, the rolled-up flap of the backside window opened and fluttered. On it was a red heart with a white flying pigeon, a yellow rose between its beaks. Inside, Maya sat with crossed arms, anxious fingers holding on to the familiarity of her own body. She wanted to reach the camp before nightfall.

Maya sat alert, ready to jump out if the driver took the wrong route, even when there was no way for her to know if it. There were no sideboards to direct them and no streetlights to illuminate the area. All she could see were long bushes, fresh from the recent rain, surrounding the rutted mud road. Hanging between the knots of trust and fear, like an amulet on a black thread, she sat.

Maya was in the kitchen, light filtering through the window, her burgundy hair parted in the middle, shining like a crown of ruby. She was standing near the sink and chopping vegetables to prepare for the lunch box she had recently started taking to office.

Behind her, on the shelf, was a ceramic plate with an old Nyishi man painted inside a black circle, sitting on a bamboo stool in a white and black *pomo* (a traditional sleeveless shirt worn by the men of the Nyishi tribe). He had intense eyes and a soft smile. His head was covered in a cane hat with a hornbill beak and feather. Maya planned to hang the plate in the dining hall and kept it in the kitchen to remind herself of the task. She had found this piece at the North-east fest held recently at Palace Ground. It had been years since she had visited the place of her birth. Yet, feeling nostalgic with memories of her childhood, she had gone to the kiosk of Arunachal Pradesh. She had boasted about her connection and inquired about the recent developments in the towns she knew—Zero, Pasighat, Tezu, Namsai, Anini, Changlang, Bilat, Yingkiong, and Lumla. She had shopped for herself and her friends, especially a traditional cane hat for Kevin, which stayed in her wardrobe. He had admired the hat's coiled weaving and its boat shape and semi-elliptical centre, but citing his girlfriend's probable suspicion, he had left it with her, like every other gift she had gotten him.

Next to it stood a red speaker which Kevin had left last night. It was playing Karthik Iyer's violin composition—*Rejoicing in Raghuvamsa*, the one with which she would often begin her mornings. A classic violin piece, *Raga Kadhanakudhukalam*, a usual raga to conclude Carnatic concerts, gave her the start for the day. With each of its ebullient notes, her fingers too bounced in rhythmic excitement.

A light green bottle-gourd lay in front of her. Finely sliced onion sat in a plate next to it. On its side was the marble mortar with crushed garlic inside. It was then that the mobile rang. Keeping the bottle guard aside, now in two halves, she paced to the hall.

Her phone, attached to the charging port, was balanced on the window grill. Outside the window, on the service road, a black bitch—aptly named Kaali, was roaming around, waiting for her morning offering of four bread slices soaked in milk. She picked it up and sat on the chair nearby, upholstered in a worn-out green fabric with a detailed paisley pattern that came with the house, along with a centre table, a four-seater dining table, and a TV cabinet—one of the reasons why they'd agreed to a rent higher than their initial decision. They—Ma and her.

'Maya *beta*!'

It was a call from her mother, who was on her yearly trip to meet her brother. The time of the year Ma looked forward to, the time of the year she couldn't repeat more than once. Dependency on the host was a key influence here. She'd called to inform that she was travelling to Guwahati, to visit Kamakhya

Devi temple. The one Maya had visited when she'd turned a year old. A family trip. At least she believed so.

The temple was important to her mother, for reasons Maya didn't bother to know. Yet, when she pointed the fact out, she could hear her mother smile. A smile of contentment to know that her daughter remembered her likes—clearly not a frequent occurrence in their lives. Preferences changed with place, and for many years now Ragigudda Hanuman Temple had turned into their favourite. For Ma, it was because God listened to her. For Maya, it was easier than taking charge of her mercurial faith, and calmer than confronting her mother over it.

Tips were shared on how to reuse the leftovers, to keep the milk in the fridge before leaving for office, to eat and sleep on time, reminders on keeping the house locked, to ask the maid to get groceries and treat her well, to order online if needed, to check blood pressure and sugar levels more often than usual, to drink only bottled water. Each ushering the other towards a management of her affairs, their preferred way of living. The call continued in its usual pattern whenever one of them was away, until Ma informed Maya about her additional trip to Itanagar. To attend the wedding of a colleague's daughter, with her husband.

'You are going with Father?' It was less of a question, more of voicing out a shock.

Maya looked at the picture that hung in front of her now, on the wall above the door leading to the dining room. In its exact centre was an old picture of her with her parents. Both young, in their late twenties, while she, a five-year-old girl with a different sock on each leg, sitting on her father's lap. Too old a picture to hang; the only picture too. Seeing it, occasionally a splash of doubt would dilute her thoughts. After all these years, why had her mother still decided to hang a reminder of her past? Maya often wondered if Ma longed for a life with her husband, or if she missed him. Believing in its improbability was the only way to end those questions.

Maya had just returned from school. She was at the door when she saw her father packing his clothes and books in huge trunks. Next to it, a canvas bed roll lay open, a mattress and a pillow resting on it. A thin blanket and a few folded bed sheets were folded and tucked into one of its sides.

She saw her mother standing stiff, a thin stream of tears trickling down her chin. The first and the last time she saw her Ma crying. She stood stiff, her left hand holding the edge of her saree in a tight fist while her right hand just hanging, as though lifeless.

Maya slowly entered, unsure of what her expected role in that situation was. Seeing her, Ma smiled and told her to freshen up and be ready for the onion pakoras she would fry soon. Father greeted her with a faint smile too, informing her of his upcoming official tour. But there was a sense of foreboding in their words. Somewhere deep down she knew he wasn't going to return. Since that day, Maya kept an eye on her mother, but maintained a distance too. She felt responsible, but wasn't sure how. Yet, she believed herself to be at fault, the reason for her mother's struggles and heartaches. It continued even when her mother had finally come to stay with her in Bangalore, a shift as sudden as the previous one.

'Haan, beta. He is staying at Barua Uncle's house,' her mother reconfirmed.

'Okay. I didn't know.' Maya then disconnected the call, feigning to be in a meeting.

'Might as well get a new family picture now,' she mumbled while looking at the frame for a while, then put the mobile back for charging before returning to the kitchen.

IndoSoul's *Boundless* had just started playing. Her heart quivered with the drums, an ongoing internal *Korappu*, just like the rhythmic interludes of Carnatic music concerts, while she peeled the skin off the bottle-gourd. Her focus unshaken and face turning pale as she nibbled on her lower lip, her fingers worked on the vegetable with enviable precision. Her mind moved away from the musical beats to the past, which she was sure Ma too didn't like.

Maya thought of the words she had to live with, words implying emotions that felt far away. Customary praises and burdensome gifts; smiles that appeared forceful. She was irked. *How can they talk now? If they had to reconcile, why did they make my life so difficult? How can they be happy now? Do they ever think of me?* She wanted to scream and shred everything around her to pieces.

Long shreds of skin mounted in a heap. She was now slicing the remaining gourd into small pieces, then smaller and much smaller. She clasped the knife, moving it with increasing speed.

She wanted to know what they talked about now. The topics of their discussion. Whether she was one of them. Whether they were telling each other everything. Were they remembering and laughing at their child?

Their child, who was now executing her parents for the situation they'd brought her up in, placing her expectation right in front. A child, grown now, still brooding over the injustice she believed she had had to face. A daughter demanding her right to be loved and cared for. Nothing in words, everything within. Soon, the slices of bottle-gourd turned into a paste. She threw the preparation into the dustbin and dropped the plates in the sink, the sound of which resonated around while she went ahead to get ready.

Kevin would be coming in with his change of clothes. She left the main door open. At times, when she was alone, he would come without any pretence of privacy. It had been a year since they'd started dating and a month of occasional living-in. Not very inclined, she had agreed for Kevin's sake when her mother went for her yearly vacation of two months. His excitement, his insistence, and then his proclaimed love for her were the reasons. *I did what any reciprocating girl would have done*, she had reasoned. About the other one who was also reciprocating to him, she didn't probe. 'I need both of you da,' he had told her, and she'd chosen to believe him.

2

Mridula walked into the hospital. It was an old, recently whitewashed building, standing alone. Stalls sold water packets, packaged fryums, and biscuits, and a few auto rickshaws waited in a queue. With open vastness of green and the diminutive stalls around it, the mere four-floored building emerged as monumental. The receptionist at the hotel suggested that she should check into the hospital first. He had called a rickshaw for her too, a voluntary act of kindness that Mridula was in half a mind to refuse. To her, kindness was a civilized form of control.

A massive French door, the glass inside the wooden frame with a finishing glossier enough to reflect her, marked the entry into the hospital. A watchman, a blue woollen cap bordering his wrinkled eyes, smiled to everyone who went in, a habit Mridula hoped he would set aside for that day. The stool on which he sat was equally aged and rickety. His one hand was on the door, another on his left knee, and his legs were between the four-legged stool. A set of six spindly legs holding themselves firmly on the floor, their fight against the doom that loomed over them.

Entering the hall, Mridula found no reception desk. A wooden table, a lone chair and an open register on top, its pages the colour of shrivelled cardamom, scribbled with names and time of entry. Finding nothing on the ground floor, she ran to the first floor.

Her heart galloped like a horse left free, the boundaries of its stable no longer binding. She was excited—sure of finding him. Yet, a fear of the unknown overwhelmed her—not a fear filled with sadness, but the anticipation before a surprise was disclosed. A fear of it turning out to be inadequate, failing her expectations.

She too was hoping for a pleasant one, hoping to find Priyom sitting on one of those side benches, waiting for her to rescue him. Rescue him from the life he led, from the person he was, from the husband he had been to her, and the kind of father he continued to be. Waiting for her to release a new life on him. A hope to see him waiting only for her, for her to claim him, to take him back—a hope she was not ready to acknowledge.

On the first floor, many people were on the benches, but not him. Some slumped on the floor too. Not him. They all had the same look of disbelief, a perennial shock looming over their faces. Everyone, including a young girl around Rimi's age, looked time-worn. Their eyes were the shape of dried pecan, dirt sticking like freckles on wrinkled skin. Nurses were bandaging their bruises right in the alley; beds were for the serious victims. Involuntarily, Mridula started praying for them.

Hospitals did bring out compassion to some extent, often making strangers wishing for each other to recover. Emotions would take a different form here. For an ailing, if known, sadness would mix with love, with a higher level of intensity, birthing tears or even words intending good. A cocktail of faith in science and God would resurface, the willingness to help others would take a paramount stage. Defying the habitual tendency, people would go and wish a stranger well.

Hospitals are indeed enigmatic, Mridula thought. She pushed herself inside the ward where new beds were brought in to accommodate patients; rot-iron cots were placed in two rows, each a few inches away from another. Saline stands, oxygen cylinders, stools mounted with medicines, a child clenching one pole of the bed, a relative standing in attention, nurses bent downwards, a doctor filling up the injection, men and women lying on makeshift beds, children on ground, a woman barely conscious, and many losing theirs.

Standing on the side of the door to ensure the least possible hindrance to the running nurses and doctors who weren't prepared for this sudden rush of patients, Mridula looked at every patient, trying to find a familiar one. Peering over others, 180-degree rotation, dazed, she searched as her hands clenched the door frame. She had seen it on the news channels but hadn't anticipated its impact to be so distinctive and soul crushing, its pain too apparent to ignore. Yet, she looked at the faces again. An attempt to end the pain, at least hers. She couldn't.

So, she stepped away from the door and inquired about the other passengers. A man in his early thirties, his clothes still carrying the grime of his life's (probably) biggest catastrophe, told her to check in the second and third floors.

She went upstairs, reigniting her hope. It was also packed in a similar way, people waiting for aid outside and inside the wards. Cries of pain, hunger, and discomfort filled the entire place. She didn't find the face she was looking for amid the ones she saw. So, she went to the third floor, her hope diminishing gradually. By now, she was mechanical, like a robot controlled by the player standing afar. Mridula went to look inside, to search within the crowd hovering around. This floor had fewer cots; some patients lay on a negligible floor mat while a relative or two squatted near them.

The hospital, with its limitations apparent, had brought everything out and put everyone to use. But still, it failed to cater to such a massive demand for medical attention. A camp was being set up to offer basic medical assistance, but till then the hospital had to accommodate all.

Finding no trace of Priyom, Mridula stopped a panic-stricken doctor. He, annoyed from being stopped on his duty, told her to check at the desk and the relief camp. Before Mridula could ask further, he walked past her, running down the stairs, covering two at a time. Mridula then searched the entire hospital once again, scanning every room and face, just to be sure. She couldn't find him.

Outside, the smell of food from stalls around reminded her that she hadn't eaten. A hawker sold lukewarm tea from a steel kettle in flimsy plastic glasses, another sold poori and a greasy curry of mixed vegetables. There were a few more, selling almost similar breakfast, each with a long queue in front. Maggi was being sold for thirty rupees a plate, and forty rupees for luci and saag, while those who couldn't afford these stalls' luxurious produce went to the ones selling white, papery chapatis and curry from tin boxes, fifteen rupees per plate.

With a maroon umbrella still shielding her head, Mridula went and sat on a wooden bench, damp from the light drizzle that hadn't stopped since early morning. Ordering her usual omelette and tea, she thought of their road trips. Jeypore rainforest, Dehing-Patkai rainforest, and even a stay at a tea estate, just like tourists, newly-wed, high in love. The trips would invariably end at a tea stall where he would order egg Maggi and she would go for an omelette. She knew that Priyom would have never sat here and eaten with her. Hospitals scared him. An easy lie or a genuine problem, she wasn't sure now. Hospitals had started to affect him more in the later years of their marriage.

Mridula's mind went from one memory to another. It was in a similar hospital when the realization had struck her. She had thought that he would smile, hug her, kiss the baby, their one-day old Rimi, and things would change. Hugs that would be warm and soft with a gentle touch, the way one would hug a puppy or a bird, caring for its delicate self and spindly feathers.

He did come. He smiled as expected, but his stare ruptured something in her. His hand felt like ice, sending tremors within her. His apology to be a day late felt stuffed with brashness, oiled with the luxury of repeated disappearances, even when Mridula was in labour. She had cried, but not out of joy. Her tears—they weren't warm. They were cold. Cold enough to freeze emotions. And she had tried her best to walk past her frozen emotions. But soon, summer came, and the ice melted. Rivers of arguments overflowed. Issues which were buried deep under the ice started flipping their tails.

She planned her next course of action. *He must be at the relief camp,* she decided. She mulled over the possible reasons for not finding him till now. The drizzle outside didn't seem to be stopping anytime soon. A leaking cloud, with no one to fix.

Sometimes,
the idea of hope is more comforting,
than the feasibility
and
reality of it.

Reality is
a thing to create.

A painter's canvas,
writers on papers,
and sculptors on stones.
An intuitive reality fuelled with hope.

3

Causes and Prevention of Frequent Railway Accidents in India

By Deepa Mehra

Delhi

8 June 2015

The recent Maajorghat-Guwahati Express derailment has raised questions on the safety of travelling in trains. This derailment is already being termed as one of the worst train accidents in Indian history.

Indian Railways has been instrumental in connecting the country from one end to another. Given its vast usability, with more than twenty-three million people travelling every day, and 19,000 trains—12,000 trains to carry passengers and 7000 freight trains—operating each day on rail lines that can circle our Earth one and a half times, it is impossible to think of a replacement for it.

However, the number of accidents have raised a lot of concerns. In recent years, efforts are being made to reduce the number; yet, accidents continue to claim commuters' lives. And 63 per cent of all train accidents in India are because of the train derailments. Let's take a deeper look and evaluate the causes.

Excessive traffic, announcement of new trains without parallel track expansion, delay in track renewal, and overall under-investment in railway infrastructure is adding to the burden of already over-used tracks. Lack of updated facilities and diminishing manpower could also be attributed as some of the major concerns.

For the North-eastern part of India, its challenging geographical make-up and demanding terrain does make it difficult for the railways to start new lines and rebuild deteriorating tracks. A hurriedly laid out track without enough geographical consideration would create a riskier, and not a safer, travel route. The concerns about the North-eastern terrain and the need for fitting technology and designs have been raised by the Northeast Frontier Railway and Commissioner of Railway Safety time and again.

If rules are to be followed, three to four hours of time is to be dedicated for maintenance of tracks every day. However, owing to factors such as increasing numbers of trains with fewer rail lines introduced in every rail budget and frequent train delays, not many options are left to the railway zones than to reduce their allotted time for track maintenance, leaving many potential hazards unattended. More attention to increasing freight traffic, and in turn the revenue, also affects the time that must be given for track maintenance.

Adding to the tragedy are the decades-old systems that are being used in Asia's oldest railway network. Indian railways, for example, rely on gang-men almost to a level of blind faith. Gang-men, most of them ageing, walk up and down a track, manually spotting irregularity on the rail tracks, if any. They are assigned stretches of six to eight kilometres that they must cover, while carrying almost bags as heavy as twenty kilograms full of spare nuts, detonators, wrenches, and other small parts. They go about replacing missing bolts, loose keys or fixing the fishplate on the rail. In spite of their best work, one cannot deny the chances of human error. To depend on a person's judgement to spot even the minutest of defects in a track is surely not a fool-proof method.

The gang-man who claimed to check the track near Maajorghat Bridge has blamed the officials for not providing him with a SIM card. He has stated that due to lack of a mobile phone, he couldn't warn the officials on time, nor could he fix the track that morning due to heavy rain. His claims have been rebuked at the higher level and we have to wait for the final report to know. However, his complaints have raised many concerns. Loss of several gang-men's lives on tracks also questions the continuation of this outdated system in place of modern technologies.

The solution could be to fill up the vacancies and empower the RPF to handle accidents better.

Another could be the use of LHB coaches, which are technologically more advanced than the conventional coaches. With the use of LHB coaches and tight lock centre, coaches can be prevented from climbing over each other, securing many lives in case of any accident. There is an urgent need for new lines to reduce the pressure on existing tracks and to provide more time for their maintenance.

Technologies like track monitoring systems, anti-collision devices, and rail fracture detection systems are being considered in order to reduce the number of train derailments. T-CAS (Collision Avoidance System), which is an anti-collision system, is already under trial. Indian Railways is also looking into Ultrasonic Broken Rail Detection System from South Africa which, after being attached to the track, is capable of sending real time alerts to officials.

A properly laid out strategy that can strengthen the weakening segments while creating space for new systems to be built, as well as thorough following of the IR systems and procedures, and no meddling with the time allocated to the operation department for track maintenance are a few steps to begin with.

To avoid and reduce the number of accidents in future, major investment towards maintenance and development of railway infrastructure is required.

Deepa Mehra is a Delhi-based independent journalist.

SECTION 4

DRIFTING BACK AND FORTH

When shadows lurked around
in wretched magnanimity,
and lives eluded,
they sought a mirror
of reason.
The mirror that replied
in a fickle reflection
of the fears
they had kept hidden.

1

Amid the ocean of searching eyes, Mridula's too were searching. Desperately. She was at the relief camp where relatively less injured passengers had been shifted.

She had walked up to here from the hospital. Clouded with confusion, with love and hatred blurring the lines between sanity and insanity, she needed that walk before encountering Priyom. As she treaded on the winding paths, their elusiveness somehow calmed her. Those curvy paths were further enhanced by the strokes of monsoon green. She saw fresh leaves, born out of love, an odd yet inevitable union of rain and trees. Rain, that arrived in fiery urgency to meet and imbibe the love induced metamorphosis. Distributing itself—a part to the trees, few drops to the earth, and the rest to the Sun, that would take them back to the clouds, to repeat the cycle. Rain on a tree, Mridula, and Priyom; one willingly transmuted, another quietly waited.

Now standing outside the camp, Mridula thought of all the possibilities. She had been to the station to check the list of passengers, but his name was nowhere. The surety of his travelling, being in town, was turning into a fog. Although, she was not sure if that could be possible.

Priyom had informed her of his travel to Maajorghat. Before reaching Kranti's house, she had sent him a text message too, wishing him a safe journey. He had replied as well—his last communication to her. To confirm, she checked her phone; to her shock, she couldn't find any message. She had read it. She had replied too. She tried searching thoroughly. She re-read each message, even those that did not bear his name. She didn't even skip those she had sent to herself—texts she would've preferred not to read again. Yet, she couldn't find his text message.

She was sure that she had read it. Not finding it made her restless. *It was real, not a dream*, she told herself. She remembered her heart skipping a beat when she had heard the news. She must have known he was travelling on the same train. She must have feared losing him. *Why else would she come searching?*

What I understood and felt, what I had been told and shown, should I believe it or not? Mridula wondered. She had often been confused about reality. Mridula was questioning herself again, a habit that was instilled in her childhood and strengthened by her husband, who would often make her doubt herself with his self-assured lies. It first started when the man she had seen in her parent's bedroom was deemed non-existent by her own mother. In what way could she claim her versions to be true, to be sure of his presence and absence … Mridula still did not know.

Last night, while looking at the stars, she had wondered how old the light reflected from them was. It was not their current flicker; it was the glimmer of the past that she saw as present. The sparkle of a faraway star reaching her could be its last light; the starlight decorating the sky could be long after its death. The existence she saw could be out of its non-existence. Even light could take millions of years to make an appearance, mark its existence, and eventually simulate the past as the present. When even light could lie to her, how could she trust anyone else? When even the cosmos was hiding so much, how could she be sure that he wasn't?

The blurring boundaries of her dreams and memories had often left her doubtful, but this time she was adamant to not let it dictate the course of her actions. So, she went to the inquiry desk and submitted his name and hers for them to announce whenever he was located.

She wrote in a paper:

Passenger name – Mr Priyom Phukon

Coach number – Nil

Seat number – Nil

Travelling with – Alone (he had to be alone, as far as she believed)

Person to be informed – Mridula Phukon, 98******80

Mridula handed over the sheet and was about to leave when they told her that someone had come looking for her too. She thought it was a mistake on their part, until they mentioned the name of the person searching. She wasn't surprised by the name, but by the act.

Unprecedented act at an unprecedented time.

Nevertheless, she stood by as they announced his name, asking him to report back to the desk. Fatigue was apparent in her demeanour—hair tied up in a bun, fringes swept to the left, bag slumping down from her shoulder, fingers tracing the nails.

After a while, she saw him walking towards her. His face looked fuller and a shade fairer. His ever-famous curls didn't bounce as they used to, though. His steps hurried to reach her. His athletic limbs, as they once were, indicated weariness. The clothes covering them were crumpled. His puffy eyes indicated that he hadn't slept at all.

Looking at him, she realized, *he was searching too.*

Kranti came and hugged her. He was overwhelmed at the thoughts of losing someone at one moment and finding them unscathed the next. His face brightened with a smile, and in the process relaxed her too.

Their hearts swelled with emotions, like high tide on a full moon night. Two portions of the same tide, each rising with a floating moon of its own. On one elevated wave surfaced those who survived, shining white under the silvery light; another wave levitated the fear of death, the coldness of loss and loneliness of night.

Surprised with his show of affection, a rare occurrence they both knew well, Kranti stepped back and asked in his usual composure, 'How are you?'

Taking him by his hand, Mridula started walking. He continued prodding her with questions, to which she answered as calmly as she could. They walked outside the camp, away from the people who were looking at them with part happiness and part jealousy—hoping for their endless search to end as well, yet resentful of their reunion.

For Kranti, at that point, the search was over. He had found his sister. He wasn't going to let her go. Hers, on the other hand, wasn't. But the quest went on. His, for experiences of life, and hers, through images of her fancies.

2

Kranti and Mridula reached a restaurant named Bamboo Hut. The bamboo walls surrounding it justified the name. Suggested by the hotel receptionist, it guaranteed the best lunch in the town.

'You didn't tell anyone. Why?' Kranti asked as they took their seats.

'Didn't want to worry them,' she lied casually, for both of their benefit.

They wouldn't approve of a woman sobbing and shivering in shock for a husband who, not long ago, was compared to a devil of the worst kind. Questions would be asked and answers would have to be fabricated. So, saying nothing more than what was strictly necessary, Mridula had left for Maajorghat.

'At least you could have called me.'

'How could I? We haven't even spoken since last year,' she snapped.

To avoid scraping out the years of irritation embedded in her, he asked, 'Achcha leave it, what do you want to eat?'

Kranti prepped for an elaborate meal, his preferred way. For starters—chilli fish, to be made fresh and crispy, and manchow soup, one by two. Chicken noodles, fried rice, and veg. Manchurian for the main course, and chocolate cake for dessert, because *Komolar kheer*, an Assamese delicacy, much to Kranti's irritation, wasn't available in the restaurant trying to (almost) specialize in Indo-Chinese cuisine.

Kranti always took control and ordered whatever he thought would and should be liked by the one dining with him. Ordering for all the courses was his way too. Kranti didn't like referring to the menu-card in between his meals. After a few minutes of careful consideration, a detailed order would be placed, with instructions on the timing and temperature of the food.

Soon after, while devouring fish fritters and slurped the manchow soup, they inquired about each other's life. Both gave answers they had prepared for everyone; both were not yet ready to divulge more than necessary. They were testing the waters before taking the plunge. Both knew the kind of flooding the other person was capable of hustling out.

After a bit of hesitation, Kranti finally asked her, 'Hmm, so what actually happened then? Like, why divorce? I mean, I didn't know. It wasn't that bad, was it?'

Kranti would never say Priyom's name out aloud. Same was the case with her other male friends—even the one whom Mridula wanted to elope with. By mentioning their names, he feared to give them the validation they didn't deserve.

'We never spoke about it. Don't know why.'

'We both know why. And no one bothered to inform me either. I am family, after all…' Kranti was back to shifting blames.

'And who is responsible for that, Kranti?!' Her anger was mounting again.

Divorce was a painful process for Mridula. A prolonged one, like an operation that lasted for years. Skin shredding slowly and painfully every minute, needles piercing her skin, tearing every inch apart till nothing remained for any sensation to be felt.

About the divorce … what could she possibly tell him? She had wished Kranti to be there. He would have if he wanted to, but he wasn't present. Neither were reasons for his absence enough, nor were the lack of them.

Everyone had questioned her, which they thought were crucial. Questions about Rimi and her future. Questions on abuse (physical), affairs, demands of additional dowry, and on salary. Inquiries about her freedom to shop and on the decency of clothing. Suggestions on drinking, on satisfying, beautifying the house, and herself. There were assumptions. She was advised based on those assumptions. If he had accepted his mistake, then she was required to forgive him. Anger would dwarf her. She needed to grow above whatever the reason was. Forgive and forget.

But what if Mridula didn't want to take the higher moral ground? What if she wanted to find a corner—and stay in that selfish corner of hers? What if she didn't want to forget, nor forgive? No one thought of it. And how could she? She couldn't lessen the frigidity between them even with the heaviest of quilts. And that occasional warmth of marriage became unbearable, burning her world and identity to ashes. She couldn't rise from those ashes. Even if she tried, she couldn't turn into a phoenix. So, she kept quiet; the reasons wouldn't be enough.

'You just didn't come, not even later!'

'You know, Mridu, only you can answer me this way.' He smiled to mollify her.

'Anchal cannot?'

'How is Rimi? Must be all grown up now, *hain na*? Got lots of gifts for her.'

'You should visit more often.'

'Why are you still in Dibrugarh? Shift. Come to Delhi. Stay with us for some days…' he said to pacify her again.

Mridula nodded. As she was about to speak, the waiter arrived with the main course, balancing three serving bowls on a sleek melamine tray. While most of the dishes stayed put within the bowls, Manchurian gravy defied balance and dripped out freely. A journey from the base to the edges, and then finally to the table. The waiter, apologizing, wiped the drops as soon as he placed the dishes.

'I thought you loved him. He also liked you, right?'

'Ah Dada! Our love expired a long time ago.'

Mridula had often smelt the stench of its decay.

'No, yaar. How can love expire!' The sentence came out more defensive than he'd intended.

'I don't know. Ours is dead,' she said while praying for his words to be true. She felt as though her words were brawling on the floor while Kranti's idea of love stood tall, with a smirk, assigned to the righteous.

'Hmm, that's one way to look at it.'

'The only correct way,' Mridula replied.

What was love anyway, Mridula thought. Love didn't come to help her in her daily struggles, didn't give her company on the days she felt lonely, it didn't come to lessen her pain, or hear her thoughts. Love was not a companion. It was a feeling, and a feeling without a person in attendance was nothing. It was non-existent.

The absence grew each day. Initially, she managed for a few hours, but soon she learnt to handle a lifetime of absence. Hours turned into days, days into a week, and weeks into months, which felt like years. It wasn't a year since they officially separated yet, but the drifting apart had started many years before.

'Anyway, how are you these days?'

Mridula didn't know how to answer that. She still felt those tremors, as though there was a waterfall within her. Mostly she would just lay in its pool, but sometimes she would try to move against its flow. Try to cut its current into half. She had been trying, repeatedly. That was how she felt, like nature mostly, but sometimes its captive too.

'So, what have you been doing since morning?' she asked, while the same young man in a milky-white uniform cleared their plates, mounting the leftovers on his tray. Fresh dessert plates were brought in, their sweetness to cover their blank shine.

'I was volunteering. Helping here and there. There was so much chaos ... No proper guidance, and everyone looked confused. I had to help,' Kranti added after a pause.

Help—an innocent, almost angelic motive. Also, a hegemonic offshoot. Help, because he could, because he had the privilege of being a giver. The power of giving, to control, the power as addictive as any psychoactive drug.

Kranti had to help; he knew no other way.

Post lunch, as they stepped out, Kranti stretched his arms, straightened his back, and in a long breath filled his lungs with the air of his land. His face, relaxed now, looked like a cool breeze surprising the summer sun.

Throwing a tender look at his sister, he spoke. 'See *bhoni*, I am here now. Right? So, you go home and chill. I will find out and tell you. *Theek hai na*?'

It was a pleasant monsoon afternoon. Clouds cleared up, giving way to the Sun that shone bright, sprinkling its golden happiness on everyone below. Mridula felt her skin burn with the heat. Rain was what she was more used to now.

Mridula wanted to stay back; she told him too. But Kranti's why's and how's didn't give her enough space to explain. He winked, looking down at her as he spoke, and tilted his head sideways. His persuasion had the precision that came from years of rehearsal. She nodded as they walked up the stairs of the hotel.

'Listen, one more thing. You know it, right? That you can talk to me? The love between us is not dead,' Kranti said as he stood in front of his room's door. Wooden doors polished in aqua blue, the blackness of the doorknob balancing its sheen.

Mridula remembered her marriage and divorce (both of which Kranti had missed). She remembered things she shouldn't have, or maybe should have. She remembered a lot, but she didn't remember it enough—linear enough to share.

'Dada … I have started meeting Priyom again,' she admitted finally, straightening the edges of her ironed tunic.

'Hmm, I guessed as much.'

Why don't we talk like we used to? Kranti thought as he entered his room.

Kranti and Mridula had grown up together, filling water, plucking oranges from Dutta Aunt's house, sharing dreams and events of the days, guarding the secrecy of those dreams from others, and solving the confusion those dreams brought in the lives of a young boy and girl who were more or less figuring out life as they grew. The angst between her parents felt almost similar to the love between his parents, the hierarchical love that he blamed to have instigated the angst in him. A usual teenage predicament with an unusual fixation.

It had been five years since they met last. In these years, they had spoken not more than a few times, calls lasting no longer than a few minutes. There was no rift between them. Kranti moved out for his studies and Mridula moved to another city after marriage. They merely became too busy with their lives. Too busy to acknowledge her marriage and later divorce, to send invitations of his marriage scheduled in Delhi, to call him after his wedding, to attend her father's funeral, or to inform about her daughter's birth. They both became so engrossed in their lives that even when his yearly visits and her occasional trips occurred, they could never meet. It was just that their different worlds pushed the bonds farther away. This time, Kranti had decided to meet her, to rebuild the bond they had. He needed that bond of relations, a recent realization.

Few hours later, Mridula left for Guwahati, leaving every possible detail about Priyom with Kranti. This time, the wait was sure to be over soon. This time, her Kranti would bring Priyom back in her life, she hoped. She hoped Kranti would restore her life, despite his absence when it had been uprooted.

3

In spite of the passing weeks and circumstances telling her otherwise, Mridula waited, convinced that Priyom would come back—that it was just a phase which would soon be over.

This was because Priyom's steps, while walking out, were so confident that they flashed an ease of routine, a calm composure of surety. He had walked out like any other day, to be back like any other day, in the evening, or the weekend, or in ten days.

Priyom didn't take any of his belongings either. He just walked out as if nothing needed to be changed, as if everything was as it had been until now. His books, half read with bookmarks between the pages, still lay under the centre table; his shirts hung in the closet, by the side of her mekhela and tunics; his toothbrush stood with hers atop the washbasin. The set of crockery they had received on their first marriage anniversary, his favourite brand of tea, his bottle of Old Monk for his daily dose inside the wooden closet behind her Rooh Afza and Coke bottles, hidden from the prying eyes, still stood firm in the kitchen closet.

Every corner of the house reflected Priyom's presence, even though it was not him who had built a home inside those four empty walls. Even though it was Mridula who had spent months finding the house, or weekends searching furniture deals. She was the one who made sure that the walls and main gate were painted before the onset of monsoon. She had ensured the timely delivery of bamboo for the fence, that the fencing was made thick enough. She had dug the soil for the front garden and the vegetable garden at the back. Even then, it was he who had brought the change, the change she wasn't able to reverse.

For the first few days after Priyom left, mornings were grim. Living without having him around was not new to her, but the realization that his absence might be permanent made it more unbearable than before. Waking up, eating, or even watching TV—everything felt like a chore. To get ready and go to the market or to take Rimi for walks turned into responsibilities she wasn't inclined to do anymore. But Mridula knew that she had to continue living, to prove herself on the day he would decide to return, something she hoped for, every day.

So, every day she would cajole herself into going to office, cook, walk, and even attend occasional dinners, every time with the same vehemence. With the same fervour she had started waiting for him to return, to end this uncalled-for separation, although she was the one who had asked him to leave. Setting him free, she had hoped for a docile return. But he didn't come; he continued to be away with equal persistence.

On some days, Mridula would act like Priyom, her way of bringing him back through imitation. She would sit on the sofa the way he used to, read a book with one leg on the couch and other on the carpet; she would eat with hands the way he did often at home; she would dip her fingers in oil, tearing everything into pieces, creating a mess on the plate, pushing the balls of mashed rice and curry in her mouth, and gulping them down with water whenever tears choked her.

The first time she had seen Priyom eat to his heart's content was during their pre-wedding days. It was during the first and only long drive they had taken before the wedding, sneaking out of the market where they both had gone on the pretext of shopping. On their way back, tired, and hungry, he had stopped at a road-side restaurant. It was the kind of place Mridula hadn't visited before, owing to her mother who considered highway restaurants as trouble-dens. Plastic tables were laid out in the open, each with a set of four plastic chairs, their whites turned into a dirt yellow over the years. Ordering a plate of chicken tandoori and boiled rice, he had transferred half of the portion onto his plate. Tearing the chicken leg effortlessly, he'd pressed it down and taken a piece out of it—everything with his fingers. Then, he mixed the pieces into his rice. Holding a large portion of the mix between his fingers, he had bent slightly forward and pushed it into his mouth with his thumb. His golden spectacles had slipped down, almost touching the large ball of food he would cup between his fingers. Mridula had sat there, looking at the way he ate, impressed with his flawless precision. His rustic ways had fascinated her back then.

As weeks became months and their divorce approached nearer, Mridula's days too took a normal stride. But then, there were days she didn't feel brave, bouts of discomfort seizing everything. There were incidents which made her feel as vulnerable as any other woman around her, irrespective of whether they were staying alone or with someone. On those days, and especially nights, even the sound of crickets would scare her; dogs she had befriended would disturb her, their howling across the street making her heart beat faster and hands shiver. With each day, she emptied herself a bit to fill up the vacant hope, like an hourglass with an unstoppable dripping of sand.

Mridula had stayed almost fine and somewhat lion-hearted, except for a few episodes of panic attacks when Priyom left her, and a few bad dreams when he didn't return. It was after that incident that even the hourglass of her resolve also broke down.

Mridula was heading to her forced routine to the vegetable market when she saw a man standing alert, looking at her, as if planning something, or waiting to act on his plan. He stood on the side of the road, his forefoot on the concrete and his heels digging deep in mud. Right there, in broad daylight, he was masturbating. His hand went behind his *lungi,* which was folded up to his knee, when he saw her walking towards the main road, knowing that she would cross his path. Mridula, as a person she thought herself to be, should have slapped him and raised her voice. She had seen him going back to the side as soon as he saw her walking; she knew it was meant for her—the public act of pleasure. The act that every woman was subjected to at least once, twice, or innumerable times in her life. The cost of stepping out in public, threatening the ever-fragile male ego of those like him. He was there, pleasuring himself at the sight of her, letting her know how she aroused him. Pleasure merging into loathsome sexuality.

Yet, Mridula didn't say anything. Just like the usual lot of bystanders, busy in their morning banters, shutting their eyes to what was happening on the opposite side, she too behaved as if nothing had happened. They did so by choice, she due to fear. Lowering her eyes, she walked fast, past the man; yet, she could see his hand jerking faster, uncontrollably. She didn't see clearly—she didn't want to. That day, she returned home by an auto-rickshaw, without any purchase.

On a cool pleasant morning, she was sweating. On a morning when birds were flying fresh and trees were gearing up for the day to come, Mridula was subjected to something she would not be able to forget for months to come. It was then she had wished Priyom to be by her side. It was then that she had decided to contact him, once again.

4

'Do you still get those nightmares?' Mridula asked, standing outside the bus.

The bus driver had started the engine. As the bus vibrated, a mild panic hummed its way to the passengers. The tasks that everyone was engrossed in started to end hurriedly—shorter bargaining at the food stalls, a quicker trip to the bathroom, and succinct goodbyes. The bus was filling up faster now.

'Haan yaar, I do,' Kranti sighed.

'Why can't we stop them? Every night, Dada. It's the same heaviness. And for so many years.'

'Don't know. How do you handle them?'

'I don't know how to. I just let them be.'

A quick hug followed, and she went inside the bus, back to Guwahati. Mridula hadn't found any clue about Priyom's whereabouts, yet she was going because Kranti had decided so. She settled herself next to the window and pushed her bag under the seat in front. On her lap sat a stuffed toy for Rimi, packed in a plastic zipper, bought at the hotel's gift shop. The toy looked like a baby goat, though it was meant to be a puppy. She covered it with her stole. It reminded her of the goats she had seen stuffed on trucks, their necks peering out, ears flapping in the wind, heads almost stuck together, and eyes sighing a collective pain—a silent cry for freedom. To come in front of an over-speeding vehicle, or to go into the mouth of a predator.

The freedom to decide. Whether for them or Mridula, freedom remained a paradoxical concept.

Hoping for stability, Mridula's mind wandered away from the turbulence that Maajorghat had caused. The cure of physical distancing, while waiting for a healing solution to be pushed down her throat.

As the bus started, Mridula started contemplating her life and imagining the worst, a habitual recreation, especially when she was agitated. *What if the bus met with an accident? Or worse, captured by dacoits?* It was a rare, but not an impossible occurrence. She pondered over it, nevertheless. *How would she go back to Guwahati? What if no one realized that she was missing? Who would come to search for her?* She tried to remember the names of everyone she knew. She imagined getting kidnapped. She decided that she preferred dying over getting raped and being left to rot. She was busy guessing the turns her life would take. She thought of ways—rocks smashing her head, a five-foot long body buried in a field similar to the one her bus was crossing then. *It would be painful*, she thought, *like pulling one's organs out while being fully conscious.*

Like her mind, the bus too was running at its regular speed. It went ahead on a lively district road, which after a few kilometres connected to the highway. It went past the houses lined in perfect symmetry, taking a detour owing to the heavy downpour the previous night.

Each house was guarded by a few inches' tall bamboo fencing and a wooden gate, a protection more from fear of burglary than the possibility of it. Each stood at an equal distance from the other, facing a similar one across the road, and between them the bus drove. Their roofs were the colour of rust, which invariably darkened at the bottom; creepers curled up high on walls and fences, and a few flowered too. Those houses stood in harmony with nature and each other. Mridula, on the other hand, wasn't, neither with herself nor with her surroundings.

Behind those houses, a few kilometres away, stood the Maajorghat hospital which, like her, wasn't holding up a harmony of life. Somewhere within its white walls, a man was opening his eyes under the broken rim of a golden spectacle, awakened by the sound of his watch falling off, gold, or the sensation of his ring, also gold, being forcibly pulled out of his swollen finger, its yellow stone covered in a crusty layer of blood. Unaware of it, Mridula was speculating the vilest.

The bus was moving fast on an uneven road that left many passengers holding on to their seats. The driver drove on his path of expertise and Mridula on hers, both of them unmindful of the jerking. As if in a trance, she was taking a flight to a world far away. Like a feather, light and carefree, but angry at losing its path because of the astray wind. It hated to be dependent, in seeking the wind's help to rise. It was angry for not knowing where it would be taken next to, for the inconsistent movements of the wind, once shoving it down on the ground and then elevating it in the air again. Mridula felt like that helpless feather which was left alone, plucked out of the bird, and left fragile and clueless, on the verge of being lost.

The road on which the bus now trod was shiny clean, having been washed thoroughly by last night's rain. Thick carpets of grass surrounded the road on both the sides, which were then lined by freshly bathed trees. Clouds still hovered, yet the light slipped out. Revived now, nature was blessing and blooming with pride.

Mridula looked at the lush fields that appeared to be running backwards, their greenery so bright that it hurt her eyes. She didn't feel blessed. She was raging. She hated the earth for showing its exuberance upon rain's arrival, sprouting coyly, as if it were not rain but liquid diamonds falling down. She cursed their meeting and branded it as a temporary union, a show off.

Soon, envy replaced the angst. She felt an urge to get down and peel the earth barren and deprive it of every single grass. It angered her to see how, despite being so far apart, they could still meet.

Pity followed envy. Now she wanted to know why her desires were not being fulfilled. Comparison came in, and she found herself at a higher ground than nature, which was creating havoc in her state. Yet, she was the one being punished. But soon again, anger found its way in. Anger, much of an extrovert, always had its way of showing itself. Pity and envy lay hidden in the secluded corners of the heart, often acting from behind.

So, Mridula started cursing nature again. It was then that she saw a farmer couple along with many others. They were standing ankle deep in the water, bowing forward and planting rice seedlings. Their heads were covered with traditional *gamocha* scarves or plastic sheets, while some even had the conical shaped, cane Japi hats on them. Hats that also had their days of glory, once adorning the heads of the rich, now gracing the ones who worked for the rich. Its nostalgic representation in cultural symbolism was still integral. Their clothes were drenched, nevertheless. They all seemed preoccupied with nature and companionship. It was the Kharif crop season, so they were sowing paddy, which was to be harvested in the month of November.

Mridula stared at the woman—her face, though receding inwards, didn't exude the dread often accompanied by fatigue. It seemed to have the peacefulness of meditating saints. *A sign of a content relationship*, Mridula assumed. She despised them too. The woman looked up at the bus, which had slowed by now. As if she could hear Mridula, she looked at her with challenging eyes, a proud display of her happiness. This burnt Mridula further. A burning coal was being pushed down her throat, and she wanted to scream. Pain penetrated from within, as though her hair was being pulled out, one by one, each strand leaving beads of blood behind.

What's the point of existing if everything has to change? Mridula was typing a long text message, her own number in the receiver's name. A message she would delete the next morning.

The person I am with, the home I am in, can change any moment. It did, too. Everything changes, everyone moves, even Rimi will. No one has or will stop for me. Out and away. All of this will slip away. She hit the send button and started typing once again. *I shouldn't stop my life too. I should run away; I should constantly run. No, I should stop it from changing. There shouldn't be any change.*

She was not looking for a future. A lifelong standstill was all that she needed. Although her fingers moved furiously, she sat still, wishing for permanence in a bus that too was under a perpetual motion.

Outside, the sky was changing too, a dull grey hovering over a pale white. Day was transforming into night.

❦

The bus drove swiftly now. The passengers were asleep, and a small night bulb blinked. Mridula too closed her eyes.

She saw a round blot of colour. It was as clear as seen with eyes wide open, but Mridula knew better than to open them. Her eyes felt glued shut, eyelids heavy, eyelashes sticky.

She saw a circle engraved on the ceiling—within its vast boundary of intricate floral patterns, lights danced as though in a discotheque. The white would turn to blue, blue to red, red to black, and black to white. Within the circle, there were carvings of innumerable human bodies, ancient men and women, bejewelled and naked, shifting their shapes with the change of colour. At one moment the circle was curvaceous, and at another a flat round. She could see a man, in the midst of acrobatics, holding a woman in his arms, and to their side was another woman staring at the man, standing adjacent, doing nothing but gazing right through him. Mridula wanted to focus on the faces of the man and women, but the light shifted and it all turned black. Then appeared two men—one standing, and another frowning from the ground underneath. His eyes were lit in blue and red. The other man hopped over him to take the woman. A face of stone, a face carved in patterns, a creeper with huge flowering and demented leaves. Both the faces hovered over each other on the ground. Their teeth glinted back the light—white, turning blue, then red, and white again.

Mridula was dreaming, like every other night.

She was dreaming of two women and one man, then two men and one woman. Entangled relations and insatiable desires. Dreams that she could never share with anyone, not because remembering them was difficult, but because understanding them was. Dreams that increasingly left her confused—more so when she saw her mother with the man who was not her father but was made to believe that he was, when she was told that what she saw wasn't the truth, that the clothes he was wearing were the new sets she hadn't noticed earlier. Mridula was branded as unreliable, her words dismissed as fabricated. Her encounter was ignored as a misunderstanding, and all questions were silenced forever. The man in the bedroom was still often spotted—his head similar to father's, but not quite.

The intensity of those images and dreams increased when Priyom too came with someone, who was claimed to be a fragment of her insecurities. Too many calls outside the house, too many bills of untold dinners. Small gifts were found hidden in wardrobes, but no one trusted her, so even she couldn't.

The illusion of relationships and vagueness of love that she was forced into, much before her father's death, continued later too. The deception she witnessed often took the form of her dreams. The one that she hid from her father, and the guilt of it she carried inside, along with the angst of having to witness it all. It all led to muddled, unreliable memories when events of her present forced new illusions upon her.

5

A traditional Hindu wedding had commemorated Mridula and Priyom's entry into the marital world, escorted by blessings and scrutiny.

Mridula had taken the last leg of her graduation exams, ready to begin the much-awaited life of financial independence, far from her ramshackle hostel. Away from trees that were decades' old and dew-soaked grass, she dreamt of settling in a metropolitan city with its airy, modern houses. A dreamy balcony overlooking an excessively lit cityscape. Away from the chapped walls with faded windows, where years of dampness turned them green, she dreamt of a new life, almost similar to Kranti's. But she was called home, to meet and marry. It was then that her dreams were put on hold and her longing to restart began.

Mridula wasn't ready for the wedding. It was her mother's melodramatic speech that had extracted a yes from her. The glory of being a married woman, emphasized since birth, the pampering showered on the bride, the excitement of events around it, and the unique appeal of wedding frenzy, also convinced her. She had secretly revelled in her sisters' fussing and dressing her in the bridal mekhela sador with its golden motif of intricate peacocks matched with the crescent-shaped gold *joonbiri* necklace, the neck-hugging *golpota* necklace with red stones, and the recently procured gold-coated *gamkharu* bracelets.

The golden tint of her off-white *Muga* silk contrasted with the red of her bindi, the green of her mother's stone-studded *keru* ring, and the black of her kohl. She was elated to be adorned in handmade traditional Assamese jewellery, often influenced by nature and music, and the durable yet smooth Muga silk that the state prided in.

Her first encounter had also gone well. Priyom, who had arrived in grey jeans and a whitewashed shirt to a meeting which was nothing but formal, had pleased her. His hair was neatly combed and parted sideways, but they had a ruggedness that his face, dotted with fine features and golden eyeglasses, lacked. He seemed to challenge the expected protocol of dressing and conduct. His face, although with no effort from his side, also hinted at disobedience, despite his sleek nose and watery eyes. It wasn't rebellion but the lack of personal interest and abundant trust in his parents' ability to find him a suitable wife that had made him appear at ease—something Mridula didn't know then.

She, on the other hand, despite her disagreement, had put on a traditional attire, with her mother's gold chain and danglers. Her short hair, put together with dozens of bobby pins, was tied in a bun, creating an impression of long tresses.

Although she had agreed for the wedding, Mridula hoped till the last moment for Kranti to come and intervene. A faint wish for it to stop—when the groom was reluctantly shelling out cash to enter the house and her cousin Kuki was washing his feet, when she was being given the holy *panchamrit* to drink, and even when her uncles were carrying her to the wedding hall and the groom's brother was bringing him in. Amid the blowing of conch shells and chanted verses, promises and offerings, she had waited for her favourite brother to come and throw this marriage out of her life. The foreboding that everyone in the world had for that year, she had for her wedding. Both turned out to be true. The world did fall apart in recession, and she crumbled in her marriage.

Kranti showed his disapproval of the family's decision through a few calls. He had informed everyone that a twelve years' older man was not suitable, citing instances of failed marriages with such a huge age gap. His parents had then reminded him of their age gap and long marriage. He had tried to convince the family about Priyom's unsuitability, owing to his family background and mannerisms that Kranti had grasped from the only time they spoke before the wedding. Disappointed with his thick accent and coarse greetings, he had informed Mridula about his perception of Priyom, with his outdated appearance and brash dressing sense. Even though he'd circulated his list of dislikes about Priyom, Mridula's parents decided to go ahead with the wedding. So, as a result, he dodged the wedding. 'It's a crucial time at office, can't leave and come, bhoni,' Kranti had told Mridula over a call. But that was how Kranti dealt with things—lending a casual shrug to other's problems. Mridula, who knew him very well, knew this too.

Unaffected by the financial crisis that the world had come upon, when many found it difficult to secure their income, Mridula and Priyom focused on securing their marriage. They appraised not jobs but Dibrugarh together. Abiding by the rules of new marriage, they went to parks, temples, tea gardens, and restaurants. Crossing the towns in Arunachal Pradesh, relishing their local cuisines, they also made a trip to Tuting. Infatuation trespassed and Priyom appeared good. He didn't smoke, and only drank occasionally. There were no previous affairs that she knew of, and he also earned well, according to her parents, something she believed initially too.

In accordance with her wishes, he had acknowledged her need for space and time to adjust. Contradicting the drops of wisdom poured over her, he had not approached her on their wedding night too, not even for a month after that. Later, afraid of his seemingly increasing coldness, Mridula had pursued him in ways suggested to her. Eventually, a daughter came as a proof of her efforts and his refusal for abortion. Slowly, attraction faded and the glitter of the new diminished. It wasn't Mridula's first love, after all. She had heard and believed that it was one's first love that always lasted; everything else eventually diminished. Even if you lived with it, it would cease to exist.

Mridula got Priyom, who was not bad, as she was often told. Though, she had hoped for good and desired the best. On days when their differences became glaring, she saw him as a misfit—whose view of life was in complete contrast to hers. The age of his friends, the songs he listened to in college, his idea of fun, and his preferences. The expectations of a husband, who was decades older, from a wife who had barely entered adulthood, added further to her frustration.

The hopes for best shouldn't be pursued, especially when you are already married, Mridula was reminded on every trip home.

Since then, Mridula had been constantly searching. But what was it that she sought? The sound of the river, often flooding her state? Some days, she also longed for the sky during the golden hour, a hint of orange smeared with blue that she couldn't see but knew existed. She sought the sky where clouds gave way to her imagination, full of shapes of flying monsters or an angel, of a broken weapon, a five-winged bird, a dying flower, two eyes looking at you, or the one running away from you. Also, the sky with a bleak orange birthing a silver, star-studded one. The sky that the moon owned, even though the stars shone brighter.

6

By the time Maya reached the camp, it was close to seven at night. People were queuing for dinner in front of a makeshift counter under a tin shed. Three wooden desks, most likely fetched from a government school, were joined together to make it. She dragged her suitcase and left it next to the counter, requesting one of the volunteers to keep it safe.

A few metres away, a settlement had erupted under a few blue tents. Yellow flicker from bulbs illuminated it. Looking at the plastic sheets, she wondered if those feeble tents could withstand another bout of heavy rain. It was only one of the few doubts that everyone chose to ignore.

Shuffling past huge aluminium saucepans and a tall stack of paper plates next to them, Maya went inside the tent. A plain concrete platform, the stage of an auditorium in its golden days, was covered in plastic sheets that were tied to square pillars. A braided protection. Next to it were a few more rooms with bare windows that no more cared for the modesty they were once granted. A collective grumbling distilled through each room and reached Maya like a group of siblings complaining to their mother, each demanding her attention, leaving no moment for it to shift to another.

Maya went in, a heap of black-red chequered blankets still wrapped in plastic behind her, yet to be distributed. People inside, many bruised, looked pained and hungry, not particularly for food, but for dignity, for a life presumably peaceful. Hunger for that mundanity, away from the hysteria they were experiencing now, for the boredom that once defined their living. They craved for sanity—for that innocence towards life and death. An intense hunger lurked within them.

Their near-death encounter had shocked them, a seemingly harmless journey bringing such disarray in their life that now they were mourning for the ones they had lost and the deaths they had seen.

Amid them, Maya searched for a chiffon or a cotton saree with blooming flowers. She scanned every woman to get a glimpse of that confident gait. She looked for grey strands in black ponytails, wrinkled hands holding a brown handbag, and black leather slip-ons. Her gaze raked at every red suitcase for signs of familiarity. She searched for that meditative composure that was capable of bringing her misery to a halt. But nowhere could she find her mother.

A family next to her was eating, their silent heads bent in focus while their hands mechanically pushed morsels in. Somewhere, a kid was being beaten up for spilling his meal; a distant laughter; a call for attention from a husband to his wife; a mother nursing her baby; a feeble hello; a loud wail. And next to them were water bottles, accumulated and stationed, packets of biscuits, torn clothes, and bare feet.

She looked around and thought, *accidents like these bring everyone together.* To her, it appeared as a leveller too. Whether you were in a general coach or a first-class compartment, nature would strike equally on everyone. Yet, when she realized the probability of her too being among them, Maya couldn't call the leveller nature kind. *They are in better condition, they are fine*, she reassured herself.

'Hey,' she said to one of the families. 'Uh … can you see

these photos, please? Have you seen them?' she said, extending her phone to them.

'No madam,' the man of the family spoke as he handed back the phone. His expression mellowed for a fellow sufferer.

'Can I see?'

A young girl approached Maya. In her early teenage years, dressed in torn jeans, with a long shawl thrown over her shoulders, she sucked her lower lip as she glanced at the picture. Her face resembled a deflated ball, and her eyes were pushed into a pitiful deep hollow. Her inclination to help hinted at an understanding of the situation, of Maya's pain—a maturity she'd gained within a few hours.

'Didi, ask in those rooms too,' she said, trying to sound reassuring.

As she stepped out of the last room, Maya felt a violent surge of hunger. She hadn't eaten in more than twelve hours. She looked around and saw that food was still being served.

Two massive hearths on which the food had been cooked were still flashing with red embers. A light smoke rose from them, reminiscent of the wood that was burnt a while back. She held out her plate and two scoops of porridge and a watery curry was poured on her plate.

'Hey, hi … uh … I need some help,' she said to the man filling the water can. His curls were covering his eyes, face tense but not grim. Something in him told her that she could approach him. He appeared to be not as affected as others but still involved enough to help.

He smiled. His gaze held hers while his hands filled the cans. His manners were brisk.

'Have you … uh … have you seen them?' Maya's hands reached the inside of her bag, trying to locate her phone.

'Let me hold that for you,' he said, taking the plate of food from her hand. Two small diamonds reflected the yellow light into a labyrinth of colours as his finger straightened. His gait exuded confidence, as if he could control this entire accident if he wanted to, but didn't, only for the thrill of doing it now. The sheer gratification of solving a puzzle after it reached its highest level of complexity. His ease with the whole situation unnerved Maya.

They both looked at the picture: it was a woman in a navy-blue cotton sari with a thin golden border, slim-built like Maya, with wrinkled lips and happy eyes. Her hair was pulled back in a loose pleat, parted in the middle, with a few strands of white mixing with the rest of the black. She had a look of seniority, not fragile, but the kind that commanded respect. Maya swiped the picture to show another picture—of a man, his round face smiling, shy eyes looking away from the camera. His oiled hair, dyed in black like his moustache, was combed back. It would have been easier if she had a picture of them together. If that were to happen, she wouldn't be here, searching, a distant possibility and an inability to change the past.

'Sorry, I haven't,' he said apologetically, handing back the phone to her.

'But many passengers are also in hospital,' he said, regaining confidence in his voice, while Maya trudged towards an empty place with a few plastic chairs, one hand holding the plate and another sliding the phone back into her bag. Unmindful of the overfilled dustbin, the mobile toilets exuding a putrid smell, and the blocked washbasins with a flood of their own, she ate hastily.

After searching once again for the frail pair of humans that no one seemed to recall seeing, she decided to go to the station. The same auto driver agreed, this time without the usual bickering over money. Satiation from the free meal had improved his mood.

He once again tied her suitcase on the top and started the vehicle. The *vroom* of the auto-rickshaw soothed Maya. She was thankful that he didn't play any songs. Songs that she used to find jarringly loud, all invariably with a tune that felt stolen or inspired from a popular song. In Bangalore, she often heard Kannada songs, feeling puzzled about its lyrics. Irrespective of the songs, she would always ask them to decrease the volume, a hint of shout and anger laced in her request. Once, a driver had played English songs. She had gotten down quite impressed, a privilege that she believed was restricted to her and the kind like hers. Imbibed hierarchy that we all lived by.

Recently, she had started enjoying those auto songs, remembering them with nostalgia for a time when she only travelled by auto-rickshaws, the days of college and lesser salaries, but of a younger and carefree self. Those songs were now a thing of laughter that she and her friends would recite and enact for fun. A contemptuous enjoyment, an uncouth banter about their puerile tastes. Yet, those occasional rides would feel like coming home, a feeling she wasn't used to, a feeling that she detested as well as longed for.

After what felt like many minutes of silence between them, the driver asked her, 'You are also searching, madam?' He seemed to have jumped into old age. His wilted body was so slender that Maya could see the spine jutting out of his back.

'Ya. My mother,' she replied. '… my father was also on the train,' she added after a pause.

'Too many deaths, madam.'

As he spoke, a plastic figurine of Lord Hanuman swayed, one hand holding the Sanjeevani *parvat*, the mountains which had herbs to resuscitate the dying. In his other hand was his signature mace. His legs were slightly bent, torso straight, face upright. Racing with the wind, he was trying to fly back to his Lord yet tied to the rickshaw.

'Everybody is tense now. My wife fought with me today because I was late to get my *sowhali* (girl) from school. Many passengers nowadays. That's why I got late. But she was scared ... Maajorghat was not like this. This accident has changed it so much. Everyone is coming to report. Not good for us. They will make big buildings and sell everything at more cost. People will choose taxis and not take my rickshaw,' he lamented, wondering aloud about the debatable impact of development and his dilemma about the good it might do and the harm it could cause him.

The mirage of an ideal life would become stronger when seen from a distance. Memories of the past appeared sweeter once they had changed for good. The omnipotent death and the pain of loss were ignored when an accident caused them, when there was an outside source to be blamed. A reason that would leave his town free of blemishes.

'Ya bhaiya,' Maya said finally. She wanted to tell him that she knew how life in this part of the region was. She, too, was one of them, but not anymore. Instead, she sat in silence. A town like this was her home too, before 'home' transitioned and continued changing from one city to another.

As though trying to resist any kind of change, the auto stopped. The tyres were stuck in mud, of a light-coloured ash. The path was narrow, with puddles after every few metres. The weight on the tyres created a shallow cleft on the mud, making it difficult to move the auto-rickshaw further. Bamboo fencing ran along sideways with small, whitewashed houses inside, their tin roofs still wet with droplets of rain. He had taken a by-lane.

He got down and smiled at Maya. She couldn't smile back. She anticipated his veiled intentions. Was it the fear of loot, or something worse? When uncertainty hovered, even the chirping of crickets sounded like a wolf's howl.

'Should I get down?' she asked reluctantly, holding her seat tightly. *Should I run away or sit inside?* She was weighing her options.

'No madam, you sit,' he said as he pushed the rickshaw with practiced ease.

As they moved further, avoiding another puddle through a dirt track between thick bushes, he said, 'I heard that accident, *Baideu*,' addressing her with an honorific commonly used for an elder sister or older woman. 'We all get up early na. I heard it then. Very loud sound. I thought it was a bomb. My wife thought our neighbour's gas cylinder had exploded!'

He laughed at the last comment.

'Some people saw it too. There was fire. As if train tyres were burning. And then, the coaches started falling! Just like that! We all ran towards it. I saw one coach; it was hanging. Really bad, madam. Everyone was screaming. It was scary! I saw people falling in the water. They opened the gate and jumped. We swam and pulled some out. Took them to the hospital also. Even in my auto, madam.'

'We helped, but no TV showed us,' he added after a pause.

Maya didn't believe that the bridge had caught fire, or that iron tracks and train tyres could ever trigger one. She knew people wouldn't have just stood and watched passengers falling out of the coaches. But she could hear their cries. She could imagine flames, drop-shaped, setting everything ablaze. As he spoke, she could see the fire's golden tongue swirling, licking everything out of existence. Billows of smoke, stronger and fouler than odious morning breath if charred flesh mixed with metals and plastic dropped like saliva. A fetid rareness. She prayed for her Ma and father.

Maya reached the station.

7

Two platforms facing each other and a rail track between them constituted the Maajorghat station. Rusted log of a rail's life. Tin roofs covered the platform on both sides, under them a few scattered benches and a yellow stone slab in the far end, with its name in bold and black. It was around nine at night when Maya entered the station, mostly dark except for a few tube lights, one of which quivered every now and then. The platform was packed with people unlike the night Maya had come two years ago. A visit equally tumultuous and sudden. Visits outside the purview of Ma's knowledge, a rarity in her life.

Shrugging off the thoughts that were seizing and dragging her back to that time, Maya went straight to the office but found it closed. A ticket collector, in a black suit and cap, still displaying faint creases of that morning's ironing, with a leatherette bound black register in his hand, ripped at the edges, asked her to try the next morning after eight.

It was a long wait, from that moment to the next morning, to know where her parents were. Whether they were safe, comfortably sleeping somewhere, or waiting for her. *I will find them.* She shoved hope down into her heart, unaware of the coming times when she would have to fill this constant depletion.

Hesitant to search more, Maya placed her suitcase next to a wall in a corner and sat hunched on the station floor. With one hand on the purse in her lap, she slowly crossed her legs. Around her, many were settling for the night, each choosing a place best suited to them. Some, like her, had taken a wall or door to lean on. Those who'd arrived early chose a bench as their shield and spread their shawls and sheets around it. A few preferred the frenetic fan above them, regardless of its threats of falling with each rotation.

Almost every family created a human circle, with children and women in the middle, luggage on the side, and men surrounding them. Societal structure was being enacted on a lesser scale, one gender protecting the other, one age guarding the other. Sense of ownership led the way and fear of loss forced itself in. Or maybe the awareness of deceit lurked within the protectors. Reasons could be any, but the structure remained the same. Dread rumbled around them, like the buzzing of bee swarms in an overcrowded honeycomb. Sound of a tap leaking drops of water into a concrete basin reached her. It was soon interrupted.

'Didi, how are you?' a young man greeted Maya with a smile, the kind that created ease and regenerated hope. He stood in front of her. A lean figure with sun-kissed skin and an exceptionally sharp nose concealing the blandness that his eyes exuded.

'Oh you?' Maya said, noticing his bandaged hand. He was the same man who'd gotten her a ride to the camp.

'Sunil.'

Maya nodded, deciding against telling him her name. An impotent protection. Protection, nevertheless. She raised the handbag over her chest now, an armour offering a sense of safety. In a similar fashion, she had often drawn comfort from a cotton stole, encircling it around her neck in a loose long wrap, covering her already strapped breasts, to avert the otherwise piercing eyes. An unfailing but futile attempt.

He inquired about her parents with a familiarity that should come from years of acquaintance, not from the few hours they had known each other. He suggested more ways in which Maya could continue her search. He then came and sat next to her. She shifted, sliding towards the door. He smiled again, an unfeigned amusement at her show of distrust. He appeared to know how she felt, as if he too had gone through years of unsettling gazes and lurking tongues. His smile annoyed Maya.

'You called their friends?'

'Yes, da. They know nothing.'

A pause filled the air between them, long enough to pick a book and read its blurb, but not enough to go past even a single page. Maya looked at him. He was sitting cross-legged, one hand on his lap, the soiled soles of his shoes pointing outwards. His bandaged hand lay lifeless on the side.

After a while, Sunil ran his good hand on the bandaged one, his face tightening when he touched it. His hand looked paralysed, and he appeared tired.

'My hand broke. I knew it then itself. Because of the pain, you know.' He was looking intently at the stained white of his bandaged hand.

'When I was young, I once broke my leg.' Maya felt a need to connect. The memory of which she had successfully pushed in the vault, meant to be never opened, until today. Her vault had many such memories, and a few dreams too, where soon memories of this search would be thrown in. Alongside the pain of a father's slap for a broken leg, and of a mother who had carried her to the hospital, running in a threadbare cotton saree and rubber slippers. Buried in the vault was also the heaviness she'd felt that day and on many such days in later years. It was a heavy burden for a child to force her mother to live on, to shoulder responsibilities, when she would have preferred a flight away from the life she had. The load a daughter carried upon seeing her mother stare at empty walls and wallets, greeting her with a hearty laugh nevertheless. The load of knowing the paradox a mother could live and the guilt of inducing it. Maya had learnt early on in her life to segregate memories—for the vault, for sharing, and for hopes.

'When I was in there, you know, I thought they would never find me. But they pulled me out,' he said, to make the reality of his escape more real by repeating it.

'Sometimes I feel it was a nightmare. As in … what if it was just a dream you know? Just waking up, all curled up in a blanket, and simply waiting for hawkers, for tea and all. And to look down and see other passengers getting ready to de-board, putting their stuff back. But I see blood all the time. Not while dreaming. Like, even when I sit, I see myself suffocating, falling, crawling. I try to forget it. I keep opening my eyes wide, but it doesn't stop.'

He paused for a moment and continued.

'I saw it. All of it. Was sitting by the window when it happened.'

Maya could feel the trauma he was in. He repeatedly widened his eyes, as though trying to wake up from the nightmare he'd lived a day ago. He could still see bodies hanging, being brought out, detached limbs, and broken skulls.

'It was weird. So strange to see coaches falling one by one. All those sounds of cracking and dropping.'

As Sunil spoke further, he could see it all again. He too squirmed slightly, the way the train had done a while back. Pieces of bridge falling down, splashing the water around. As it fell, it toppled the coaches that were on the bridge. At first, they fluttered like a bird taking its first flight, then losing the struggle, they plunged, one after another, twisting and twirling as they lost balance, unable to remain still on the shaky bridge. Sunil told Maya that he could hear the screams of the people in those coaches. He too had shrieked when death felt so near. Maya had heard similar screams when she saw relatives refusing to acknowledge the few recognizable bodies, in their desperate attempt to deny reality.

'I saw it. So many people were inside…'

He rubbed his right palm over his face.

'My coach hung on that last pole of the bridge. It was still very strong. Some *jawaans*, they tore our coach and pulled many of us out. Lots of bags fell on me and my hand. I thought I would die but didn't.'

His expression was grave now.

Maya wondered where her parents were. She thought of showing him a picture of her parents once again and seeking his help in her search.

'Where were you going?' she asked instead, placing her handbag beside her now.

'Nowhere else. My home is here.'

'Then why aren't you going home?'

'Uh … my mother. Not able to find her. She works here … at a Baideu house. She is a maid there,' he added as an afterthought, as though to fight his initial reluctance. 'Raised me alone, you know. But we managed. I also tutored younger kids when I was in school.'

Maya could see a hint of pride on his face. There was an honesty to it, for creating a space which even he thought was impossible. He had blurred the boundaries in a society where social status decided the food one could eat, the people one could marry, and the places one could enter. Maya, too, felt the same pride.

'Baideu told me that Ma went to that bridge. She didn't take her phone, not even her bag. It is so crowded now, maybe that's why I can't find her. Home is locked too, even now. I went in the evening, to keep my bag.'

Maya now saw a bag on his side. A huge jute cover, torn at the top, was placed next to his feet. 'Jayalakshmi Sarees and Dress Material' was scribbled over it in bright ink, with the store's address below it.

'Got everyone gifts—for Baideu's family too. They paid for my admission. Good people. It's all broken now,' he said, casually caressing the bag. Maya was surprised to see how nonchalant he was, as if everything was in control; as if he had prepared himself for tragedies like these, long before the actual act.

How can he act so normal even at this point? Maya sized up the young man in front, who was clearly in his early twenties, a decade younger than her. *He must have already faced a lot in life*, she concluded, looking at his unperturbed gait in the face of trauma. Assuming the lives of other people was an old habit of hers. Maya used to try and peep inside the houses that looked like a hole to her. She would then compare her life to them, in her attempt to make herself feel better. She would gaze into the intimate details of their lives for her emotional stability, a liberty she had taken without reluctance, without letting its awareness reach her carefully secured self-worth.

A modern liberty, created by her education, that allowed a generous dose of justifications, keeping intact the stature of her superiority, education, and newly acquired class. Of travelling in cars or trains, while they stood outside, staring with dreamy eyes. The subtle yet eternal difference that she wouldn't erase. The difference of places that she wouldn't swap if given a chance.

She wanted to know more about Baideu and Sunil's lives with and without them. Instead, she asked, 'You are a student?'

'Got a placement. My first job. In Bangalore,' he said, abruptly getting up to leave.

'Hey! You're leaving?'

Seeing him leave, Maya felt the same tension she experienced when he'd arrived. His presence had eased her. She wanted to know more about him, to seek hope out of his conviction.

'Ya didi. Will search for my mother. She will be somewhere. You know, she is my everything. So much she did.' Such heightened sentimentality showed his fear of losing his mother.

Flushed, Maya heard the story of his love for his mother. A desire hankered within her too. A wish for a similar bond, for a love-filled childhood. Soon, jealousy stung that desire.

Sunil continued as he stood to leave, 'You know, there was a man, he was sitting opposite. The night before, we played cards. Very nice man. His head hit the window grill when our coach shook. Immediately started bleeding, too much. His child kept screaming seeing all that blood. Weird cry. Hearing him, I felt we all would die. His hand was stuck too. I pulled him out, but then we all were upside down. I don't know what happened to him.'

'Don't even know how I got out so safely. I think I have some major injury. I guess I feel it, not sure. But after I find my Ma, I should go and get myself checked,' he said with a hint of guilt in his voice, as if surviving was his fault. He stopped speaking and briskly walked out, his jute bag lugging beside.

Looking at him, she knew that his memory was going to be permanent. An indelible ink stain on a white shirt. The rhythmic sound of water droplets hitting the surface reached her again. A lullaby for a night that puzzled all of them.

She had a close relationship with her mother, but it wasn't like those shown in media, be it in advertisements or books. Neither was it like the one Sunil had, the kind that could exude warmth. Her mother too had endured a lot, especially in raising her. Maya was aware of it, yet she didn't feel the profound gratitude that she'd heard from Sunil. Its realisation brought guilt, which then piqued her.

She didn't grow into a woman under her mother's womanness. They didn't have their first talk on menstruation when she was thirteen and had seen a patch of blood in her underpants. She had gone to her friends, not Ma. She didn't tell her mother about her first crush, or when a boy from her tuition had proposed to her, threatening consequences if she rejected him. A young Maya didn't know how to react. Even though scared, she kept it to herself, eventually forcing Ma to change her tuition teacher. It wasn't Ma but her friends who had shown her the kind of brassiere she could and should buy.

Maya's understanding of her parents' equation and her father's absence fuelled the distance between them. She moved away from the dead dreams she saw in her mother. Although she presented a strong self, Maya could see how fragile Ma had been for a very long time. It was a reminder of her failure in protecting Ma from the life she didn't deserve. It had persisted since childhood, when she sought solace in inanimate objects. As an adult, she found peace in solving others' problems, the problems she wasn't experiencing, which made hers look smaller, less significant.

As she grew, their world expanded, and their relationship changed further. Maya fulfilled Ma's needs with the luxuries she hadn't asked for. There were no inconveniences for her, but nothing beyond convenience too.

Although they stayed together, Maya retreated into herself even more. She couldn't give Ma the normalcy she deserved. It wasn't intentional. Heeding to oneself felt natural, like the sea gearing up for a tsunami with the intention to rise a bit more, but killing even its most honest admirers in the process.

Maya had received the news the only way she knew. And to that perceived reality, she'd reacted in her expected way.

When the derailment seemed to have altered everything, this search was her way to change the reality that might have engulfed her mother—and this time her father too. It was more of preserving what was left of Ma.

8

The continuous honking of a truck jolted Maya out of sleep. The station had taken a different look altogether. Constant muttering of passers-by replaced the night's silence, and the glistening streak of the sun dimmed the flicker of tube lights.

For a while, she stood looking around, lost, like a lone calf separated too early from the mother. Gradually regaining herself, she checked her belongings and headed towards the office. Rushing inside, she pushed her way forward to the man who was sitting with an open register in front of him. His table was cluttered. A pile of documents and three mobile phones lay near the register. On its side was a folded copy of *Asomiya Pratidin*, the local daily, with a strategically taken photo of an NDRF soldier carrying a bleeding passenger, with fallen coaches and the broken bridge as the backdrop covering the left section of its colourful top half.

A heavily built man with a thin moustache was sitting on a timid chair, his sides exploding out of the chair's frail arms. He threw a hasty glance at Maya, only to return to the register the next moment. He continued to check his register, the pen in his hand swiftly hopping from one column to another, from one page to the next. Maya greeted him enthusiastically, as if her parents' lives depended on the rapport she could establish with this man, who was sprawling over this sudden splurge of power. The power of hope that made the relatives queue in front, the authority of information, of divulging their fate and their loved one's lives with just a quick glance at his paper. His access into their unforeseeable future, the power of certainty at a time irrefutably uncertain.

Not getting any response, Maya pleaded again.

'Call the helpline number,' he finally replied. 'Go see the news, madam, it's everywhere,' he added before Maya could respond. Seeing her unwillingness to budge until he offered something substantial, he took out a printed paper and handed it over to her. The same sheet had been published in the newspapers too.

As Maya stepped out of the office, her eyes remained fixed on the paper with the names of passengers found or reported so far. Her heart was pounding so loudly that she could hear it clearly, even amid the honks and thunder.

LIST OF INJURED PASSENGERS TRAVELLING BY TRAIN NO. 011188, MAAJORGHAT-GUWAHATI EXPRESS.

Another page, much dreaded, had the **LIST OF DEATHS – PASSENGERS IN TRAIN NO. 011188, MAAJORGHAT-GUWAHATI EXPRESS.**

It was a comprehensive list of passengers, dead or hospitalized, with their address and age mentioned next to them. Maya went over the sheet twice but couldn't find the names she was searching for.

The list ensured that her search was not going to end soon, like an eternal quest for illusory happiness. A search that often left one aged and frail.

Not everything aged, though. Nature delighted in its nativity, and greenery often sneaked itself in. At the peak of its beauty, a verdant earth gleamed in pride. Trees in their prime flirted with the rain. Rain came down and took a walk of vigour; flowers blushed in coyness when a breeze caressed them, while the demure shrubs waited for their turn and sighed at the affairs. Bees flew and kissed flowers, butterflies emerged out of caterpillars, leeches revelled in the abundance of hosts. The nature, unaffected by misfortune that had befallen them, appeared to be celebrating. This revelry did reach the platform where Maya stood. She could hear it, in spite of her heart's pleas.

Looking around, Maya also saw many young volunteers from colleges and NGOs. They were distributing water bottles and food packets, requesting everyone to form a queue, and shouting at the ones not adhering to their rules. They were trying to calm the mayhem, but becoming a part of it nevertheless.

However, they couldn't help everyone. Nor did everyone seek their help. Maya accidentally nudged one such with her shoes as she walked past. She turned around and saw a kid, four or five-years old, sitting with a loaf of bread in her hand and a huge bag on her side. Apart from the gloom that'd settled over everyone, including Maya, like a thin layer of sand, the kid appeared at ease, unaffected by the chaos around her.

Like a sparrow on the lookout, her dry vigilant eye gaped at Maya. Her hair, pulled back, was parted in the middle. She had crimson lips, with breadcrumbs around their edges, strangely reminding Maya of the wine she would have drunk at one of her usual dinner dates with Kevin, if she were not here today. The young girl shouted 'Papa!' upon seeing a man who was walking towards them urgently, a water bottle and food packet in his hands. He picked up the kid in one hand and the bag in another, and walked away. His behaviour baffled Maya. *Why was he so worried? What was happening to the kids who were left unattended here?* She knew that not everyone had a Papa to rely on, with or without accident.

She then saw a group of people standing and listening to a middle-aged man who spoke with feverish speed, as though chasing time, but with utmost authority, like a classroom teacher during a dictation. He was a government official. They were hearing him attentively, expecting him to say a word of hope. Seeing the expressions on their faces, she could guess that he wasn't.

Everyone in that station seemed to be guided by a sense of loss. Like them, Maya's walk was also crippled with the tragedy. She slouched under the roof of cries and anger, burdened with the sight of pain.

Overwhelmed, she walked further and found herself standing next to a pale woman. Under different circumstances, she would have distanced herself immediately. Avoiding the triggers of emotional distress, which included feeling pity, had been a way of survival for Maya. She would reflexively look away, busying herself in matters she could control instead.

But today, she looked at the woman and saw a look of devastation on her face. It was making her look perpetually sick. She was sitting listlessly, oblivious to the commotion around. Tangled hair fell carelessly on her shoulder, and her swollen face, mournful eyes, and parched lips breathed out soft sighs. Her saggy shoulders seemed to plead for some sleep. Maya was intrigued. The woman seemed to have led a content life in the past. Maya could guess as much after noticing her diamond ring and leather bag. Her hands were on her knees. Two metal bangles hung loosely from them. Two silver toe rings shone on her bare and immobile feet. Her feet resembled her face, but with intensified coarseness. Their enormous size seemed to cover more space than they meant to. They were distracting for Maya. She stared at them, their nakedness giving away a vulnerability—a compromised modesty. It passed on to her.

Yet, when she looked at this woman as a whole individual rather than an assimilation of parts, she found her humane. An accumulation of emotions similar to hers. The colour of her watery eyes held Maya's. Their brown, that now appeared red, enticed her. Two balls of sun held within the white sky of her eyes. Like a floating fire.

'Hello,' Maya heard herself addressing the woman while looking for a place to sit beside her. To look into oblivion, the way she was doing.

The woman nodded, although her eyes continued searching for something familiar. She eventually shifted her gaze from the rail tracks to Maya. She looked at her as blankly as a doll's glare on a dark night. To Maya's relief, she shifted her gaze back to the iron tracks in front. The tracks that travelled together, but remained perennially separated. Between them were used cups and plates, some broken, some undamaged, and a few crushed bottles. Faeces were piled at regular intervals and crows hovered around the rotten food. The tracks that were constantly running away from them. For a while, Maya, too, looked at the tracks, hoping they would signal a path to her parents.

'Uh … hi, you were on the train?' Maya asked after a while, without looking at her.

'No, no. I came to search.'

'Oh. Okay. Got any information?'

'Yes.'

Her answer and tone confused Maya. If this was how they were to be found, then she was ready to abandon her search. In the woman's answer, Maya could hear her hope for the search crumble too. A crisp piece of life crushed under the feet of fate. The possible reality of a different outcome scared her. This unknown woman's 'Yes' had given her a reason to abandon everything she knew until then. Yet, when she tried to think, Maya wasn't sure what to leave and what to live with.

She focused again on the prospect of finding her parents alive. Looking at everyone fervently, Maya searched for those two figures of flesh and blood whom she had resisted until now, in her guarded way from the probable hurt.

Maya got up and walked away from the woman. Above her, under the blue sky, a starched flag fluttered, as though just out of the box, eager to show its bright colour and creased rim. She felt cheated, wronged by nature, by her fate.

If they were travelling, why weren't they in the hospital, or even in the camp? Why? I should check the mortuary. No, I shouldn't. This list is wrong, Maya concluded.

She decided to go to the camp again, to the hospital, and this time to the hotels as well. She wanted to defy that yes. 'They are fine. Yes, they are. It's my fault. I am bad at looking,' she told herself.

SECTION 5

STATIONED AT MEMORY

1

Scared at the possibility of losing them, Maya tried to erase it with forced optimism, seeking hope through a staged, vocal surety of finding them. *Ma is a fighter. She is fine. They must be fine,* she affirmed again. She put her entire faith on affirmations. Praying for them to come true. The power of words to turn magic into reality.

Walking on a cramped lane, she was surrounded with freshly sprouted shops and hawkers. Shouting here was different from the screams she heard a while back. These makeshift stalls, with their occasional call to attract customers, provided a voice of familiarity, negating the quietude that many were succumbing to. These shops sold everything a passenger would need—from water bottles, tea, Maggi noodles, poori and curry, to packets of potato chips and biscuits. Umbrellas with plastic handles, translucent raincoats with imposing black buttons and toys too, to keep children from distressing their already dismayed parents.

Maya judged the shops for flourishing out of an accident, feigning ignorance that these same stalls catered to the needs of those like her. Dissecting those in front helped in diverting herself from the fear that was transforming into grief.

She eventually went up to a man standing under a wide umbrella, with many hanging on to his arms. Two-fold, three-fold, and a few five-fold umbrellas too, while some were long and straight. Some bare, few with their individual cover, colours in black, red, and green. Most of them plain, a few patterned, floral, and chequered. A limited few were transparent too. Yet, they were nothing like the one she used to own once upon a time. Her satin umbrella, in the colour of gold, flowers embroidered on it, with a matching handle. Even though it was unsuitable for the rain Sigo Dolung received, Maya would carry it everywhere. This time, she had forgotten to pack one. Haggling for a while over the price and eventually paying the amount he'd quoted initially, she bought one.

Umbrellas here had personalities of their own. They too reflected the widening economic gaps, symbolizing access, taste, refinement, and the coarseness of it. The differentiation, like everything else of society, was decided by the ones using them.

Umbrellas, once a part of her identity and a reflection of her choices, became an accessory of occasional need when she started her life outside Arunachal. In Bangalore, it became an option, only to be brought out in the monsoons. The city received a comparatively shorter period of rain, most of which she would witness from her office window or car. She opened her three-fold black umbrella. It had a silver lining on the inside, as though to counter the grey everyone seemed to live in.

Maya then walked away from the commotion at the station, on a comparatively peaceful path that lay ahead. Wild shrubbery on both sides of the road, a light drizzle, and a pale mist surrounded her. For a moment, she felt that she was being enveloped within the soft hug of a quilt.

After almost fifteen minutes of walking, as the mist was slowly clearing up, she saw a fair of umbrellas, going to and fro. She could hear a distant sound, like a cable signal gone wrong. As she approached nearer, it turned into a hum of pain, like hearing a tragic play on the radio, the images replaced by a cumulative sound of shrieking. Maya was crossing the derailment site.

For a second, she thought of the coaches as helpless inanimate objects, believing that they couldn't do anything to her parents. The next moment, she cursed them for their deceptive innocence and cruelty towards those who trusted them. *How could these coaches be so heartless?* Maya looked at the derailed coaches just beneath the bridge. A sprinkle of blue dust, seemingly innocuous. She knew that in one of these her parents must have struggled. *They must have come out,* she told herself.

A man in crushed linen and waving curls crossed, glancing at her. Maya noticed him too as he passed by, hopping back into a minivan, this time not with the injured but with supplies and jute bags loaded with ration. She was thinking of asking him for a lift, when her phone rang. It was Kevin's tenth missed call since she'd landed.

Just then, Maya saw a woman. Amid the awnings of umbrellas on each head, she was standing without one. Her deep, sunken eyes captivated her. She felt drawn towards her petite build, which seemed to have shortened further. An aging through loss, fastest and persistent. Her sari shrunk to her ankle, patches of mud on it, which she was dusting repeatedly. She pouted her lips, while her eyes searched for someone in the crowd.

Maya went and spoke to her. She informed Maya about her son and pointed towards the bundle of coaches that lay chaotically over each other. The woman blathered again, 'He will come. I know this. My son always does what he says. I am not able to find him. My mistake. Old women like me cannot search quickly. Too much crowd also na. My eyes are also not good anymore.'

Behind the woman, the coaches were slowly getting submerged in the glaucous swamp with a desire to engulf everything. Its carnivorous-ness hidden beneath its gullible, slushy shelf. Those mutilated coaches looked incapable of having any life inside them. Maya felt a tinge of dread talking to someone who was clearly at the place she could be, or already was.

'*Aei* swahili, why are you here?' The woman paused for a few minutes and looked at Maya, as though assessing her. She had an undeviating manner of speaking without using any unnecessary words, not even the customary ones.

Not waiting for Maya's response, she continued animatedly, 'I am leaving with my son. He has a good job now. I will go and live with him. In Bangalore city. There is a big house and balcony too. Won't work at Baideu's house anymore. I will be a baideu of my house.' A slight smile appeared on her face at the prospect of being the owner of a house.

'There are many big buildings there, big markets and restaurants too. Sunil told me yesterday, I can shop and eat there. When I meet him, he will show me pictures. On my mobile, I don't get pictures,' she explained to Maya in between her soliloquy. 'Don't know where he is. Not able to find him. But he will be here only. I know. Did you see him? Thin boy, very nice smile. He's this tall.' She raised her hand a few inches above herself.

Cranes were now lifting the empty metal shell of drowned coaches, depression on sides, discoloured, bleeding paint and mud. Whatever or whoever remained under the bridge, those that couldn't be brought out, were being left unsearched.

And then, after a pause, as if those few seconds of silence revealed reality to her, she said, 'If my son doesn't return, I will go to Baideu again. She is good. Like family. What else to do? I am already old. I don't want anything. I lived here all my life. Not good to shift in a new place anyway,' she muttered to herself and walked away from Maya, who just stood and stared at her.

Silence or relentless speech, both prerequisites to pain, were at work here. As the woman walked away from her, Maya felt an urge to inform her about a 'son' she'd met the previous night, who spoke about the kind of love she could never get, and a relationship she never had. The love of a mother, that she didn't take when offered later. Thinking of the collection of unfulfilled relationships in her life and grieving over the probable loss, she decided against informing the woman.

She stood like a stone etched on the ground. Because sometimes, it was envy that won.

'Papa, look at this!' A young Maya came running with a newly acquired sweater that mother had sewn for her. 'Ma made this. For me!' she added.

'Hmm,' came a curt reply from a well-built man, who was still undoing his shoelaces near the wrought iron shoe-rack.

'Papa, it's beautiful na? Look … it has a flower too,' she asked in an ecstatic voice.

'Yes, it is.'

'You are not seeing it,' she reproached him. 'Papa, Look. Look Papa. Papa!'

He, giving in to her constant whimpering, looked at her and said, 'Yes, yes, it is beautiful. Very nice. Oh, this flower is extraordinary too. You look amazing, my *gudiya* (doll).'

Though his words were loaded with praise and love, his tone wasn't. His hands would pat her, but she could feel him standing miles away. Though a girl of ten years, she could still understand the depth of his reaction. Eventually, Maya stopped approaching him for acknowledgement and soon learnt not to reward him with hers.

'You are using Maya to show your talent? You are great. Hain na!'

'Now what happened?'

Her mother was kneading the dough for that night's chapatis.

He went and stood at the kitchen entrance, but she didn't look up. Raged at this indifference, he said again, 'You are trying to win her over. You are luring her. Trying to become great in her eyes. And making me look bad.'

'Don't think I am a fool. I know it. And stop wasting my money. Very clever,' he added, in an effort to provoke her.

'What is your problem?' she replied, finally looking at him. She knew that if she were to get peace, she had to let him fight with her. To satisfy his ego, reaffirm his manliness, and reassure his right to go away. Only then he would be satisfied and retire for the night.

'Maya was showing her NEW sweater, praising you!'

'So what?! She needed a sweater, so I made one!' The contempt was clear in her tone.

'You are trying to show her that you love her more.'

'No. I am not.'

'Don't fool me. I know what this is all about. Trying to build your little army against me.'

'Are you crazy?'

'Yes, now call me crazy. This is exactly what you want. You want to drive me crazy. That is why I should go away,' he added. 'You love Maya more. You don't love me; you don't even respect me. Never did.' He needed an excuse to part ways, and these presumed and carefully placed misunderstandings served them on a platter.

'No, I don't love her. I don't love anyone!' she said, fuming. She gave him what he waited for to end the fight.

Maya stood a few inches behind him, listening to their arguments. She didn't say anything. Neither did she try to protect her mother from his false accusations, nor did she confess that it was she who had asked for the sweater. She didn't try to understand her mother's words either. But later, she would often wonder why a mother would cry and proclaim that she didn't love her only daughter. That day, a young Maya couldn't understand their conversation. She had simply walked away from the kitchen door. A child, who didn't know if her mother loved her, or if her father wanted to leave her mother.

2

Maya had returned to the camp. With the change in time, the camp too had undergone a change of appearance. Desk and chairs were now placed in the open, and a loudspeaker stood next to them, grumbling announcements every few minutes. *Arrival at the desk, person found, person sought, reminder to maintain queue, preferably peaceful.*

In a loose shirt and skinny jeans, Maya stood transfixed, listening to the names—Krishna Sarma, Ameena Bora, M.R. Srivastava, Lalita Devi, Venu Gopakumar, Udipti Saikia … but not the names she was waiting for. With each announcement, she tore a piece of the tissue paper in her hand. She wanted to stay put and learn about her parents, yet a wish to run away was growing stronger. She wanted to end this wait.

The inquiry desk was overburdened with photographs piled in one corner, handed by relatives with their personal numbers and addresses. Everyone was trying to have privileged access to information—to be the first one to know. Volunteers and officials, in turn, showing solidarity, took whatever the relatives had to offer and piled everything. They, although overworked, staged calmness, only occasionally bursting with bouts of impatience. Bewildered with such a surcharge of questions, they too wished to be understood, their predicament acknowledged and not rebuked.

This mayhem would gradually clear out, leaving nothing but an eerie silence. No human would stand in the queue for food or information. Used plastic bottles, forgotten slippers, scattered papers, blankets, and sheets, torn and soiled, would soon lay in silence, as though guilty of their existence. Crows would fly and peck at the leftovers. Dogs would hurl to look for food and scare the crows away. A cow or two would walk in search of something to eat. A bird would fly and sit on its back while the cow would dig its nose deeper in the garbage bin and swallow a plastic or two.

Maya stood in the queue now, her burgundy hair tied in a high bun. She crossed her hands in front, fingers intermingled. She stood with her legs set slightly apart, head held straight, suggesting her readiness for anything they would disclose. Yet, her heavy breaths and the deep shade of anticipation encircling her eyes divulged the turmoil she was trying to hide.

Approaching the inquiry desk, she gave her parents' names, their ages, her mother's recent picture, her father's twenty-years-old photograph, and coach number. Receiving no information, she further inquired about the other survivors of the B2 coach.

Maya didn't know details about their journey until she'd reached Maajorghat. Her mother hadn't shared any information. She hadn't asked, either. This wasn't the nature of their conversation. They usually called to inform each other about their plans and whereabouts, mostly updating about their well-being. Their calls didn't last for more than five minutes. It was from Mr Barua, at whose place her parents had stayed for the night, that she'd found out the coach number.

After asking them to check the information twice, Maya moved away and sat in front of the camp, like a devotee in front of the deity. Surrendered, yet hopeful.

Twilight had darkened into an early night. Nature, like time, prided in its continuity and refusal to remain the same. So, the sun had set, and stars slowly made their way into the sky, as they did every night. The sky was as it had always been—aloof, yet attached to its promptness. Isolated, yet impactful.

Residents would start for their home as soon as the day faded. Absence of streetlights, muddied roads, unabated rain, and the onset of nightfall by six or seven would lead to early abandonment of the chores. Even that day, around five p.m., most people had started leaving for the places they were to retire in for the night. This town, bearing the burden of a calamity, was also sketching an image of desolation, of a disquieting menace. Now there were frequent talks about small-scale robberies and snatchings—rumours or reality, one couldn't tell. A touch of frenzy lingered in everyone's actions.

It was past seven, but Maya still sat cross-legged in front of the camp. Amid constant buzzing of vehicles and human voices that floated around, she was still hopeful of hearing her parents' names.

The camp was slowly transforming back to what she had seen the previous night. Tables were joined and massive saucepans brought and arranged on top. Maya's gaze was still fixed on the poll and the loudspeaker, like a hawk watching its prey, although she lacked the precision of its movements. Her torso appeared to have drooped between her legs. Her hands were around them, as if in support.

When she turned, she didn't find any of the people who were sitting by her side till now. They were gone without leaving a trace behind, maybe like her parents.

'Madam, I hope you are fine?'

The voice startled her.

Turning around, she saw the same man from the previous

evening, standing a few inches away. His big, dreamy eyes diverged from the brutal sharpness of his nose, an angular face in congruence with the softness of his lips. His appearance made her trust him instantly. His unkempt hair gave an air of weariness, while his voice had the sharpness of a robotic machine. Severity embracing modesty. His humility didn't give away any weakness; it appeared to be his biggest strength. His brusqueness was an asset he deserved imperially, not to destroy but to save.

As he spoke to Maya, he moved towards her. His movements, though slow but precise, were in full control, as if they were not a part of his weary body but an illustration of his mind. He pulled her upwards, helping her to get up. Their gaze holding each other, they stood as if hypnotized. And then, with a sudden jerk, he steadied himself and pulled away his hand.

Even I used to be like him, thought Maya when she saw him. His sight reminded her of the recent past where, presumably, she also had the same control over her life.

'Yes, I am,' Maya replied, taking a step back.

'You are also waiting for someone?' he spoke again, pointing in the direction of the loudspeaker. With everyone gone, it stood in absolute silence, a characteristic so unnatural to it. To Maya, its silence was more clamorous than the announcements.

'My Ma and Father,' she replied, glancing in the same direction. Mother, who was hers, whom she called Ma. A father who had willingly walked away from the world of Papa, whom she had eventually refused to consider as hers.

Kranti nodded, understanding her plight. It was a nod of solidarity, yet she felt it was not for the situation they were in, but for the thoughts that ran through her mind. Maya feared that he could see through her. She looked down to ensure that her skin wasn't a transparent curtain, allowing him a good peek inside her life. It pained her, this strange visibility, as if her skin were peeled apart, and everything concealed within put on display. His looks and his smile implied to know more than they should.

Maya nodded and turned away from the man, who seemed to strike a chord and build a bond, something she wouldn't give in to. He ran behind her. After knowing that she hadn't booked any hotel, he offered to take her to a decent one in the town. 'People of this small town haven't seen women going alone and asking for rooms,' he explained with such a familiarity that it irked Maya.

He had taken charge of her situation without even seeking her permission. 'I don't even know you,' came a sharp response. Yet, he called a ride and insisted in such a manner that she couldn't refuse, obliging her to trust him before she could decide otherwise.

Although unsure, Maya finally handed over this search to him. Seeking a hotel or a person, peace within or silent surroundings. Sometimes, for certain things, Maya needed someone too.

3

Dropping Mridula at the bus stand, Kranti had returned to the camp, partly to seek information on Priyom as well. He checked once for an update on his whereabouts and then spent the rest of the day doing what he had decided to. Careless volunteers were brought back to work. Cooks were tutored about timing. Water cans were bought, and water bottles were set aside. Even while helping, health wasn't to be compromised. Multiple trips on ambulance and constant calls for arrangements for the dead and living alike were made.

He was offering a helping hand. A steady hand over shivering shoulders.

He felt a generous dose of kindness. His care was as patronizing as a friendly nudge to one's driver, or a well-intended joke on one's staff that they couldn't reply to. It was a superior kindness that Kranti believed in. He had been busy all day.

It was in between those acts of generosity that he had seen Maya. Standing still in front of the desk, her stance showing strength, her eyes failing her, nevertheless. Seeing Maya, he had smiled, thinking of how heroic she must be to try hiding her emotions where everyone else openly cried. He had instinctively admired her courage. Kranti knew that he would have behaved similarly. Her casual dressing had captured his attention too. A style similar to his, which, as per Kranti, was marking both of them apart from the rest. A distinction he liked.

Later that evening, as he was finishing his tasks at the camp, he saw her again. Her straight stance now bent to the ground. Crouching, with a bag on her side. Whether she was deep in thought or just blankly gawking, he couldn't tell. Her hands hugged her legs, on which she rested her chin. Arms and legs stuck on to an arched back like an eggshell. An impression of wholeness with a definite frailty. Yet, to Kranti, her presence felt like the thunderous sound of a waterfall that he wasn't able to ignore.

Approaching Maya, he asked if she needed any help. Her glance felt familiar to him. She too was trying to recognize him. He extended his hands to her. She slipped her fingers into his and got up, but immediately started to walk away from him. He felt a compulsion to stop her. As to why, he didn't bother asking himself. He couldn't understand such an abrupt end to their meeting. For a second, this urge confused him; yet, the next moment he ignored it and went ahead with a casual assurance. When she told him that she didn't have a hotel, he offered to find her one. She reluctantly agreed.

Kranti took her to the main market of Maajorghat where all the four hotels of the town stood next to each other, defying the very logic of exclusivity. There wasn't any need for more hotels. Even the ones operating didn't see many guests, apart from travellers who would come for a night's stay and leave in the wee hours of the next morning to catch a train or bus. Once in a while, a couple or two would come and ask for a room, which they would invariably refuse.

He took her to all the hotels. Maya rejected the first two after a mere glance at their deteriorating buildings. The remaining two mimicked each other. Tall, white buildings, dotted with rectangular windows, equally distanced from each other. Flashy sign boards on top that would light up at night in twinkling colours. Both the hotels had a small parking area in front where a security guard stood on duty. Attractive entrances, lined with flowerpots, bright coloured sofa sets at the entrance, and receptionist counters covered in different colours of mica sheets. Both displayed their loyalty to the elected leader on their walls, a smiling middle-aged man holding a flower bouquet in his hand, gamocha on his shoulder, and tea gardens in the backdrop.

Maya chose one with the name 'Blue Hill Hotel'. Abiding by the name, it had blue walls and its windows were adorned in blue curtains. A blue nameplate shone on the wall, and in front of it was a receptionist in a blue shirt.

'This looks fine,' she told him. Handing over the suitcase to the receptionist, who had now transformed into a bellboy, she ordered a cup of tea to be sent to her room. She then turned back to face Kranti.

She didn't thank him; she didn't feel the need to. A pull of familiarity. Not a rush of emotions, but the subtlety of comfort, as though they had spent their entire lives in each other's companionship. A look enough to understand each other.

They stood facing each other. Kranti reciprocated her smile with his.

'I am also staying here,' he finally told her.

'Oh. Okay.'

'Actually… I didn't want to come across as some *chepo*, you see. Anyway, it was better for you to see everything and then decide,' he said with an air of finality.

'Maya,' she said after a while.

'Kranti.'

They felt a strong desire to know each other; a faint wish to spend time in each other's company, although they weren't ready to accept this misplaced attraction. A blur of dream and reality, one leading into another.

4

The tea at the hotel, insipid and cold, hadn't been of her taste. So, after a few trials, Maya complained like always, asserting her issues and making her unhappiness known. This time, she didn't call up beforehand but waited for their call, and when they did, she politely informed them of her displeasure. She expected nothing but an ear to vent. What she received surprised her. She heard an apology from the other end. It was not how things went in her life usually. She had to fight to be acknowledged. She was also offered a free pot of tea again. She refused it. She wasn't prepared for such generosity.

It was when she was sitting and smiling at the apology that she got another call from the hotel's cook, inquiring about the issue and offering to mend it through one of his signature dishes. She politely declined. She didn't know how to behave if her wishes were fulfilled, especially without a fight.

Later, post freshening up, she called the receptionist, who also handled the room service, and ordered a plate of samosa which she planned to pay for. No acceptance of generosity. No place for unnatural emotions unsettling her further. She was trying to stay in her usual reality. However, the moment she opened the door, it was the cook who had come personally to offer his apologies and the plate of samosas. She fumbled upon seeing him. *Should she smile and praise his cooking, or should she complain more to validate her dissatisfaction?* She did neither.

Oh, the pain,
pulling you down into its cavernous pit.
You gasp for air, your hands shiver, fear throws you
up and down.
You splatter tears. You want to come out, but you fall further.
You feel that ache. But there's no injury to show. Yet,
something hurts.
An earnest hurt.
You cry out for the pain you can't see.
Sometimes you seek the pain for comfort.
You get up and forget,
but it comes back, crippling you.
Yet, when someone asks where it hurts,
you can't show.
Oh, the pain,
stabbing you, without spilling a single drop to show.

Perturbed, she took the plate inside, keeping it on the small table. It was then that she heard another knock on the door.

She was pleasantly startled to see Kranti, although still preoccupied. They had been meeting every day, to exchange information and sometimes a meal or two. His presence felt comforting to her. With no one to speak to and only dread in her mind, Maya felt relieved whenever she met him. Listening to his impersonal details on the accident, she would also forget how it affected her personally for a few moments. His willingness to spend time with her, often shown in his unannounced arrivals or requests to explore Maajorghat together, flattered that child in her who still waited to become someone's priority.

After the basic greetings, still standing in the hallway, she asked, 'Can I ask you one thing? Not sure if it's relevant but… uh … have you ever felt that you are not entitled to good treatment?'

'No. Why? Can I come in?'

Apologizing for her abrupt and loud contemplation, she invited Kranti in.

'Care for a samosa?'

'Too salty,' he said, keeping the half-eaten samosa back on the plate and spilling the mixed vegetable stuffing, unusual to the rest but common to this side of the country. Maya didn't touch them. She couldn't.

'Actually, I was going for a coffee. Would you like to come?' Kranti finally asked.

Maya agreed to join him downstairs. Before leaving, she called up the receptionist and asked him to inform the cook that the samosas were exceptional. A natural lie for the exceptional generosity.

Standing in front of the mirror, Maya looked at herself. She chose a purple shirt. Purple brought out her complexion, Kevin had told her. An open suitcase on the floor. A few shirts scattered on her bed.

She now regretted for not being careful in choosing her clothes and stuffing her suitcase with everything from that day's laundry, which were mostly her gym and shopping clothes. She hadn't got the good ones she wore to office, which were always washed with hands, as Ma had specified. She wanted to look better. After arranging her hair and putting a thin line of kohl, she looked at herself once again and went down to meet Kranti.

Maya and Kranti took a walk around the market. A cemented shopping complex shone in white light, with buyers and pedestrians walking in and out. A few people idled around the snack vendors, while some sat on the stairs. A few independent shops sold everything, from shoes and clothes to utensils and toys, keeping the area busy.

Walking further, they crossed several restaurants, wooden benches, and tables lined inside, all with billing counters displaying a collection of sweets under a glass dome. They eventually stopped at the one with cane chairs, warm golden lights hanging over each table. Bamboo Hut, the sign board announced.

Once in, Kranti called for the menu while Maya went ahead to make a call, to assert a decision that was pending for months now. A call to Kevin. The last few days in Maajorghat had heightened the feeling of impending doom in her. She now felt devoid of any energy or interest to even elongate their relationship. With the probable loss of Ma, she felt it was the time to lose him as well. This accident had not brought this feeling, it only strengthened it. Although she had long prepared a list of justified reasons to leave him, she didn't give him any. Uncomfortable with anything overly emotional, she informed Kevin in a few words of finality, disconnecting the call when he questioned her. It was a quick call, but long enough for Kranti to place their order: black tea for her, when it was cardamom tea she would have preferred, and a plate of cottage cheese dumplings for her and fish fry for himself, when she was looking forward to an egg sandwich. She came in, deleting the record of twenty missed calls from Kevin and his messages next in line, in an effort to erase reminders of the past to stabilize her present.

Settling in a secluded corner, they dipped their toes in the pool of conversation. Obama's visit to miraculous wins, Kranti's disappointment with the Cricket World Cup to Maya's reluctance to give up her LPG subsidy, their fear of the fast-approaching flood to anticipated blockage. They discussed everything they could think of, until Kranti started speaking about his reason to stay back, which he hadn't informed her until now.

'My sister,' he told her. Giving details which he didn't need to, about Priyom, the divorce, her child, his responsibility, her house, her career, and so on. As Maya heard him, her mind went back to Kevin and his girlfriend, whom he referred to as the 'good friend'. The distancing he had been speaking about, and the marriage she had been planning. The life that now she was not sure if she ever wanted.

Sipping his coffee, Kranti also complained about it. He looked at the six slippery dumplings placed around a small bowl of red sauce. The stuffing inside could be seen through their transparent skin. Like six corpses draped in white, soon to be buried in the red liquid earth. He couldn't eat them, not even the fish fry he had ordered. The table in front turned into a sepulchre he had seen a few days back.

Maya gulped down a dumpling, thinking of the food that was being served at the camp. A lump of porridge topped with claggy curries, cold luci, and watery tea. She wondered whether her mother could eat or not, and whether her parents could get proper food. She couldn't eat anymore. Her black tea lay next to her plate too, untouched.

Unable to tolerate the food in front or the thoughts within them, they shifted their focus again on each other. Their reasons for search were discussed further, the purpose of waiting or staying back, and about the life that they had outside Maajorghat. Just then, Maya noticed the ring with two diamonds, sparkling on his finger. The sight of the ring urged her to speak about Kevin and her call to him, though not about the content of the call. 'It was still unsure. He isn't ready. But … I mean there is someone else too,' she added abruptly to her monologue.

'Oh … by the way, I am married,' he said, surprised by his own urge to inform her.

'That's nice. Love marriage?' She looked into his eyes, observing her minute reflection in his shiny pupils that moved with unease, as though scared that she might get a glimpse of his thoughts.

'Hmm, ya,' he replied, lowering his eyes.

For the rest of the meal, they didn't talk much, except about the derailment and its impact, about which mostly Maya spoke, and also about the arrangements and the reason for derailment, which only Kranti spoke about.

Hearing him speak about the technicalities, about the responsibility that none was willing to take, changes that could, and should be done, Maya thought of Kevin again. He would have reacted in the same way, taking practicality as the sole parameter of behaviour. Like Kranti, he too would have tried to even out this situation with logic. For him, there would be a reason even for the lost love, to behave distant if in case she was among the victims. She toyed over the possibility of his presence—whether he would be here too, waiting for her to come back, or if he would have accepted it easily that she was gone.

Upon reaching the hotel, Kranti told her that he often visited Bangalore, and asked if he could meet her there as well. Seeing her approval, he asked for her number. 'I mean, just to catch up in case I am there. As in … you never know, right?' he said, justifying himself.

5

Going out with Kranti had left Maya more distressed than she was earlier.

Tonight was the time when she ran out of emotions. She would have been unaffected had news of her parents reached her by now. She felt numb, disconnected from this world, wishing to unshackle herself from her body and fly away. She lay listlessly on the chair, with her head tilted sideways and hands resting on the arm-rest. It felt relaxing to her—the persistent thought of leaving and going away.

An irritation, fear, and longing thumped in her heart while she was trying to escape them all. She closed her eyes, trying to shift her mind to positive thoughts, hopeful ones, of finding her parents. She started taking slow, long breaths, to calm herself. *123 breathe in, 456 hold, 78910 out.* Soon, she dozed off for a few minutes.

While dreaming, she felt as if her lungs were under siege. Her body seemed to cramp, as though she was being pushed down into a hole. She slumped against the cushioned back. She felt as if she was drowning, going deep into the sea, waves tightening their grip, submerging her further. The water, soft on her skin but resilient. She wasn't able to fight; she was going deeper. It was dark. She could die; she wasn't able to come up. She was restless. She couldn't breathe.

Maya was sweating and shivering when she got up from her chair. Unable to bear the heaviness, she paced around the room.

After a while, she went to the balcony. It was raining. It had been drizzling since evening, but now the rain fell heavily, without a break. Clouds seemed to burst open, and the sky veiled in a thick grey blanket. The houses stood oblivious to the havoc outside. The darkness within them merged with the one outside, slowly sneaking out of the windows and hugging the sky above. Maya stood still, looking at the dark sky. Darkness had become the only shade clouds seemed to acquire. Dark. Enormous. Black. Black, the colour of her life, as she felt. *No, that's not the colour of my life,* she thought instantly.

Why did we brand dark as bad? Why couldn't the light be wrong? What if it was the light's mistake of illuminating the wrong side? It might be the one that plotted the accident against her, and everyone involved. Maybe it was white, and not black, who had wronged the right, she thought.

She was questioning herself, her decisions, and even wishes. But nothing presented her with any answers. The uproar inside had prevented her from hearing the clues laid out in front of her. The derailment had struck not just the town but devastated her inner world too.

Memories shifted from one instance to another. Her life with her parents, and then with just one of them. Their faces appeared in flashes, as though she was hallucinating. The innocent, fragile smile of her father; her all-embracing mother. At one moment, she felt she could hear Ma calling out, 'Maya beta, this remote is not working.' When she turned, she saw an empty bed. She remembered the things she should have done for them, but didn't. Solo travels, adventurous hobbies, and differing preferences, otherwise normal, felt wrong to her now. She questioned herself for not taking any more trips with Ma, for not spending enough time with her, for cultivating hobbies that her mother either didn't like or couldn't do. Maya was blaming herself even for things naturally human.

There was a knock on the door. Kranti stood outside.

'Maya yaar, do you want to go somewhere to eat? The food is pathetic here,' he said, entering.

'Sorry da. But not tonight,' she replied and asked to be left alone. Rejecting his offer and ignoring her inclination felt appropriate. She couldn't let herself enjoy someone's company when her parents had suffered alone. She couldn't laugh at his jokes when she was on the verge of losing her family. Tonight, Maya wouldn't add more guilt to her bundle of emotions.

6

Survivors recount the Maajorghat-Guwahati Express Derailment

Maajorghat:

Image 1: *A young man leaning against a pillar, with a middle-aged woman standing beside him. His one hand is bandaged; another one holds a black umbrella.*

Mr Sunil Saikia (23) was thrown out of his upper berth due to a sudden trembling. The coach shook like a swing, and he, along with many others were thrown left and right inside the coach. He held tightly to the lower end of the metal ladder, trying to stay as close to the seat as possible—the effort that has left him alive today. 'I saw one of the coaches falling down,' he said in shock.

His mother was missing for two days. She was found sitting near the bridge. 'I was waiting for him to come,' said Mrs Parvati Saikia (55), clearly shocked by the derailment.

Image 2: *A girl lying on a hospital bed with an amputated hand, a white bandage covering her left side. Her head rests on a pillow, looking at the camera. Face blank.*

'I was sleeping on the lower berth. I woke up because something hit my head. When I tried to come out, my hand got stuck in the door, and then someone pushed me,' Nancy (13) said, recounting how she lost her hand.

Image 3: *An old woman lying on a hospital bed. With a grave expression, she is looking at the camera.*

Ms Aarati Nath (60) suffered multiple fractures. She has refused to speak. She has not spoken to the other surviving family members. She was travelling with her husband, two sons, and one sister-in-law. She lost her younger son, Mr Pranab Debnath (20), and husband, Mr Harideb Nath (65), at the derailment site.

SECTION 6

A BANISHED DREAM

'What is love?'
'Yours is a fictional love,' he added before she could reply.
'What do you mean?'
'Love is not to run away from everyday struggle or real life. Love is that everyday struggle, that real life. The day you understand this, your love will transcend from fiction to reality.'
'But what if I call it degradation rather than an uplifting transcendence?' she retorted. 'The love that is as flawless as a perfect work of fiction—that love can surpass any reality. It is better than everyday reality.'
'It is not an everyday struggle then.'
'It is an everyday occurrence that makes even struggling an enjoyable story. Reflecting pain and peace in the same measures, treating them with the same passion. That is love. Yes, that is love. So yes, my love is a fictional love.'
His love was of the practical kind; losing and gaining had been an equal part for him, none affecting beyond a limit. So, he found hers to be extravagant, as glossy as a fantasy, the shimmer she was always proud of.

1

They were down at the restaurant for breakfast. Maya glanced at Kranti, who was talking to one of the waiters in his insufficient yet functional Assamese, a bit of childhood still lingering in him.

Yesterday, while listening to a Punjabi song, Kranti had offered Maya his earphone, one part still stuck to his left ear. There was a casualness and intimacy in the act which had alerted Maya. She'd immediately declined and walked away. Her sudden reaction had startled Kranti, who wasn't sure what he had done wrong. She had walked away smiling. She liked the control she had on that situation, no matter how inconsequential.

Now thinking about it, she felt angry at herself for liking his attention, when she should have been worried about her parents.

Leaving Kranti mid-conversation, she had left the hotel to resume her search. When Kranti went to her room, he saw that it was already locked. Later in the day, when he was walking towards the camp, he saw her at the station. Her hair was now pulled back in a ponytail, and her white cotton shirt hung loosely over a muddied denim.

She reminded Kranti of a wildflower, an uninhibited prodigy of jungles. He wanted to know her more, as if to resolve something. Although he didn't know what he wanted to understand. Yet, he hoped for that unresolved interest to linger in her too.

Approaching her, he asked if she'd received any information today. 'I want to search more,' she replied as she looked at him. His physique towered over her; behind him the sky cleared to a soft blue. His eyes had a tint of yellow, like a retreating jaundice, somewhat translucent, thin enough to reflect the nerves inside, their manner zig-zigged, as though reflecting his confusion.

'True. I will … uh … I will definitely search again, and in other places too, maybe more thoroughly this time,' she replied to his suggestion of searching in places she already had.

Looking at her trying every day for the last week to present a sorted self, he decided to show her the impact of the derailment she was refusing to acknowledge. Guided by an obscure instinct, he asked her to accompany him. He soon started walking ahead, and she too, in an equally inexplicable manner, followed.

She followed him, a stranger until a week ago, without asking where he was taking her. She felt dragged, and allowed herself to be, sometimes placing her feet on every imprint of his, sometimes speeding them to match his. Her feelings confused her, which, as usual, she ignored.

His presence gave her a sense of protection. Oblivious to the ache in her feet, and the blazing sun that on any other day would have given her a headache, she walked as he did. Occasionally, she would walk faster, as if challenging him and herself. Challenging the fate that brought them together, and the nature that started it all.

The wind hit her harder as Maya quickened her steps. Instead of resenting it, she wanted to open her hands and let it run all over her. She wished to be a feather and fly with the wind. To be taken to any direction the wind would decide, to any destination it would choose to. To fly and land on the person walking in front of her. But, as the realisation of her wish struck, she folded her hands, and unfolded them to untie and tie her hair again.

Maya found her happiness out of place. Yet, she couldn't stop herself from noticing the measured movement of his shoulders, from admiring his rugged skin and its healthy gleam that his sweaty arms reflected. She stole glances of his scruffy hair that he would push back with his slender fingers, and their perfectly chipped nails. She stared down at his shadow, equally strong and in control. The shadow that also fell on her, as if hugging.

Maya felt a sense of ease and lightness, something that only complete devotion could offer. She was a Sufi in trance, immune to the noise around, dancing to the music that only her heart could hear. She was feeling at home, a long-forgotten feeling.

But soon, she reminded herself of the reason for her trip. She was there to find her parents. She had to. She wanted to unite with them, at least with her mother, and maybe see her father one more time as well. Yet, even in guilt, a festive feeling fluttered around. She wanted to celebrate life. Which of these feelings she would keep, she couldn't decide.

With each day, a void was deepening in her. A void that her mother's sudden absence left in her. A void she wasn't fully aware of but could sense. If not her parents, she would be left with no family. Would she ever go to Delhi and meet her mother's brothers to find a home, a glimpse of Ma in them? She didn't know. She was trying to fill that void with Kranti's presence. Proximity with him comforted her. The distance from her parents and Kevin didn't affect her with the same intensity when she was with him. She felt reassured, as though something good had happened—not a loss, but a gain. Whenever this realization stuck, it left her more troubled.

Looking at him, she wondered what happiness was and what one needed to create it. So, she asked, 'Do you think happiness depends on one's situation?'

'Not always. But why do you ask?'

'Was just thinking da.'

'And what do you think is love?' she spoke again.

'You are like those big thinkers, yaar. All these heavy questions out of nowhere! But to answer you, I don't know.'

'Ha-ha! No, da … then liking someone is also love right? A tiny little form of it? Like a prelude to something bigger.'

'Hmm, yes, I guess. True actually, liking can become something bigger, more serious types. You know right what I mean?'

'Like marriages?'

'Not always. Liking can turn into love. Same way that love can turn into something else too. But ya, some people think marriage is the final goal. Like an end destination of their love.'

He paused, giving his words a second thought, and said, 'See, love is not all about finding the "one" in your life, and then marrying and just living all your life with that person. As in, I feel love is also a choice, right? A choice to not spend your life with that person. All for the very sake of love. I think its definition changes with the person.'

'Profound, da! And you were calling me a thinker!'

They didn't talk anymore throughout the journey. They both were at ease with the silence and the conversation they just had. They walked, crossing the small bridge, the railway tracks, and a hamlet. They walked till they reached the other side of the hill.

Although the day's sun had partly dried the grasses, the soil was still damp. A lone streetlight lit up; it was almost time for sunset. Crickets hummed, playing a game of hide and seek. Crickets, that she used to call helicopters, the same that her friends used to tie on a thread, creating their unique kites. It reminded her of times when cruelty took a playful touch. Times of innocent games, where childhood gave licence to pin up, tie, or even stab, for the sake of curiosity. The place looked ethereal, apart from the stench.

Maybe some animal is decaying nearby, she thought. The smell penetrated her head, hitting her hard. It wasn't like something one would come across every day. The contrast was unfathomable, like a clock rotating in reverse. It was then that she saw white logs kept side by side. Logs that turned into bodies as she went nearer, enshrouded, tied with ropes.

Puzzled, Maya looked at Kranti, her pupils dilated in incredulity. He held her hand. Standing sideways, he told her, 'Some are buried here. Those passengers.'

Releasing her hand from his clutch, she turned and walked away. Overwhelmed, he waited for her response. Telling him that she was going back, she left without the reaction he was expecting, the vulnerability that he was hoping to protect her from. All he got was a cold shrug and an expression that refused to divulge anything.

A proper disposal of bodies couldn't be done owing to the persistent downpour, and birds and insects were already feasting on them. To prevent any further catastrophe, these decomposed bodies were being buried at a ground cleared for this task.

2

The farther Maya went, the greater the desire to stop her overpowered Kranti. The desire to hold, and preserve, to wrap and hoard. Like a longing to shop, where he bought control, for brands which labelled his swank. His collection of watches and perfumes, latest phones and designer bags that gifted him a costlier worth, unmatched to those in clothes from festive sales. A desire to claim and collect. Like the wish to hold a firefly, bringing its light into the room. To cage its sparkle in a glass jar, that would eventually fade away in his walled admiration.

A display of vulnerability from Maya would have affirmed a similarity to the emotions he felt at the burial ground. And his act was in accordance with that wish.

So, he wished for her to let down her guard. A chance to know her, to provide an end to her search, no matter how gore. An end that everyone wished for, even him. He took her to the burial ground, to show the option she was running from. He had then expected her to seek solace in him. A vague imagination of embracing him as she cried. Still affected by what he had seen, he was also looking for validation for his fright—a justification to rationalize his vulnerability.

'Why the hell did you take me there?'

'You should consider all the possibilities. So, I thought …'

'What possibilities? Who are you to decide what I should do and think about?'

'Arey yaar. I am not deciding for you … you are misunderstanding …'

'Stop it! Who do you think you are? I will consider WHATEVER, WHENEVER I want!'

Maya couldn't find any logic behind Kranti's decision to show the gore of death, especially when she was trying to find hints of her parents' safety. She couldn't bear looking at it. The inability to do so made her feel helpless. It made her vulnerable, which until now she had successfully shielded. And all of it birthed rage. Rage, with which she wanted to push Kranti in that very same pit, to jump in it, and end the search. Rage, with which she wanted to scream, loud enough to shatter all the windows of the hospital where the injured lay. Rage, forceful enough to snatch clouds by her bare hands and squeeze them over this very town, further flooding its overflowing rivers. Rage, capable enough to light a fire on that river of tears too.

'Maya, please yaar. Listen …' Kranti started, but she walked away, paying no heed to the approaching darkness ahead of her. Night was creeping in. She didn't stop. He started walking behind her, and then slowly by her side.

Kranti was eager to be a part of her search, or wait, if that was what she was planning to do. And in that eagerness, there was also his inclination to forget the ones who were waiting for him, in Guwahati and Delhi. Since the time he'd seen Maya, his mind, much to his ease, had dimmed the area where Anchal and her memories stayed. The darker the area got, the easier it became for him to follow Maya.

On some days, his attraction towards her flabbergasted him. *Why was the thought of not being near her troubling him?* He didn't know. Yet, it didn't feel unnatural. She invoked something strong in him. The kind that would have made Michelangelo paint Sistine Chapel; the kind that would have made Thomas Hardy write *Jude the Obscure* and then leave writing altogether. Kranti felt a passion as strong as theirs, and its intensity could make him lose everything too.

3

It was a calm morning—the kind after a heavy downpour. Whistles of pressure cookers woke up the houses, leaving roosters incompetent; morning exercises started, and so did the chattering; kids cursed their schools, and elders their offices. A usual morning in a town, just like anywhere else in the world, where the day would progress at its usual pace. But for Maya, it wasn't a usual morning. It hadn't been for many days now. Her day didn't start as it was supposed to, and even the regularity of her search had stopped now.

Maya hadn't received any official information. So, she took it upon herself. She called travel operators of the buses her parents might have taken, hotels where they were about to stay. She went to every NGO in Maajorghat. She repeatedly contacted all her parents' friends, colleagues, and every person they knew. It had been over fifteen days, but she hadn't been able to gather anything substantial. The impact of this realization was slowly crushing her, especially after what she had seen at the burial ground, and more so in the last two days.

She was haunted by everything she saw in the recent days. She had burnt herself in the process, and was left with nothing but fire to spit.

On the first day when she decided to not step out, Maya reasoned it to be a symptom of PTSD. Post-Traumatic Stress Disorder. She had consistent back pain and lethargy. A pinning headache, as if nails were being hammered inside her head, added further to her reasons. At night, it was getting harder for her to fall asleep. Nightmares gave way to her fears, of her parents being amid those lined at the burial ground. She was restless even inside the room.

The night of visiting the burial ground uncovered the trauma she had been avoiding until then. Walking away in anger, she had kept herself as composed as she could. But once in the room, she'd cried in explosive rage, tearing apart the bedsheet, and throwing pillows, her phone, and the TV remote on the floor. An urge to break things. Then, she wanted to break herself. Pulling her hair with her hands, she'd cried. She hit her head on the wall until she felt breathless enough to fall down and curl herself. A volcano erupted out of her. Next morning, there was no trace of the night's rage. Instead, a silence took hold of her. And slowly, she went into hibernation.

She would order food and then return the plate untouched, decline the room cleaning, or even personal hygiene. Those two days she spent either on her bed or standing on the balcony, where she went only when she was sure that Kranti had left for the camp. Maya wanted to be invisible, and with Kranti there was visibility. A parade of emotions would follow her, making it difficult to find the seclusion she wanted. So, she had cut him off as well.

She would spend her time thinking. A buoyant train that was moving with eagerness to meet its station, and a journey that destroyed it. She thought of the fate it gave to those relying on it. Because of a stubborn bridge that wouldn't stand for a minute more.

The stories of a lifetime were over in less than ten minutes. The train's, Ma's, and hers. Every life seemed predestined to Maya.

She didn't see the point in getting up from bed, speaking to Kranti, or replying to Kevin's pleas. As she longed for those regular escapes into her own world, she instinctively decided to avoid reality, at least for a few days.

She read to distract herself. But, in between the pages that on any other day would have taken her deep into the stories, where she would have floated with the words, she would lose track and look up. Book in hand, she would stare at the blank wall in front. She would think of Kranti, or even Kevin, but reliving those moments with them failed to arouse anything in her.

Indecisive, she was waiting for answers. Answers that were as complicated as a Rorschach test, but equally simple too. Just spilled ink, or a bat set free to roam at night but caged in the day. A bee with its stinger ready to bite, or the painting of a heart gone horribly wrong. Emotions deranged. Was it a girl in a frock, standing firm but hiding behind, or the face of a demon? Four eyes but no lips, spying every move, no words, and no smile to comfort. A man flying in the smoke of freedom, or was it a life escaping out? Dancing death. *Should she see it as a whole, or fragmented? Was it one thing, or many clubbed together?* Answers were to be found as per one's understanding, imagination—under one's controlled kingdom of thoughts, and perception.

It was the fourth morning in a row that Kranti had come and knocked. This time, Maya opened it. The room smelt of sweat and tears. A side lamp was switched on, yet the room appeared darker than other days. Without uttering a word about her sudden disappearance, he stood at the door and smiled.

She asked him to come in.

'Finally! I have been calling you every day,' he said as he hugged her, relieved. He noticed her crumpled chequered shirt over a dhoti pant.

'Sorry. Wanted some time off. By the way, I am… I am actually leaving.' she said, freeing herself from his embrace.

'Oh! Bangalore?'

'No, da. Sigo Dolung.'

'What! But why?'

'Because … I don't want to go to Bangalore.'

'But why are you leaving?'

'I don't want to stay here.'

She was seeking the comfort of home, no matter how fragmented. Kranti did understand that, and, in a way, understood her too.

Since the day she left for higher education, she had consciously tried to forget her association with the place—with her past. She filled the vacant spaces of her life with new experiences, allowing new people to take up greater space. She had deliberately allowed the new life to take over the old one. She wanted to rewrite her life. In Maajorghat she'd realized that it was never erased. So now, she planned to go into that past to reclaim the life in which her parents resided too.

4

Tiredness gripped her, discomfort transcending from mind to body. Pain flooded her heart. A tempestuous deluge restrained her search. There was an unease in the air, a tension clouding her mind—beyond her reach to put it away, but close enough to suffocate her.

Tomorrow, around the same time, Maya would leave Maajorghat, aborting the search. If it was any other time, she would have busied herself packing. Travelling, an opportunity to see something new, and to associate and dissociate within a span of a few hours always excited her. But tonight, it was different. Her things were scattered all over the room, and the suitcase lay empty on the floor.

She sat still on the bed, staring straight into the immobile, unshaken wall. Her body rested limply, yet she focused on it, wanting it to break its pledge of silence and tell her parents' whereabouts. She wanted to put an end to its constant hearing and coax it into speaking from what it had heard all these years. Setting the wall free from its eternal stillness, she wanted to free herself from the shackles she was bound by.

There was a lethargic touch in everything she saw and did. Outside her room, the trees, which until now prided in their greenery, seemed subdued. The sky spread a blank sheet, its vastness empty and lifeless, devoid of even a single star to brighten it. Around her, the walls looked paler. The ceiling above her stood silent, apart from the fan which too was trying to flee, away from its monotonous life, spinning rhythmically. Yet, it repeated the same pattern with the same intensity, losing itself and its characteristic appearance in the process.

Intuitively, she took out a pack of cigarettes she hadn't touched since she reached Maajorghat. Finding a matchbox in one of the side table drawers, she lit it without much thought. She had been trying to quit. She had reduced. Her recent body check-up indicated weak lungs—the one that Kevin had forced her to go for after frequent episodes of breathlessness. It was one of the few times he had surpassed her expectations, by fulfilling them.

She took one long puff, letting its smoke clear the fog in her mind. She took another, a short one this time. Watching the burning cigarette between her fingers, she relaxed. After a few more puffs, she dropped it on the floor. Its butt, still ferocious, burnt red.

It had been more than an hour. The phone blinked, indicating several missed calls and messages. She didn't read; she didn't change; neither did she pack.

In spite of his repeated questions, Maya hadn't informed Kranti anything more than her decision to travel. The thought of going away from him brought a strange heaviness in her heart. She couldn't decipher it, nor could she tell him blankly. This departure, although intentional, seemed as sudden and unacceptable as their first meeting was. Even when she met him for the first time, she'd felt closer to Kranti—an indescribable feeling then. Similar to then, even now she didn't dwell deeper into that uncensored emotional territory.

It was as though she had a parallel reality, like the surreal fiction she recently read. Its story, although away from logic, pulled her in. The story had become like an addiction she couldn't leave until it was finished. The story that made her want to know its author; to get into his mind and see why he wrote the way he did. Kranti, to her was that story, pulling her into a maze. She had to find a gateway and step out.

To her, his presence was like dreaming with open eyes, with no expectation of credibility, or even appropriateness. It was a dream, after all, that she hoped not to share with anyone. Maya lay thinking of him, freely, in ways that she reserved for dreams. Imagination taking an uninhibited ride. No guilt to smother her desires. No past to obstruct her way to him, or his to her. Their selves extended towards each other, away from the pile of missed calls, unanswered text messages, forced waiting, and the blinding light of diamonds on a ring. She felt as if he was next to her. Quivering, she hid herself in him, a rugged caress, complementing a soft smile. She fell asleep, and as she fell deeper, images took different shapes and vivid forms.

Deformed bodies, rotten and torn like pieces of used cloth. She saw a baby, his body swollen, his eyes bulging out. On her side lay another, in a condition much worse, hair entangled beneath the hand of another that surfaced from nowhere. The bodies turned into a fluid, mixing into each other, falling without any definite shape. They decayed into a combined mass, fused together. A few lumps here and there, few eyes, some hands, and a few legs stretched out. The heap looked unquenchable; a never-ending void ready to take more sacrifices. Sacrifices of humans to nature by the technology he'd created. She was standing on that heap and trying to search for her parents in it. Their faces—or even a hand. Maybe a forehead or a nose, similar to hers. She couldn't, so she decided to step into that mass of bodies.

Maya woke up gasping for air.

A knock on the door brought her out of the pit she was gradually slipping in. Relieved to be away from the bodies she felt were so near to her, she thanked Kranti as she opened the door.

Unable to understand her gratitude, yet encouraged by it, he asked her out to dinner. He spoke urgently, as though pushing the words out of his system.

Throwing a cotton stole over her shoulders, she immediately stepped out. She still wasn't completely ready to show him the feelings her room carried at that moment.

5

'Alang dalang khelise
Raja Rani aahi aase
Kuuk jhok jhok'
'We are playing Alang Dalang
The King and Queen are arriving
Kuuk jhok jhok (the sound of a train)'

Although it was late in the evening, a few children were still playing the game of train Maya and Kranti had grown up playing too. They walked past them, feeling nostalgic at their song. Both reminisced about their turn to form a train or to parade under the bridge of hands, when they too stood holding hands with their counterpart, making an arched bridge for the others to pass while singing *Alang Dalang*. They thought about their turns to capture a coach or two as they would collapse their hand bridge. The game of train played on, filling the surroundings with laughter, while they both thought of another game of train that was being played at a distance not too far.

Past and present intermingled, creating a game they were neither able to understand nor share.

'I used to play Kith-Kith more,' Maya said. *Mostly alone*, but she didn't tell him that. The game of skipping, jumping over a few boxes, landing on a few, all to reach her destination; the game she could draw anywhere and play even alone.

'I was more of a Kho-Kho guy.' The ancient tag game of India, where he would often be the captain. The game of virility, on the field and off the field, in which banter would last for hours about who'd outdone whom.

They further spoke about other childhood games, happy at finding similarities that wouldn't have been possible if not for their shared experience of displacement.

About *Alang Dalang* they didn't share. How could they? It was the game that Maya wasn't invited to play, after her father had pulled her out in the middle of the game, crashing the bridge long before everyone was ready. It was the game that Kranti and Mridula played with others, tricking their way into making the bridge at the start and crashing the game altogether once their chance was over.

Soon, they were at the restaurant. It was on the terrace of a hotel located just a few blocks away from theirs. Casting a hasty glimpse at the menu, Maya ordered a plate of steamed rice with plain yellow lentil soup, while Kranti asked for a plate of fried noodles.

'You are leaving for sure? Because of that day? It wasn't my intention yaar, I only …' Kranti spoke after a while.

'No. Not for that,' she said, looking at him. The moon above him shimmered with a halo around.

'Then what?'

'Some other reasons, man. That's it.'

'See, it happens to many. We can't disregard reality, right?'

'What reality, da?'

'All this here is real yaar. This town, that accident, your parents. Everything is reality, na?'

'You know about that painting by Salvador Dali? The one with a melting clock?'

'Arey, what about that painting now?'

'What exists and what doesn't. How do we know what we see is real, and what we don't is not?'

'Surreal madam ji! But let's get back to *this* reality. Around us,' he said and gestured to show the world.

'No ya, we see it differently. This life is just a living totality of all these tragedies.'

'No. We feel about it differently. But what we see is the same.'

Before Kranti could add further, the waiter arrived with two plates, both balanced in one hand, and a set of cutleries in the other. He then brought a quarter plate topped with salad – onion and cucumber forming the base, while sliced lemon and whole green chilies sat on top. Unlike the restaurants they both have gotten used to, they weren't given the option of bottled water. Without asking for their choice, a young boy in his early teens, dressed in an apron over his jeans and shirt, poured water from the already stationed jug on the table.

'Bhaiya, bring one water bottle?' Maya asked.

The water poured, boiled or directly taken from the water tap, was unacceptable to Kranti too. They couldn't risk drinking that water with its potential threat of bacteria and illness, he asserted.

Kranti's phone rang. He decided to receive it at the last leg of the second ring. It was Anchal's call, concerned and angry at Kranti for being unavailable. The call he'd received to inform that he would be calling soon, turned into an explanation of his acts—a dash of lies, pointless reasoning, and a tinge of frustration, which he immediately camouflaged, owing to the listener sitting opposite to him.

'I am out for dinner.'

'Finally you are free?'

'Jaan, I will call you soon.'

'You are with someone?'

'No, nothing like that.'

'Then why can't you talk? We haven't spoken in days. *Bolo na*, who is there?'

'No one, yaar.'

'You are lying.'

'I am not.'

After disconnecting the call, Kranti said, as if explaining, 'Anchal worries a lot for me. I am here in these conditions you know.' Meanwhile, continuous beeps notified them of messages being delivered to his phone.

She nodded, gulping a spoonful, looking at the white corner of her plates that were still clean, while the centre was burdened under the mounds of steamed rice clad in yellow dal. A detached slice of onion lay on the side, ogling at their union.

They ended their dinner with a cup of black coffee and lemon water while talking about life as they saw here amid the accident. Display of strength and the lack of it; heightened emotions and honest care; corrupted help and forced hopes.

Even though he too was volunteering, Kranti couldn't stop himself from seeing the pitfalls that took it far from perfection. Mediocrity frustrated him. He couldn't take pride in it. Maya, contradicting herself, was appreciating the rescue efforts, hoping for it to reach her parents too.

As they returned to the hotel, Kranti spoke, continuing the conversation they once had, as though everything between that moment and now was inconsequential.

'You know … I was thinking about what you said that day.'

'About what?'

'About love. Like, I feel we cannot categorize love or find logic behind it, you know? It's not always situation-based. Sometimes it's not even right.'

'But how do we even know what is right?'

His gaze followed her as she walked upstairs.

6

Kranti was back in his room now. Putting his feet over the coffee table, he picked up the TV remote. A local channel was telecasting the movie *Bahniman*, the kind that his mother would've quietly, and often secretly, liked, and his father explicitly ridiculed. After a few minutes of channel surfing, he decided to watch National Geographic, Anchal and his favourite past-time. He dialled Anchal's number, but quickly disconnected it. He thought of calling his mother, but ignored it. He then put his phone on silent mode, leaving it on the table, and went to lie down.

Unlike his usual routine, he didn't bother changing into his night suit—fine linen to help him sleep. Though his socks and pants were coated with the entire day's dust, he climbed on the bed. He was feeling responsible for pushing Maya away. He wasn't sure if he would ever see her again.

What Kranti saw at the burial ground had brought a sense of ending in him, the end from where his journey of search began. The search that he had continued even after finding Mridula. A farewell to what had been dead since long. Death of a child's wish to get his father's approval. Farewell to the end of his youth, to the wish of renewing a dying trust. Parting from love and its stagnation.

Taking Maya to the burial ground was also to share these endings with her, which she also became an instigator of. But her reaction had caught him off-guard. When he suggested meeting her in Bangalore, she didn't give a hearty approval.

My marriage must have pushed her away, he thought. He was mulling over the probable happenings of tomorrow, when she was to leave. He was unable to find reasons to stop her. He was failing at this attempt of acquisition.

Even though Kranti had seen her for only a few days, he felt a monumental sadness at her sudden departure. The intensity of his own emotions baffled him. He had Anchal in his life, and for all these years he believed that they loved each other; but never had he felt this way for her, as he was feeling for Maya.

Classmates then, he and Anchal spent their entire college life in each other's company. Going to movies, bunking classes, exploring hidden corners of the campus, and then priding in their discoveries, spending nights in long walks, driving each other crazy with assignments, creating mayhem, and then resolving it. They were the Siamese twins of the campus. He knew Anchal loved him; he liked her too. Nothing had happened to make Kranti question his feelings—until now. As far as he knew, he loved Anchal, but Maya fascinated him too. With Maya he felt a pull stronger than gravity. He wanted to be by her side, even if that meant just following her everywhere.

'But I am married,' he told himself.

He thought about calling and telling Anchal everything, but he didn't know what to say. Kranti was already finding reasons to not be with her—to leave her out of the goodness of his heart. Although, a part of him knew that he had already wronged her. He then contemplated speaking to Maya first. He was sure that she too felt the same. He wanted to believe it. He interrogated himself more than he could answer.

I should tell them both, he finally decided.

SECTION 7
DETOUR

Who is she? Who is he?
What will she be?
A shadow born with the light
or
a shadow dwarfing with the escaping light?
Its existence doused as he goes down into the dark,
a shadow that is left unaware.
She wonders
if she should wait for the light to reappear.
Can shadow ever strive if not nurtured by the light?
Though she knows she must try and survive.

1

Though Maya had come to the bus stand, the clarity on her further actions was still bleak.

She had walked to the stand, crossing a small market, catering to the residents nearby. A small kiosk sold products varying from condiments to washing soap. Even shrivelled vegetables were mounted on its counter. The restaurant was a concrete variant of the tea stalls around it. All of them were covered with tin roofs that inclined downwards. A permanent remedy for stagnant rainwater. Even though she was craving for her evening cup of tea, she decided against buying any.

An appearance of cleanliness of not only the place, but also of those working in it was a deep-seated parameter for Maya. With a brief glance, she decided against entering the restaurant. Signs of destitution, presumption of dirt, were visible on clothes and their being. The eternal hierarchy of cleanliness. The parameters that wouldn't fit in the world she was going back to.

The past few days had perplexed her too. Appearances to disappearances, she had been left to deal with unprecedented things. Kevin to Kranti, love played out, taken away too. Parents came together. As they travelled on a cobbled path, memories rushed back in. Ma to father, they to her. A temple visit, belief resurrected. Faith lost and gained, in kinds that shifted, in ties that stayed. God for everyone, love for her mother. Ma to Her, the ever powerful, the Supreme.

Maya dwelled on the years spent with Ma. Small acts of love, the chocolates she would surprise her with, the dresses she would buy for Maya, frocks with frills and skirts with side slits. Culinary feasts presented at father's return, which continued even when his returns ceased.

Maya thought of the distance that grew with changing homes. It started in Sigo Dolung, and never shrunk back. The distance from which she tried to escape, but inevitably found it in every new home and city. It stayed in her, like a stone thrown at her heart, and her heart bled a well. A well so deep that darkness went past it. So did her emotions.

With what she faced in the recent days, a realization, although meek, struck her. Maybe it was not Ma, but she who had widened this gap.

The Past Roared Again

The Past comes knocking, in fact roaring.
An unexpected roar of a caged puppy, when, in the end, he knows his day has arrived,
or that it would never arrive.
He who has been kept hungry and beaten, stunted under the iron cage, roars his last roar,
And his first too.
The past comes like that.
It hits you with its claws while it's often meek, once a brave cry rings in your ear,
taking a permanent place, like the bird who builds a nest in your balcony, one after another.
While you, never having enough heart,
Or often having too much of it,
let it stay.
So, half of your balcony nests the eggs and birds, spilled hatch, and the warmth of hatching.
The past becomes an uninvited nest in your heart too.
Now, when it comes to roaring,
You squeal a silent roar, the one that you fear sharing.
So, you leave it, plugging your ear with an
intentional deafness.
You stop the voice of the past with yours,
louder and hoarser.

2

Somewhere inside a state in the north-eastern parts, a town lay stagnant, no train or plane stirring its repose. Maya embarked towards it in a semi-sleeper bus, the way she and her parents used to. Past too stayed still in this town. Nothing to move it towards the future. Shops stuck barren where they were, bridges still broken, walkers still crossing the river on foot.

Maya could have opted for a train. But the train, at this point, felt too raw to experience. She chose a bus. 'Night super,' they used to call it—even she used to, till names became embarrassing, and the conditions nauseating. Night super, with shrunken seats and rusted handles, chipped paint around them. Its silent aging seemed like a graceful acceptance of the changing times. Maya too wanted to free herself from the pain, but prolonged it through this fleeing.

Her nomadic self was transiting homes. A reluctant soul wheeling on the road, towards life as it was.

As the bus started, Maya examined her surroundings once more. She was searching for someone, or a few, maybe. She saw a child whining for a toy—a yellow teddy bear wrapped in transparent plastic, hung with some other toys at a makeshift shop, while his mother was unsuccessfully trying to cajole him away. Soon, they blurred and those in her vicinity became clearer.

The world inside the bus took precedence over the one she passed by. A woman next to her and a couple on the other side.

A shawl unfolded and spread, shoulders to toe. The couple, Maya saw on her windowpane, settled with a commotion, their curtain drawn. Invitation to an early sleep, presumably comforted by each other's touch. From her back came the rustling of a chips packet, its sound tempting everyone. A smell wafted soon, possibly of curried rice, overwhelming her.

She was waiting for a different smell, a slight hint of fresh citrus with a woody finish, a specific aroma which, to her surprise, felt close to her. She knew this smell; it evoked familiarity. The smell of the accident, and its ambiguity, of possible loss and unattained gain. The smell that she was running from. When she turned around to search for the source, she saw Kranti.

Standing upright, bringing in the smell, he crossed his hands, as if by closing himself he could hide his feelings too. A deviant gesture for an unprecedented moment. His pants, unusual to his suavity, were crumpled now, and had traces of mud.

She looked at him. Though brightened by his sight, she became tearful. He stood, guilt and eagerness paralysing him. His mind went back to Anchal, her expectant face waiting for him to return home, her open smile when she would see him, displaying a perfect set of teeth, her short hair freeing themselves from the hair clip, the hair that she would often brush aside between their kisses. His mind went back to her, acknowledging her wait; yet, he walked towards Maya.

Getting up, Maya took him to the back door.

'I will come with you. Just to help you set up and all,' Kranti told her.

Why was he helping her? Why did he suddenly leave everything and decide to join her? She had many questions, but asked none.

Clasping the door handles, they stood opposite to each other. Her hair was flowing, and a calmness descended on her face. Kranti stood with a plain, honest smile. His eyes, though, displayed confusion. After a while, Maya closed her eyes. The sound of the wind and the leaves were amalgamating with those of the birds, chirping away in excitement. Her heart fluttered too. She could feel their excitement.

The bus was now running on the tarmac road, common in these areas of heavy rainfall. It crossed a series of small, hunched houses with tin roofs and planked doors. These doors were painted in bright colours, while a few were left in their initial rawness. Washed clothes were drying under the receding sun on the mud-polished ground. A few houses had their doors wide open; most had open windows, allowing the light in. Some had bulbs already flickering in the veranda, wires invariably hanging around each of them.

They then saw a wide open ground full of children engrossed in their games, screaming, running behind each other, and rolling old tyres with bamboo sticks. On the same ground were goats, many, of different sizes and colours, white, brown, and black. They were lost in their own world, unmindful of the children's presence or the bus's; there was a pair chasing each other too.

The bus gained speed, fogging the views they were watching, blurring the reason to stand in silence anymore, and reducing the time to contemplate their actions in the last few days and for the days to come. A blur of women walking to the sole water tap at the corner could be seen, smudges of plastic pots in striking colours in their hands. A blur of men standing by the road; men on cycles, on the way back from their daily labour. Hazy bodies sitting hunched, or standing bent, looking at the bus go by.

They now sat together on the back seats. Feeling self-conscious, Maya fiddled with her phone, while Kranti observed his fellow passengers. The rexine-covered blue armrest in the middle placed them in segregated worlds. Apart from the initial tears and basic communication to tell their intent, they had not spoken at all.

Even though they weren't, they both felt tired. The accident and the search had left them drained, the impact of which they could feel now. And soon, they both were asleep.

After an hour, the bus halted, halting their sleep too. It had made its last stop at Maajorghat's main market, crossing the hospital building, the small market around it, a few colonies, patches of fields, and a ground that had now stopped taking in the bodies.

Looking out, Maya spotted a young man with a familiar aura of warmth waiting to cross the road. He had a vigilant gaze on the vehicles approaching, and cast a fleeting one at her bus too. Through a translucent layer of frost and dirt on the windowpane, she saw a faint resemblance of a calm composure. Plastered in a creamy white cast, his hand hung through a blue belt encircling his neck. On his other shoulder was a cloth bag filled to its capacity. He held a transparent polythene cover with vegetables in it and bundles of *Dhekiya* leaves. She could see the fragile fern struggling under the weight of a curvy bottle-gourd, while some spiny gourd rested around it.

As he walked towards her, the haze of his figure cleared. He had spotted Maya too. His tight-lipped smile drifted in a greeting, to which Maya nodded. Guilt overwhelmed her, but soon it settled with the news that Sunil gave her. She felt relieved.

Sunil informed her about finding his mother at the station, and also about the well-being of Baideu's family. He later shared his plans to leave for Bangalore in a week, without Maya asking. He inquired about her search. 'It's going on,' she replied. No further explanation was needed.

Later, as the bus left the stand, Sunil disappeared from their sight and the town restarted its run opposite them.

'Who was he?'

'No one, da,' she replied. Maya wasn't yet ready to divulge herself entirely to him.

3

Once the initial shock of separation and the high of union had subsided, they grew awkward with their emotional display from a while ago. Emotional hangovers seemed to be over, and the sobriety was making them aware of the current situation they both were in. Avoiding each other's glances, they maintained a considerable distance, praying for time to provide them with clarity. Unsure of what had gotten into them, and what should be their next step, they sat in silence and observed their surroundings.

But soon, Maya wasn't able to see much. The moon had overpowered the reluctant sun. For its arrival, the sky spread a carpet, much like the green around, but grey instead, the usual occurrence of every night. Nothing to see, she drew the curtains. Dust-laden, smelling of dampness, unaccounted years, neglect, and intended busy schedules. Closing her eyes, she relaxed to the rhythmic lullaby of a moving bus on a rocky road. A bumpy ride with a thundering sound, like the humming she had been used to—still was.

Dreams, though, took away that rest, for she was to jump, bury, be buried, and of course, run. Dreams, a resting reality to the exhaustion within.

Soft snores occasionally escaped from her flaring nostrils, while she slept curled up. Her head rested on her elbow and hair fell on her cheeks in a free escapade. Through a slight parting,

Kranti could see her eyeballs move under the lids. They were escaping the pit in which she was jumping in.

Maya was dreaming of a pit. It was not the kind of pit she'd dug once with her hand to bury her dead doll, but the kind that grew deeper with every second, with corpses, each attached to their suitcase and coach number.

Confused, she jumped inside and lay herself on top of them. Alive and awake, with surrounding deaths. When she struggled to come out, her feet brushed against a blood-smeared flesh, like a bird inside out. She shook her feet, and a few drops of blood spilled over. When she looked to the left, a swollen face lay with eyes closed, like in deep sleep. She could smell its foulness. It had a bindi, intact, hair parted in the middle, white strands on one side while the rest were black. She felt suffocated, but wanted to touch the face. She couldn't. It was stuck under a broken limb. She then tried to get up, but a hand rose and pulled her in. She descended further; the sky she could view till now vanished too. To understand how deep she had gone, she tried to peer in that darkness.

She opened her eyes wide and found Kranti next to her. His eyebrows wrinkled slightly, but he smiled as she woke up.

'Sorry, I just dozed off,' Maya apologized and soon felt frustrated with herself. Her need to apologize always flustered her.

A mirror to her inner reality. *Should I try to note down my dreams?* Maya often thought, but never did. She would sit back and let it control her, without acknowledging its impact. Blaming everything on fate, while the things happening were with her own intent.

It was similar to the dreams she had often seen. She would wake up with it, realizing, sometimes thanking, and occasionally trying to comprehend. *Was it even a dream, or did she just see a distorted version of what she had seen earlier in the day, week, or even years?* She didn't know, and didn't want to understand either.

If Freud was to be still believed, then her dream was nothing but a manifestation of her innermost desires, fears, memories, and experiences. Her subconscious in a nutshell. But hypothetical analysis of a perceived notion was not something Maya would do. Not knowingly, at least.

SECTION 8
FAMILIAR ROADS

Search for a home

'Where is your home?'
'A difficult question indeed.'
'Aren't you from the Hindi belt? You are a Hindi girl na?'
'A Hindi girl?'
'Oh, sorry yaar, your hometown. I guess it's in some part of Northern India?'
Both knew the extent of everyday racism rooted in all of us.
'I don't have any. Maybe I don't belong anywhere. All the cities and towns I have lived in are my home—and aren't, too.'
'I feel it every day. I came here feeling nostalgic, and now I long for the homely comfort of Bangalore. I go to Delhi missing my cousins, wanting to hear a language I would understand, to speak and sing in a language that everyone knows.
But when I go there, I realise that I don't speak their language, nor do I understand theirs. Even with my Hindi I am an outsider there, the way I am everywhere else. Once there, I wish to return to Bangalore, to hear those sentences that I try to understand, to eat food which only recently entered my life. And the moment I touch down the city of Bangalore, I miss being among people whom I can call family. You know, I call

cities and towns my home that aren't so. I long for a love that is not mine.'

'But then you are here?'

'Because this was my home too. Maybe, it still is.'

'You have a place to call your home?'

'Yes.'

'How is the feeling? Of homecoming?'

'I can't recreate what I have left behind, many years ago. I don't seem to want it anymore either.'

'Then which city do you call your new home?'

'My home is changing with me. My concept of it is growing with each experience.'

'So, I guess, one never feels at home.'

'Maybe one does. Like everything else, feeling changes, and so does the concept of home.'

'Maybe. Like everything else, even to feel at home we need to put in effort. I haven't, I guess.'

'Maybe this feeling of home is a myth too.'

'Like the feeling of fulfilment?'

'Maybe.'

1

The journey remained uneventful apart from the time when they got down at the state border to show their inner line permit for entering Arunachal Pradesh. Maya had forgotten, but Kranti applied online and got it within a few hours. 'Connections,' he informed, winking at her.

Even though their documents were in place, Maya tried to use her Hindi to interact with the officials in a futile attempt to feel connected. The usual unsuspecting case of appropriation. The failed recreation of a language forgotten by the young woman in front of them. Apart from this, they didn't notice much. Yet, they humoured her.

'*School ka samne mein; Bangalore parai ke liye giya tha; mera father rehta tha Sigo Dolung mein; abhi Itanagar mein hai; hoga; malum nai; uncle log hai wahan par; tora friends bhi hai.*' ('Next to the school; went to Bangalore for studies; my father used to live in Sigo Dolung; now he stays in Itanagar; Yes; I don't know; a few people I know are there, friends and uncles'.)

She used phrases that were framed right as she intended, yet they sounded alien. The touch of nativity was missing—the sound that came from living the language, and not imitating it. It was apparent to them, but not her.

Maya had mastered the art of switching between two Hindis—a puritan touch for home, and an assimilated one for outside. Shedding her skin, she would don a new one, as if there was nothing before to it, leaving behind a thin, transparent scale that she often came back to unknowingly.

As they returned to the bus, she told Kranti how her father, and later Ma, would renew their inner line permit for their yearly visit to relatives in the plain. Although she understood the reasons behind those requirements and the state's geographical vulnerability, it still disintegrated her carefully assembled wholeness. Seeking approval to enter the state she called her own did leave a scar.

It gave way to alienation, a feeling that was induced by society and cultivated by her, making her life a long episode of nostalgia. The feeling that left her displaced emotionally, dissociated from the place she lived in. There were times, like today, when Maya wanted to belong. To have a body that would merge with the crowd, to have hair that could fall as flawlessly as her classmates' used to, to have a skin that couldn't be differentiated.

Yet, there was a side that would hide that longing. Whenever asked, she would say, 'I am from everywhere. I carry a hint of every place I have lived in.' She convinced herself that not having to wait for a particular festival, or having her childhood associated not just with one, but many celebrations, was a blessed aspect. Different experiences shaped her and aided in her individualistic growth.

After an hour, the conductor shouted Sigo once, twice, and then thrice, and the bus halted for a minute.

Sigo Dolung, the town where Maya would watch fish swirling under the clear river water; where walks meant nudging the touch-me-nots, plucking flowers, and following the wind. Her town, with an ancient temple atop a hill, mostly built in stone and later renovated with cement, where she would go to gaze at the view. Taking in the vastness and its misleading stillness, she would admire the sturdy mountains hiding a restless river. She would stand there, feeling peaceful, and often inconsequential too.

As they neared her childhood home, a faint wish for a permanent home rose in her again. For a physically permanent home, in an unmovable town. A home that would go back to generations, where everyone like her had also lived. A town where she could go and map their lives to decide her future. To know what to fight for and imbibe, especially during times of confusion, the likes of which had been repeatedly increasing.

There were times when she wanted to celebrate Diwali more than Durga Pooja, and to have that one festival celebrated in the entire town, when going to any house would lead to an extension of it. She too longed for the innocence of a child, not the burden of exposure that came with shifting homes, from the understanding that the world was bigger than a city, and so was the idea of home. Back then, this realization had made her feel smaller. Even now, she often felt invisible in the maze of hometowns and her associations with them. Her early life was not a recollection of childhood indulgences but episodes of leaving, settling, and leaving again. A forever entanglement of transiting homes.

'Pretty town.'

Kranti's words brought her back to the present.

The bus had dropped them at the town's border and drove ahead to the next one. They chose to walk a few kilometres than take an auto-rickshaw.

A walk was as pale as the sky above Maya. Uneventful too. No hello's, or running into someone known, contacts that were lost long ago. A by-product of wish and fate. Not that she was resenting it; the journey to this town had always been this way. But when was the last time she had made a similar trip, Maya couldn't recall. After all, so much had happened, mostly planned, but not all. Like this trip. Nevertheless, she continued her walk.

An eagle to its cage, a prophecy of wrath.

Coolness floated in the air, the sequel to rain. Clouds parted away, giving way to a timid sun. On the leaves dew drops shone, a hint of silver amid the golden hue. Sigo Dolung, even though a modest fragment of the state's exceptional scenery, felt ethereal to them. It appeared to be celebrating its youthful greenery, while Maya, a resident turned into a visitor, had aged.

'We all turn into tourists. At one point or another,' Kranti ruminated. His experiences had taught him too.

'Still, travelling is not the same as shifting, da. It's entirely different to visit as a tourist than to live like a resident. I mean, even our needs will be so different. Everyday life is not a holiday, is it?' she countered when he attempted to connect.

Maya too had been a tourist, but believed herself to be one with a purpose. Shying away from popular sightseeing places, she would return within a week, with a sense of greater understanding. Its irony always escaped her. At the same time, she knew shifting cities was also like a long tour, but with graver emotions. An understanding of the difference between a native and a settler. At times, she felt like a migrant without being so, for staying at a place for years without any past to associate with.

They were now walking on a kutcha road covered in moss, a thick green layer on its black, clayey self. Their eyes were fixed on the mountains, and steps so focused as though they were walking right into them, while their minds strayed into memories.

Hopping over a shallow stream to reach the market; balancing rubber slippers on the water-smoothened stone. Following a snake to its hole. Daring each other to eat the wild mushrooms and being beaten at home due to the resulting allergy. Making a ring of the tortoise beetle, their golden shine sticking on her finger, and displaying it to envious classmates. Saving fireflies in jars, then feeling guilty and freeing them. Killing the carpenter ants in a fit, but leaving the fire ants to roam freely, their red selves being admired secretly. Later, handing them with a swipe of a leaf, to be eaten by those she cared for. Love consuming the loved. A motto they lived by.

Although it was close to only nine, activities were in full swing. Maya also used to go for tuitions at five in morning, which seemed impossible to her now. The houses were similar to the ones in Assam, Kranti noticed as they crossed them. Slanting tin roofs, bamboo fences guarding the rose bushes, hibiscus trees, clothes drying in the lawns, and backyards with vegetables flourishing under the watery sky. Their walk was halted constantly. A cow crossed, a hen hopped, or her suitcase tumbled over the stones.

'I am seeing Lai Xaak and Dhekiya xaak after so long. Used to hate eating them.'

Maya glanced at the bundles of mustard greens and fiddlehead ferns as they crossed the vegetable market. It was set up on a raised concrete platform, open on all sides except for the tin roof. Every seller had their designated area. Each with a sheet of plastic spread in front, varied items arranged neatly on it—dried fish, chilli, banana flowers, ginger, and bamboo shoots. Cane baskets and a few plastic ones were kept next to each seller, containing a few extra portions of each item. Each with an umbrella resting nearby and a pair of slippers or shoes, either in plastic or rubber, she noticed. Packets of bamboo shoots reminded her of her school days. She and her friends would buy bamboo shoots mixed with salt and chillies to savour in the classroom. Hiding behind the desk, they would hope to go unnoticed by the teachers.

'Did you know even ferns are depleting now?'

Kranti interrupted her reminiscences. With each passing moment, she was drifting further into her memories.

'Expected, da. Climate change.'

'On my last visit, we couldn't even get a good Poniol (coffee plum)!'

He spoke about many traditional Assamese vegetables and fruits that were on the verge of extinction. But when he started feeling the heat within, a disruption between the loss of nature and the want for luxury, he softened his stance. 'But what can we even do? Development is also necessary na.'

'Man! I miss Lateku!' She remembered the time when she and her friends would hide and pluck the Burmese grapes, just behind the principal's office.

'Have you ever tried Silikha?'

They giggled at the thought of raw black myrobalan. Despite its herby and astringent taste, they would often forcibly consume it for its nutritional value. The taste, however, couldn't negate the sweetness of the memory. They laughed with the pleasure of sharing, swinging on the thin thread of familiarity.

Now, at a slower speed, Kranti carrying his backpack and Maya dragging her suitcase, they crossed a school building—the only school in the town. The wall was still surrounded with flowering plants. A few Jackfruit and Otenga trees could be seen on the open ground. Bells were ringing for the morning assembly. Maya thought of morning assemblies, with brief morning talks, a short speech by the principal or a teacher, an oath of loyalty to the school, to the state and the nation, concluding with the national anthem. The green metal gates were wide open, with students walking in and a few walking out. Students, in navy blue and white, wearing black shoes, marched towards the assembly ground. Among them, two rows had girls in navy blue *gaale*, which were hand woven traditional wrap-around skirts, and white tops.

'They are from the eleventh and twelfth class. You all call it intermediate, right?'

The intent of belonging made clear by distancing.

She then informed Kranti about the time when the traditional attire of gaale was introduced for girls in school; for boys, the uniform remained the same. The burden of culture varied with gender. The responsibility of keeping it alive was often attributed to one, not the other.

'Almost home!' An excited Maya nudged Kranti on his shoulder, who had walked a few steps away to receive a phone call.

The cotton tree, standing solitary amid the vast field, still as strong as it was and reaching the sky with its branches, greeted her. It was the old silk cotton tree in front, not in their lawn, but far away on the ground.

When they had first come to Sigo Dolung, Maya was informed that it was more than a hundred years old. Its height had made her believe it. It soon became her favourite, and its consistency was a comfort. She would often dream about perching on its topmost branch and touching the fluffy clouds, pocketing some of it and later showing it to her mother. Although not clouds, she did collect cotton threads out of the fallen buds. Holding them, Maya would run fingers over their smooth texture, sometimes brushing them on her cheeks too. She would save them in a plastic cover, hoping to make a pillow with it. Its softness kindled warmth.

2

Although the borders differentiated the states and brought changes to the native languages, and the lifestyles too differed in minute ways, even then, the nature, Kranti noticed, remained almost similar. The earth seemed determined to ignore the divisions we had created.

The houses too reminded him of the one where his parents had chosen to stay. Their home, in an area where an open ditch flowed, where until recently a bridge of four bamboo poles was used to cross it. The ditch that would often overflow during monsoon, where he, much to his embarrassment now, used to float paper boats. 'Shift, Ma. This house will fall soon. At least now we will get decent rates,' Kranti would often coerce his parents to shift from Malegaon. It baffled him to see their happiness being limited to an aging home when there were better ones available in the locality that he deemed fit. He would often suggest suitable properties, and they would invariably reject them.

The train of his thoughts derailed when his phone vibrated. Anchal was calling, the first time since last night. The frequency of her calls had decreased with his responses, the cues she had finally decided to understand. He had informed her about his visit to Arunachal, but not the reason. A curt call of a few words. *It is better to give some time before telling her*, he had reasoned.

'Hey Anchal,' he picked up the call, still juggling between the nostalgic love he felt for the houses he saw and the contempt with which he had covered it up.

'The signal is weak here,' he explained plainly over her probing.

She countered that his prepaid roaming was functioning, a service approved only recently. Until then, no SIM, except the ones registered in the state used to operate. Their conversation moved further. About their plans to visit neighbouring states, even Arunachal, about trips to Guwahati. Anchal's first visit post marriage, when they had visited Umananda temple. Fond remembrance of the Brahmaputra, while they left the family boat ride undiscussed. Angry stares and eventual screams, comparison of rivers in the North and North-east, of life and quality of living, echoed in their minds. So, soon they shifted their memory to the Peacock Island they had been to three years ago, her last visit. The past incited a few smiles, but soon it mutated into frowns.

'Arey no, no. Not justifying, patni ji. You judge too fast. Yes, you are too quick to blame. Yaar, I was drunk then, you were too. Why are you talking about that now? I don't care. Yes, I will not have any problem. If you don't trust, it's your problem. I am not shouting! Oh yaar, I am tired. Yes, tired of you only! Give me a break!'

Kranti said and disconnected the call.

They had discussed breaking up in the past too. Every time, a fight would lead to claiming how they didn't want to live together. Initially she used to disagree, but with each passing year, she too started agreeing to it, but never wholeheartedly. Willingness was never shown.

When angry, they would avoid each other and stay in different bedrooms, experiencing a simulated world of separation. Every time, they would come together, coercing each other's imaginary partner into leaving the other person. They would claim loyalty and imagine growing old like in the movies, with just each other's company. They would come and confess their love for each other. The last bit being true.

Such was their love. Imaginary, often quarrelling, always conciliatory and, until this trip of Kranti, together too.

Kranti had married Anchal without informing anyone in the family. Anticipating the angst it would provoke, Anchal wanted to involve his family and even invite them for a short stayover—an intent that dissolved soon after seeing his stranded relations and the experience on her limited visits. Visits, where conflicts were avoided by days of shopping, bamboo jewelleries, metres of Muga silk, and even a brass xorai (bigger than the one Kranti had gifted). Her first visit—when Anchal couldn't hide her surprise on seeing the pigeon meat curry, when her mother-in-law brought out her signature *Jalukiya Koldil Paro Mangxo.* Her second visit—when her father-in-law had left the dining table offended, refusing to look at Anchal, her knee-length frock inciting his fury. Visits before which she had expressed the desire to settle in Guwahati, provided she got a view of the Brahmaputra from her window. To Kranti, the very thought of shifting back felt preposterous. The extent of its unrealism had startled him.

Seeing an excited Maya who had brightened up at the sight of a tall tree, Kranti was about to join her, when his phone rang again. It was Mridula who was calling now.

'Arey *bhoni*, I came out of Maajorghat. Not coming anytime soon,' Kranti told her, but not the location or reason for his absence.

Her life until then, and from now onwards. Maya was getting ready to trace a new path. Leaving Kranti, and also her parents, she was hoping to find them at a place they'd left many years ago. To experience love, or to lose it, she wasn't sure. Seeking love with a hope to receive. To receive comfort and then, maybe, to leave it. To return to the base or scratch it out.

Like a slingshot, she was being pulled in such suddenness that there was no time to control her feelings. She, who had been stretched to her maximum, was now going to snap back, to throw the search as far as she could. She, like a sling, was waiting for her fingers to lose their grip. Undecided, Maya was brooding whether she should leave her parents and Kranti behind, or go and pursue a life she never had the courage for. One part of her wanted to take shelter in Kranti, even though it wasn't what she had planned.

Lost in these thoughts, Maya went towards the bus which drew nearer. Dragging her suitcase, which had stamps of all the places she'd travelled, except the one she was leaving now. The thought of Sigo, and the proximity to it, pulled out a lot of other thoughts too.

Her Ma circled in her mind. Her love for Kamakhya temple, for which she had undertaken this trip. To worship the femininity of a female, and the godliness in her. The temple of her favourite Goddess, the one Ma grew up hearing about but saw after her marriage; the temple Maya saw in her childhood and never since then. *What else would her mother have liked to see? How was Ma, as an individual, without the baggage of a child to raise?* Maya tried to guess the kind of desires that would've kindled in her mother. *What would she have felt while taking this journey? How did she manage to run a marriage of absence and then deal with the sudden presence of her husband?*

After learning that she was going to the hospital to meet Priyom, he offered help. Although, when in Maajorghat, he often forgot about Priyom. Despite Mridula's daily messages inquiring about him, he didn't try anything more than a few general inquiries at the camp and station. 'I am waiting for the officials to update me,' he would often tell Mridula, as well as to himself.

His offer to help now was a distant possibility. It was just the empathy cropping up from his guilt of absence. They both were aware of it. So, Mridula changed the subject and told in detail about Priyom's survival, when most of the passengers in his coach had died, especially about the old woman who had advised him against jumping out of the coach. However, Kranti cut her narrative short and disconnected the call, promising to talk again. He then followed Maya, who had almost reached her home.

3

The phone number, the sight of which used to bring excitement to her mundane days—which brought pain too. The number which, in due time, stopped inciting happiness, but carried an unease that still loitered within Mridula. A feeling of loneliness that his presence brought with him, and an unease from that realization.

Mridula stood, staring at her phone. Priyom's number flashed in front, and so did the memories of moments with him. She thought about the day when she had seen him for the first time. His dazzling loudness had given solace to her determined silence. Intrigued by the imprudent ways of leading his life, she too had thrown herself upside down, only to find herself enduring it all alone.

Now seeing his number, she saw him. Leering out of the phone, commanding her, demanding the same dedication to his decadence, cajoling her into submission, expecting an unwavering obeisance.

In a similar way, his number had flashed on her phone screen a few months back as well. The number that did a lot more than call. It sneaked out at night; made her mornings blurry. The number that again denied holidays, selected boarding school, extended Rimi's stayover with friends, invited his guests, and embarked her in love and anger. The number that made promises, this time to keep them.

Still suspended somewhere in the web that entwined her love with his sadism, she picked up the call.

Priyom sounded ill, his voice devoid of any emotions. His tone, not his words, pleaded with her to see him. His imperious tone, even though feeble, was apparent to her. Mridula couldn't say much, apart from confirming her visit. By the time she disconnected the call, her forehead was burning, and she sweltered. Breathless, she searched for her inhaler, while her mind searched for valid reasons. At a time when love and fear were both at play, she decided to pack and leave immediately.

In love, even anger betrays. And so does the accuracy of a judgement.

But was it all his fault? She had believed it was. Was the onus on Mridula only of willing submission? Maybe, but her childhood conditioning had been at work too. She carried the learning of a home where love wasn't displayed and hands or hugs weren't offered—at least not in public. She had grown up seeing a marital life that functioned on fights and accusations.

Mridula had bellowed when Priyom stated his unhappiness in calmness. She didn't want to recreate the past, yet she would elongate fights and her show of anger. Often controlled it too, but the deep-seated dissatisfaction would eventually sneak out, right in the open for everyone to see, creating a cycle of embarrassment. And it would lead to a cycle of promises to herself. Promises of refrain, of refined calmness, and cycles of breaking that promise.

A childhood re-enacted itself. For Mridula, marriage meant being angry at each other. Their disparate personalities added to her belief. They, too, showered each other not with tenderness, but with chores to be done. To her, marriage meant being unhappy. Acceptable behaviour that she saw in marriages around, which she wanted to abhor but enacted with equal resignation.

She did contribute to what their marriage became—an increasingly frequent realization. Her actions did add further to the issues., not to the monstrosity that he embraced later. Neither was she ready to leave hers, nor was he ready to leave his.

4

Miraculous Survival in India's Worst Train Derailment

Maajorghat: Maajorghat-Guwahati Express (011188) Derailment, which caused sixty deaths and 250 injuries on Sunday, led the entire nation into mourning and shock over the loss of lives. However, many survival stories have also come up. One such is of Priyom Phukon's, who survived to tell us what had happened inside the coaches that fell.

A tiny sparkle of victory over fate, Priyom Phukon (35) experienced what very few would survive to share. Travelling in coach B2, one of the coaches that got derailed, Priyom had no idea what fate was to bring when he boarded his train at Guwahati.

'I was sitting when the train jerked. Everyone was preparing to get down. It was then we all heard a loud sound. We thought that the train had hit something. I immediately thought of calling my friend, but as soon as I pulled out my phone, the train shook, and the phone slipped from my hand. I felt that the train was toppling down. Like an earthquake. Everything was trembling. It was impossible to be steady. We all were moving from one side to another. A man in front of me fell from the upper berth. His head started bleeding, but then I also fell on the ground.

'I thought of crawling forward and jumping, but an old lady stopped me. She pulled me towards the seat and said it was safer there. I don't know what happened to her. I have been here, in the hospital, all these days.

'I thought I would die. I was under the rubble for many hours. I kept screaming but no one heard me. I had also lost my glasses, so couldn't even see clearly. A body slid over my right hand; I couldn't move it. My left hand was free, though. I removed some bags. There was a small hole through which I could see.

'I heard voices, not just cries, from inside. Some voices were asking all of us to hold on for some more time. I knew some help had arrived. People were trying to pull everyone out. They tried to create a hole to bring all of us out. Some even managed to cut the iron rods with their household tools, but no one noticed me. Some started clearing the debris. But for all their efforts and intent, the time too was running out. I fainted soon, thinking my wait would never be over. When I woke up, I was here.'

Priyom was found after six hours of searching under a seat that had gotten detached and fallen on him. He was spotted by a local resident, who was clearing the bodies near the coach window. Priyom was deep inside the coach. There was no way for the resident to reach him, so he called an NRDF personnel. Cranes were already being used to turn the toppled coaches to find an opening to enter and bring out the stranded passengers. But upon inspection, it was found that the B2 coach had to be cut open to rescue Priyom.

However, due to the risk that accompanied using gas cutters, the rescue team was not convinced to use one where Priyom had fainted. Post some deliberation, a ladder was brought and attached to the coach. A team of two soldiers climbed on top of the coach, cut it from the middle, and crawled inside. After a struggle of several minutes, Priyom was brought out and immediately sent to the hospital.

'He had suffered minor injuries and no internal injury. He had also ingested a lot of water and dust, because of which he needed constant monitoring for the first few days.' Dr Biswa said. 'Now he is doing fine, and he will soon be completely recovered to go home,' he further added.

This derailment has raised concerns over the safety of Indian railways. 'This derailment was unfortunate. Many such accidents have happened in the past too. An exceptional amount of hard work is going on in the Railways to reduce and eventually stop such accidents and loss of lives. We are working towards creating a safer railway journey for everyone,' M.S. Reddy, the Railway spokesperson said, when asked about the safety initiatives.

Honesty of Hatred

Today I see
cruelty in your eyes.
Oh, the truthfulness of it.
A remembrance of the past
and the consecutive times.

Masked in insecurity—
Yours.
Then vanished,
in our closeness.
Apparent now.

But today I see
that strength in you,
of hatred, as powerful as love,
Variability of intent.

Oh, the parade of its honesty
in your eyes.
I see once again
that
you too are capable of emotions,
with no dilution.

So today,
I love you,
and this strength
that I had searched in you
and me.
That I had waited to
denounce too.

5

The hospital was undergoing renovation. *Monsoon is an unusual time for it,* Mridula noted. In front of the main building lay a pile of logs. Pieces of wounded wood, their barks were peeled and flesh pink with cuts from the axe all over. On their side were bamboos, tall and round, in shining silky green. Both dead and uprooted from their world, and thrown into the world of buildings. Mridula admired them with a smile as she climbed up the stairs.

Love, especially the hope that it often orchestrated, could make even withered wood appear ethereal. A melodious cry within a song of ache.

The same hope performed one of its best acts at the hospital, where lives were awarded, not always, but today. The place, which even a few days ago was filled with screams of loss, now nestled in absolute silence. Maybe Mridula felt deaf to all the sound around. All she could hear was the beating of her heart. She rushed towards the sole room in the basement where Priyom had been admitted, where she had forgotten to check the first time.

A second later, gripped by an abrupt realization, Mridula stopped and headed towards the bathroom. Her reflection in the mirror looked tired. Lack of sleep gave her face a slight swell, and dark patches circled her eyes. She sprinkled her face with cold water. She then combed and tied her hair in a ponytail, all this while her fingers ran in frantic urgency. Then, her focus shifted to her eyes. In spite of the puffiness, she knew they were beautiful. Priyom, too, had praised them occasionally. Bending forward, while balancing herself on the basin's edge, she applied a thin streak of kohl, just to accentuate the broadness. She readjusted her bindi. Her lips looked lifeless, so she painted them with natural gloss. Priyom never approved of dark lipstick colours. Ignoring the why's and what's, she did her best to give herself a look he would like.

Finally, when she walked towards Priyom's room, a strong blend of emotions started brewing inside her, as though attempting an exam. Fear mixed with excitement.

His room was well illuminated, painted newly in peach, with green curtains on the windows. Its brightness was an extension of his loudness. Taking a deep breath, she clenched the doorknob. After a while, she collected herself and went in.

Once-strong-now-frail, he lay on the iron cot. The glare from his gold-rimmed glasses was missing too—something Mridula was thankful for. The air felt heavy, more so with the windows shut, as if in conflict with the lucent paint. The staleness of his breath mixed with the leftover breakfast that lay uncovered on the table. It further combined with the medicine's odour and the dried-up vomit in the bin to his side. Fighting nausea, Mridula went to his bed.

She had spent many nights thinking of him. In her dreams she would approach him, bringing him out of his pain. On the nights of suffering, she had prayed for him to suffer too. To cry, not for what he was, but for what he had done. Even then she prayed for his sufferings to be minimal. In her imaginative world, she had pictured him regretting and crying for his actions, but in good health. Today, he was in a condition worse than she had envisaged.

Seeing him impotent, incapable of moving, denied the comfort of even basic control, her heart ached. She pitied him. In that pity, she pardoned him, relinquishing the past which, until now, she had preserved as a valuable secret. The secret that she had repented, yet guarded.

Priyom was asleep with such stillness that life seemed to be slipping away. So, she sat next to him and held his hand—a tight grasp of life around him. She circled her fingers around his wrists. She was prepared for a fight. Whether it was with death or him, she wasn't sure.

As if in response to her presence, Priyom started to tremble feverishly. Neither were any nurses outside, nor could she see anyone else. Voices from the upper floors felt too distant, so Mridula tried to stop his tremors in whatever ways she could. She pressed his feet down, keeping them close to the bed, but they still moved. His hands were shivering too, so she tried to keep them still with hers. Just then, she heard his teeth chattering. She left his trembling legs and went near his face. Pressing her palm on his forehead, she tried to stop the quivering. She was terrified that his jaw would break and his teeth would spurt out. Half an hour passed, but nothing came out. His tremors continued, in spite of her holding him tight. At the same time, she shouted for help, trying to summon the nurses in vain. She couldn't stop her thoughts from rippling either. They oscillated between the Priyom of now and the Priyom of then, for whom she had travelled back and forth. Her frequent journeys into memories, and away from them too.

Memories, not of words but of feelings. Feelings that his words precipitated. Their impact was still fresh on her senses. The remembrance of senses, not the logic of the mind. Memories that she could still experience.

Memories of his nose, which wrinkled whenever he smiled, his straight gait that she felt so proud of, the laughter with which he had told her of his schedule for the coming months, and his plans to take her away. It all came back to her. Mridula prayed for his life, but couldn't stop herself from imagining the worst too. When she learnt that he was found stuck beneath the debris, heavy coaches crushing him down, she had gasped for breath. It reminded her of the time when she too had almost drowned.

It had happened on one of the ferry rides to Dibrugarh, when she couldn't show the delight Priyom was expecting. Instead, a dread had spread over her when he cajoled her into standing near the edge. The smell of the river relaxed him, he had told her. So, he pushed her into coming a little forward, and then a few inches more, until the door unlatched and she lost her balance, falling into the river. An unrest erupted, until one of the passengers jumped in and rescued her. Meanwhile, Priyom stood at the back without a word of concern. Later, he only spoke to chastise her for being careless. His own responsibility in it was confidently ignored.

Since that day, the memory of not what happened, but of what could have happened tormented her. What if she wasn't rescued? Breathless, she would have tried to float, but some big fish could have pulled her in, slashing her apart. One cut at a time. The thought of it froze her, always did; yet, she continued to think about it from time to time. She imagined herself drowning, even after being rescued, as though she secretly wanted a watery grave. Its memories didn't bring fear, but a longing that she wasn't able to leave.

To whisk herself away from those days and Priyom, who was now asleep, she looked around for a distraction. From the place she was sitting, she could see trees—not their trunks or roots, but the branches. An expansive spread of verdant clouds with sporadic curves. Adorning them were not the stars but the fresh green of newly born leaves. These clouds didn't fly away, nor did they go above her. They stayed where they had been, at her shoulder's height. A consistency that Mridula admired. She noticed a few birds too, humming around, flying in and out. Outside the window, a happy nature seemed to be welcoming everyone. An ongoing celebration of life, which ended as soon as Priyom woke up and asked for water. She gave him a few drops that he gulped with much difficulty. He looked at her unflinchingly, his head still facing the empty wall in front, while his eyes shifted to her. With his glare, her heart pounded. Fearing that he could hear it, she retreated with calculated poise and stood a few steps away—a show of confidence.

He raised his hand and gestured her to come over, his fingers not shaking anymore. His focus was like a beast aiming at its prey.

Mridula stepped further back, now close to the door. She saw a hint of hatred in him, raw and anew. The intensity of it had gathered through the years, masked by the display of occasional care. Today, Priyom didn't look for a mantle to hide it. He was getting ready to bring down all her might in just one stroke.

'Give me that bottle!' he said this time, impatient, almost on the verge of shouting. Few minutes passed in silence and then he yelled at her.

Mridula stood still. At the door. Glaring. Deaf to his words, but gazing into him. Slowly, her heart paced normally again—just a few skipped beats from time to time.

She turned back and stepped out of the door. Pulling the door to a close, she looked at him one last time—her eyes challenging him, her heart revolting against his.

She walked outside the room. Away from the sickening smell, past him, and his everything. She refused to be in that room and serve him as per his demands, fulfilling his expectations from her presence. She wasn't going to comply just because he was the husband and she the wife.

Moving across the street, she crossed him and everything that bonded her to him. This time, no butterfly fluttered in her stomach, no pounding heart threatened to pop out. She walked with the smile of harmony.

By secluding from him, Mridula hoped to unite with herself.

SECTION 9

HALT OR HOME?

The hazy nights and lifetime of memories
Of panic and wonder,
Anticipation and aspiration,
Of seclusion and companionship
Reluctant and willed.
Let's drink to them.

1

Maya?

A voice, unheard before; or she might have, way back in the past. After almost an hour of walking, frustration shone pink on her face. She was often called 'Kashmiri apple' whenever her pale skin flushed pink. *Tawang Apple*, she would retort, trying to fit in with a state she didn't belong to—not by birth. Maya was wondering whether the northern plains would have accepted her more than those mountains that ran along her side—a sight she had grown to admire, love, and occasionally detest. Murky green against the backdrop of a pale blue sky, cottony clouds passing through them.

'Garg daughter?'

'Ya, uncle,' Maya said, turning around.

'I am Paron Uncle.'

A suffix they would add voluntarily, Chowdury Aunty, Panung Uncle, Borang Sir. A suffix that took exact permanency as that of a name. Maya *Aying*, Maya *Bihari*. Even she had a suffix.

'I stay here.' He pointed to a petite cemented house, shaded by a sloping roof. Signs of habitation were apparent with the faint sounds of cooking and chatter. On the veranda, a plastic chair held piles of pillows, and a rubber mat rested on the bamboo fence. She looked at his house and the one in front, which belonged to her.

'We built it recently. Fireplace still not done. Only for meetings and cooking sometimes,' he explained, finding Maya gawking at the *Chang ghar*. Bamboo steps led to a house which was perched on wooden pillars with a cement base, a remedy for rain-induced decay. Maya could almost hear the creaking the bamboo floor would make if she were to walk on it. She imagined the rain drops that would dribble down from the roof once the *Toko paat* (Chinese palm leaves) had aged considerably, the light that would filter through its woven bamboo walls, and the smoke that would waft out of the fireplace. Above the hearth, on its suspended mud-coated platform, smoked meat would be kept warm. Beside it, bamboo tubes would be kept, promising a bowl of aromatic smoky rice. She thought of Kholams and their unmistakable difference from the rice eaten at home. During lunches at her friend's house, vegetarian versions of Pasa soup, without the fish or minced meat, were often offered, and sometimes even lai xaak. Often, she wished to try Lukter, to taste the spicy mix of dry meat and chilli flakes, but could never ask.

'Come and see it. Come for tea,' he added after a pause, addressing Kranti, who came and stood next to Maya.

'You have keys? I have one set somewhere. That time, Garg Madam gave it.'

'I have the keys, Uncle.'

'So many years you guys didn't come. Sir also doesn't come. Where is he now?'

Their conversation went on for a few more minutes—introduction of Kranti, discussion of the train derailment, the situation at Maajorghat, the condition of Indian railways, the state, the country. Maya nodded, mostly looking down, as though bowing to the truth. Uttering no words, she cautiously trod through her fears about all that they discussed.

The exchange of information would have gone further if Maya had not put a stop to it and walked towards the house. The house hadn't changed much, except for the damp patches on the outer walls. From its tin roof, rust dribbled down, a few drops every minute. It had rained in the morning.

Behind her, a cow grazed, a few cattle egrets feasting on its back. A boy cycled away, one hand on the handlebar, another raised in a wave, feeling the wind or swatting a fly—the difference seemed irrelevant. In front stood the house in which Maya was supposed to enter.

The search had paused and the wait had halted, but not the pain of displacement, neither the anger for it.

A house in which she was so accustomed to sounds, stood in a ghostly serenity. There was complete silence around her, except for the sound of plastic wrappers that were getting crushed under her feet and the clatter of thoughts that trampled without mercy. A forsaken past was scowling at the present.

The planks in the wooden gate were missing and its paint was washed out. It squeaked when she pushed it open. It was attached to a diminishing fence of bamboo sheets that could neither withstand rain nor the heat of ten long years. Their debilitated form pointed at a slow death they were awaiting as well as dreading. Like all of us, the house, too, was secretly hoping for that wait to never be over.

Many years had gone between this visit and the last. And within this gap, both the house and Maya had aged. She too held patches of time, dark and unrelenting.

A cluster of coiled hair lay on the steps—prequel to a combed lustre, holding the reminiscence of its ungainly appearance before the braided elegance. On its sides were empty packets of chips, biscuits, and a few plastic bottles, crushed and muddied.

Must've been thrown by neighbours or casual walkers in their quick spree to keep the surroundings clean, she thought.

As she approached the main door, a dog woke up and jumped outside the fence, its tail twisted, ears erect. A habitual response to ominous arrivals, of news and humans. As Maya arrived at the door, so did her memories.

Buried memories and burnt feelings, ashes thrown out in the waters. A river flowing nearby. A pile of books searched, the flicker of kerosene lamp for exam nights, a cancelled picnic, pen leaking ink, and a sweater steering despair. A plate of rice and lentils slightly burnt, served with apology, thrown in anger, a child crying, a wife sighing, a loathed love. Poorly explained menstruation, reckless blaming for sickness and health, and a house left hastily. A town hated determinedly.

The veranda, which was once made into a room, now lay bare, apart from the yellowish bamboo skeleton where a wall used to be. It had once belonged to Maya, and also to her Ma and father. All of them she had come to claim.

2

Kranti broke the lock, as the keys Maya had didn't work, and the neighbour couldn't find his.

Entering the house, Maya felt as though she could see her mother. Exactly at the point where her shadow ended. Sitting as she used to, criss-crossed on the floor, chopping vegetables while watching TV with a childlike intent. Eyes fixed on the screen, reading the news-strips scrolling at the bottom, loudly, for Maya to hear and remember. 'We all should know what is happening in this world,' she would say at times when Maya would protest and threaten to not remember anything that Ma constantly updated her with.

Maya moved further. The wooden table still stood on the left, on the grainy floor. The door slammed behind her wobbling the table, which Kranti steadied. Not an ideal place for the table to be, but it stayed where the young Maya had kept it.

It still had a small storage box on it. Layers of dust on top. Inside it used to be her once indispensables, things not to be missed before stepping out—lip gloss, a tube of Boroplus, scrunchies, keys, and a couple of chewing gums. Later, Ma used it to keep hers, something Maya had noticed on one of her trips back from college. Pins and rubber bands, a bottle of moisturizing cream, and a few neatly piled packets of round red bindi.

The rest of the hall was almost empty, except for a dull brown coffee table that was pushed to the wall. Its flaky mica was chipped at the edges, and on it were oil marks, accumulating dust, like years on an aging mother, unforgiving and constant. The cane chairs that she and Ma repainted in different colours every few years were missing, although their cushions were staked near the table. On top of them was a stack of newspapers, crumbled now, reeking of rats' excreta.

On the wall, a faded reminiscence of a once-bright picture with stone-studded jewellery hung next to a calendar. Half of the calendar was covered with a beach photo. Blue water encircled by white sand, dotted with beach-beds, umbrellas above each—the kind her parents wouldn't have seen. Spotless beaches that Maya had visited thrice and promised to take Ma the next time. The last half displayed the month of August, its festivals and holidays, and the date on which Ma shifted to Bangalore.

Three wooden shelves, perfectly aligned, were empty now. They reminded her of small figurines that Ma collected each year. Different statues of Ganesha—resting with his head on one hand, standing with a warm smile, or sitting with a bowl of *laddu* in hand. Crystal, golden, and silver figurines. They were stuck to her mind like high-definition images, with no apparent meaning, yet crediting the extent of her familiarity.

Further inside the house, the bedroom stood solitary. In it were two wooden cots arranged in an L-shape, each pushed against a wall. Mosquito-nets hung over each, dense cobwebs surrounding them. On the right was a steel trunk resting on four bricks, one for each side, covered in the same coarse-blue curtain, faded now. Like a neglected monument, they displayed false vigour from a past that remained only in the fragmented carving on its chipped walls. On the top, a TV set wrapped in a cotton sheet sat silently. The tape recorder her mother had bought with her first salary was nowhere to be seen.

One side of the wall had a wooden temple cabinet, its door open. The brass bell attached to it had corroded to green. A few idols were still there, except for her Ma's favourite *Kahna*, which she had carried with her to Bangalore.

Further inside, next to the backyard, Maya noticed the bathroom's lethargic grey door. Purple marks of crushed *Toko-gutti* were still apparent on it. Those ripe fruits of the Himalayan Thatching Palm tree, especially their nuts, were her best distractor on anxious days, but she would never eat the relish made of its peel. Father didn't approve of it.

The door was jammed, so they had to push it to open. A plastic mug and bucket stood under a rusted water tap, and a glass shelf attached over it. There used to be a plastic basket on it, with shampoos and sachets of hair colour. Absent for quite some time now. Maya saw the rectangular mirror pushed to the wall. The one that she would take down and move from left to right, checking whether her ponytail was exactly as she wanted, if her uniform had any creases that needed to be ironed immediately.

The entire house, coated with years of dust, spoke of inactivity. So, after a while of nostalgic tottering, Maya took charge. She searched for a broom, while Kranti unbolted the rusted windows. Finding a stick, she broke the cobwebs with it and collected the scraps with her bare hands, overcoming her wish for gloves. Then, she threw the garbage out in the backyard. Occasionally, she glanced at Kranti, who had already pulled the mattresses and cushions out in the sun and was now wiping the beds with his damp handkerchief.

'First, let's make a place to sit,' he told her, aware of her gaze on him.

After almost two hours of cleaning, the hall looked clean enough to spend a night. However, the house still smelled of abandonment. The weight of a neglected decade burdened the air.

The kitchen was the last to be cleaned. It still had running water. Finding a stack of utensils inside an aluminium trunk, Maya cleaned them with her bathing gel. Wiping the wooden table that used to be the stand for a gas stove, she arranged the utensils there, while Kranti washed the wooden shelves and the windows. Outside, three tall orange trees stood in a straight line, also aged, the deep green of their leaves contrasting with the monsoon glow around.

Exhausted from the work, Maya and Kranti threw a cursory glance at everything, from the trees to the ceiling, from the washed utensils to the dusted cots. A lot had to be done, but for now, they wanted to eat. Lighting the kerosene stove which she'd borrowed from Paron Uncle, Maya boiled some water to make instant noodles.

Sitting at the wooden block, once used as a door stopper, Maya reflected at the state the house was in. *Why didn't her mother give away everything while vacating the house? Why had her father's stuff been left untouched? Was it the same even when they had lived?* She tried to remember, but couldn't recall much. She wondered whether coming to Bangalore was Ma's sudden plan, whether she used to miss her father there too. *Why did Ma never tell me?* Resentment soon took over Maya, who now felt that a lot had been kept hidden from her.

'When I was a kid, even Maggi used to be a rare treat,' Kranti said as the palatable smell filled the house. He had just returned with the items she had asked him to bring, along with a refilled stock of cigarettes, from the local grocery store.

'Used to be a symbol of modern breakfast. Once, an aunt had asked my mother if we knew what Maggi was,' Maya replied, laughing.

3

It was afternoon, yet the sunlight felt soft. Slipping away from the leaves, a thin beam of light fell on Maya's feet and shone her stone-studded toe ring, something that Ma had never approved of. 'Maya, wear it once you are married,' she would say. Maya wore it, nevertheless.

She and Kranti sat on the steps. The way she used to sit with Ma, lazing under the filtered warmth of the sun, relishing garden-fresh oranges often sent by her father's friend from Changlang. A yearly gift, sent as a token of gratitude for her Ma's cooking and hospitality.

She sat as Ma would have.

Seeking Ma, Maya too was uniting with her. Somewhere in this process, she was wilfully forgetting that she was her own story, that she could neither create Ma nor live her life. Even if she tried, she would live an empathetic reality, emerging out of her memories, and assumptions from those memories.

Now they both busied themselves in discussing further tasks at hand and the activities for the days to come. Schedules were made as if they had been staying together for years in this house. It wasn't something they both overtly discussed and desired, yet they went ahead with a wild impulse. For a long time, they both had been in cages of their own build, and now they felt ready to jump off the cliff and barge into the wilderness, as if it belonged to them.

Maya had been out for years, but a bondage hung on her heart, by Kevin and every man she had allowed to treat her as they wished. Relationships depending on their convenience not hers. This time, though, she believed she was in control, and could decide the role she would take up in Kranti's life. But soon, the glinting diamonds on his ring cleared the fog of their intimacy. So, the discussion shifted to calls and helpline numbers, to the reasons validating their stay.

As they discussed the possibilities and chances of finding Maya's parents, she neither fought her thoughts nor felt the need to. This time, she stayed still, hoping for a clear vision, recalling happenings from the past with contented openness. They weren't a treasure to her, yet she remembered them with stark clarity. With all those instances came an insight from which she had often tried to run away. Every time she thought of Ma, emotions erupted, and so did a bundle of stories. She was slowly getting ready to understand, learn, and look deeper. To peel those layers of years lived, one by one.

Ma was becoming her constant emotion.

In this house of her childhood, Ma had shared stories from her life. And whenever she did, Maya would create mental pictures, associating them with the scenes being narrated. Since the day of her arrival, all those scenes had been coming back to her, like a movie being played in broad daylight. She was living that movie with her eyes open; senses evoked at one time and lost at another.

Maya saw her mother sitting; she saw her in agony, in distress. She saw her in her threadbare cotton sari, the vermillion separating her into two selves. The huge red bindi on her forehead, and her glass bangles with its fading golden polish. She saw her in every form, each depicting her marriage to Father. Every part, symbolic of the life she was leading, and obscuring the traces of the life she wanted to lead. In her memories, Maya saw her mother, the woman, who till now was hidden behind the thick sheets of life she carried around.

A thirteen-year old Maya, her socks rolled down, her skirt folded at the waist to make it knee-length, and the sweater tied over it, was running to school. The morning bell had rung twice. She had to reach before the third bell, or else she wouldn't be allowed in, which meant a slap or two from her father.

It had happened recently, when she missed the Hindi class that used to start precisely at nine. Knowing she was already late, she had spent the first hour of school roaming, looking for birds and puppies, circling trees, and touching the flowers but never plucking them. She was following a baby snake around the fence when she was spotted by a concerned teacher, who had then reported his discovery to her father. Her father had accused her of loitering and threatened to take her out of school, citing that she wasn't fit to be left free. As a few minutes passed, his outburst shifted to its usual target—Ma, who would always come in to shield her daughter. Standing between them, looking at Ma's solemn face and father's furious one, Maya used to wonder why Ma willingly took up the blame for her mistakes. Later, Maya too became accustomed to it. She knew, no matter what happened, Ma would eventually douse his anger, sometimes taking the burn on herself—traces of which were seen even years later.

So, on some days, when she was late and not in a mood to plead the watchman to let her in, she would decide to take a stroll again. Covering up the field outside the school building and chasing dogs and pigs, she would sit under a tree and open her tiffin box. Even though school was just a few minutes away, she would insist Ma to pack lunch for her. 'I want to eat with my friends,' she would lie. She used to prefer the open air outside to her home, but she couldn't tell this to Ma. Since then, Ma would fill her green tiffin box with whatever she asked for—parathas and potato fry, pickle, bread fritters, or kachori.

On a similar routine one day, after finishing what was supposed to be her lunch, Maya decided to take a walk back home, something she did every afternoon post lunch. A quick tour of the house, a hidden view of Ma doing what she always did—household chores. Every afternoon after lunch, Maya would rush to see Ma. She wouldn't go and hug her like others of her age, neither would she share the day's happenings. She would just sneak in the house, stand, and watch Ma silently.

Ma, always hunched at the water tap, washing their clothes, utensils, or her hair. Both would carry out their daily routine. Ma, out of responsibility; Maya, out of compulsion. She had to see Ma as often as possible, as if to ensure her presence. It was a duty she had assigned herself, to make sure that Ma was there where she had always been—in the house. Seeing her doing daily chores, her monotonous motions, and the same blank expressions reassured her. For her, Ma was fine as long as she was cooking and cleaning. Ma was fine, because she was still putting up a fight, abandoning herself for the family, the tasks which she associated Ma's strength with.

A comfort drawn out of consistency. A sign of support, protection from father, and the world. A slight acceptance of love that wasn't communicated. Like the morning cry of a rooster, disposal of its duty, day by day. Both required no effort from her. Both played their part, pleasing her with their presence. But time—it didn't need continuity of the present, but a change of it, if not constant then at least frequent. She came to know that later.

That day, long before reaching home, Maya saw Ma sitting with a neighbour, chairs drawn out in the veranda. They both were laughing at something. Two teacups were kept on the ground, each next to their respective chairs. Maya had returned without entering the house. She had then gone for a long and relaxed stroll. She had liked what she saw.

That day, she had taken a longer route to the main gate, balancing herself over the sleek bamboo bridge. Three whole bamboos were laid over a small canal, tied to each other with ropes. She sat on the bridge, searching for fish and tadpoles. She located one fish, and in a fraction of a second, lost sight of it. On any other day, Maya would have tried to move the rocks with a twig, cajoling the fish to swim out of their hiding. That day, she didn't. She felt content with their game of hide-and-seek. They had appeared happy to her.

4

Kranti wanted to try the local delicacies. Pehak, Pika Pila, Ngatok, Chura Pa, Amin, Ngo Dong, and Ek Adin Dong. Bresi and Khazi as well. Byak for Maya, because as far he knew, she was vegetarian. He looked it all up online and made a list, without any consideration of the local preferences or weather. He didn't think whether a dish special to Apatni, Nyishi, or Monpas would be available at a place where Galos and Adi resided. Nor did he think that a dish from the higher altitude of Tawang might not be readily available in the plain regions of Sigo Dolung. He didn't ask Maya if he could get winter specialties in monsoon. Cultural intricacies, understanding culture-specific eating habits, and the influence of weather, wasn't his concern.

'I should have explored this state too,' he confessed his regret of not seeing the neighbouring states. This time, he wanted to experience as much as he could. Maya liked his enthusiasm, but its timing frustrated her. She quickly ignored it.

So, Maya took him to the only restaurant she knew. It wasn't there, and a new one stood in its place. There were a few more, each of which they went to, upon Kranti's insistence.

As they tried various dishes, she thought of the time she had snuck out with her friends to try Wungwut Ngam at the only restaurant in the main market—and also of what followed later. A neighbour had spotted her eating the rice-coated chicken and phoned her father, who, in turn, had called and informed Ma. Maya had lied to Ma, promising that it was only the bamboo shoot fry that she had eaten, keeping the expectation of vegetarianism intact. Even though absent, her father had control over their lives. She hated that realization then—and even now. She wondered whether her mother would have understood her if she had been honest. The last few weeks made her sure that Ma would have.

Tired with the day's exploration, they went to bed early.

Maya was now lying on the bed which once used to be her father's, over it a mosquito net rolled up. Her legs were wrapped under a bed sheet, though her feet fought and escaped out. Her heels were scaled, a recent addition. A reminder of long walks, dusty roads, and a tragedy she still wasn't sure of.

Her hands were outside the sheet, palms facing upward. She slept straight, in an almost-corpse pose. Not of those she saw at the burial ground, curled up in tragedies, like hair when brought near fire. Yet, unlike hair, they didn't vanish.

Tired, she was almost falling asleep when she heard a voice. It was Ma, calling to her, walking in an old cotton sari with pink flowers still glowing. She walked briskly, like her younger version used to. She had turned younger, and looked happier too. She came and stood at the edge of the bed, running her fingers over one of its wooden stands. Maya smiled at her. She was happy that her mother was there, that she was smiling too.

Without uttering a word, this time their smile reached each other.

Maya wanted to get up and hold her, touch her hands, and feel their softness once again. She wished to hug her this time and convey her love too. Overwhelmed with happiness, she opened her eyes and looked around. Ma's presence felt tangible, as though she could smell her. She might've even heard her if she paid enough attention. But all she saw was Kranti sleeping next to her on a separate cot. His muttering indicated that he too was having his share of dreams.

Around him, the walls were contracting, leaving Kranti with no space but to lie sideways. Soon, they started to shrink further, pushing his knees into his stomach. His elbows crushed his ribs. They were pushing hard enough to flatten his nose and face into a round luci. His face detached from his body, landing on the palms of Ma, who was frying tender luci and serving it to Baba, sitting at the dining table. A huge round table, with just one chair to accommodate him.

Getting his plates full of luci, Baba swallowed, one morsel at a time, his crispy eyes, moist nose, and succulent lips with marinated tongue on the side. He continued eating till Kranti woke up.

This dream, not new but a familiar companion, had persisted, even when others had started diminishing post counselling, that he had gone on Anchal's insistence.

Nature and love

'Have you ever noticed how love changes with the change of places?' he ruminated.

'Like how lovers' quarrels pause when the sun dyes the sky orange,' she replied. She had often seen lovers holding hands and hugging longer when the waves rose to greet and the wind blew to caress. And how, around mountains, words of anger were swallowed, following the unsaid rules of silence that they bestowed. Love often became encompassing when nature beckoned it. With nature watching them, people would become timid in their expectations. Giving would come easily.

'This love, even though not as divine as nature, will become similarly elusive. It won't last long enough to be recorded or made into a habit.'

'It will last only for a moment. A moment of purity and trueness. In that fleeting moment, nothing but love will matter. Its tenderness—incited by nature.'

'The love that nature beholds for generations, that we can experience within a second. The second that will be as important as a lifetime.'

'The lifetime we will live in, just in that moment.'

5

Since the day of their culinary exploration, they had stayed staying inside the home, stepping out only to buy vegetables and once for tea at their neighbour's Chang Ghar, as promised. In each other, they found an escape from reality. The lure of a probable closeness, it felt like a new life. Maya found in him the support she needed, which she hoped to last all her life. To Kranti she gave a reason to be free from the stagnation of his old life.

It was a lazy afternoon, a surprisingly dry day in the midst of monsoon. So, Kranti insisted on sightseeing. Although it was Maya who had inhabited this town, Kranti took the lead. Now comfortable in each other's company, their guards came down and old habits flared up.

They walked around the market area where a few men were playing carrom under a thatched roof. It was a small set up with a low-lying wooden table and four cane chairs around it.

'We all should make carrom our national sport! Hockey is gone, and now even in cricket we are losing.'

'There are other sports too, da,' Maya retorted, naming Sania Mirza and Saina Nehwal and their recent wins at the international level.

'Haan right, I can watch tennis. Badminton looks like a girl's game.'

'What?'

'Arey, no, no, sorry. Not that way. I mean it's boring. For me it is.'

Why? Because badminton is not as elite as cricket or tennis? Or even football? What about kabaddi, hockey? Maya wanted to ask, but didn't. Pullela Gopichand, she thought, trying hard to remember the names of male badminton players. Eventually, she said, 'Sports also has bourgeois categories, and are gendered too. Like everything else.'

Badminton was the game that his father had taught him. He detested it, not for its lack of elitism, but for the association it reminded him of. Kranti chose not to tell her.

Leaving carrom, and the conversation behind, they moved further. Kranti decided to take a walk uphill. 'To check out the higher region,' he told her.

Kranti praised Sigo Dolung. Although it was limited in terms of comfort and facilities, the place was peaceful. The town was indeed beautiful, more so for a visitor who had come to witness nature's wild exuberance, a thick jungle even by the roadside. For them, walking in the rain was out of their will, without the compulsion of attending chores. Lighting a fire was for its exoticism, not because the roads were closed and electrical poles uprooted.

It wasn't like that when the river wreaked havoc each monsoon, bringing floods that none could glorify, or when the landslides engulfed cars and people in it. Those endless days of wait and fear, when food would be scarce and the roofs had to be rebuilt. The rain felt magical when one could leave it whenever needed; not so much when it caged everyone in their shelters, with nothing to step out with.

'We used to draw dolls only with black coals, you know. For the rains to stop. Upside down, legs up in air and its hair touching the ground. But those dolls never helped!'

Maya had a love-hate relationship with the rain. But hailstones? She abhorred them. Since the day they broke her umbrella, leaving her drenched. Making her white shirt transparent. Her teacher had scolded for the visibility of her black bra underneath, asking her to cover up. With what, she hadn't told her. So, she sat with a wet bag placed in front of her chest during the entire duration of the class, shivering. Water dripped out of her hair while her feet had crumbled to numbness inside her shoes. Yet, she didn't go back. Home used to stifle her then.

As they went further, they came across a woman doling out gaale. She sat before the loom inside the Chang Ghar, its lower beam resting on her lap, and a *gepang* (waist belt), attached to her waist. She was weaving one of the two pieces of the bright red Adi gaale—one broad and yellow, and a few thinner black stripes. This, and the other piece, would later be stitched together for a full-length gaale in such a way that the stripes would fall horizontally in the centre. Her hands moved in hypnotic precision, pushing the shuttle left and right and putting the square-shaped long *gekong* in and out with mechanical fluency. Her focus shifted from the threads to Maya and Kranti when they crossed the fenced boundary without her permission.

Talking in a language she felt they would understand, the woman asked, '*Keenega*? (Do you want to buy?)' to which Maya nodded.

Asking her daughter, who was preparing the warp for the loom, to bring the stack of gaale, she called them. Offering cane stools to them, she spread a plastic mat to display her creations. Owing to the taste of the predominant Adi community of Sigo Dolung, most of the gaale were of simple traditional designs with two or three horizontal stripes in the middle. A few adhered to modern preferences with bolder woven designs, in zig-zag patterns. Flipping through them, Kranti chose one with intricate patterns, similar to the Mishmi's diamond designs.

For whom, Maya wanted to know, but kept quiet.

'For my sister,' Kranti informed her, nevertheless.

She told him that she too had one of these back in Bangalore. What she didn't tell Kranti was that it was her father who had gifted her the pink gaale with black geometric patterns and a *galuk* (waistcoat) to go with it when she had gone to visit him. The visit and the gaale—both kept hidden from her mother until now.

Now that her parents were travelling together, she could finally wear her gaale on the next ethnic day in office, she thought.

The visit happened just once, but had Maya lying many a times. A trip that she was asked to hide from Ma, for which she had agreed after innumerable letters over the years. Meeting her father had left her as disoriented as this search for her parents. 'Come for just two days, Maya beta. I want to see you once,' he had pleaded. 'I'm going to Guwahati for a week-long conference, Ma,' she had told her mother that night. It was a lie she couldn't justify later. Its guilt still spun in her head.

A journey of two and a half days, spent in anticipation, later remembered for its excitement too, which she would have missed if not jolted out of her newspaper by a fellow passenger. The train journey in which she and others had spoken about their lives openly, for they knew they weren't to meet again. Stuck together for days, Maya too had shared her fears, experiences, and dreams, but refused to give out her phone number in the end. The journey when she had gone to meet her father.

Her father, running away, had created a world of his own in a small quarter that Maya entered once and became determined to never enter again.

He lived with minimal accumulations. A gas stove to make his morning tea, two cups, one for him, one for his friend, a few plates, and no cookware in the kitchen. A wooden single bed on which two pillows struggled for breath, two wooden chairs, and a square coffee table for guests. A small TV that was switched on only for two days when she stayed and a radio that blurted out news every morning. The windows perennially closed with rusted bolts, curtains always drawn. A walking stick, smooth with use, hung on the window's grill. Maya had noticed that his cupboards too were mostly empty barring minimum clothing requirements. It could easily pass away as empty if not examined carefully. The only activity seemed to be of the wall clock which ticked loudly, as if making up for the eerie silence that hung heavily on the house.

To Maya, his way of living appeared as an effort to not exist, except for the marks of hands on the walls, which showed his need for support. *His marriage, Ma's constant presence, and my birth are the absolute proof of his living. It must have left him troubled,* Maya had thought then.

Her father was retired, yet he'd decided to stay in a state where he knew none but one—who had also left him by death. For fifteen years, Maya was told, her father's routine was to go on walks with his colleague, who later became his sole companion for a drink or two. The frequency of which later increased and eventually became an everyday affair. He would spend all night drinking, cajoling Verma to stay back as well, adding to his already dysfunctional family life. All this continued till Verma bid a final goodbye to him and his family. A half empty bottle of Old Monk was still in the line of her sight when Maya had heard this.

During her stay, Maya had noticed that he stepped out only to buy food from a restaurant, located at a distance of few minutes by walk. The only conversation he would have was with the person at the billing counter. They would share customary greetings, asking after each other's well-being, and make small-talk about their families whom they hadn't met in the recent past and wouldn't in the near future.

What she didn't know was that there were conversations otherwise too—calls from Ma, the frequency of which increased with age, the knowledge of which would have saved her from years of guilt and anger, and a regret over that anger.

SECTION 10

GUILT OF A HOME

The wind rushed in
and whispered.
What did it say?
You wouldn't know.
To know, you must listen.
But, you got busy assuming its message.
To fuel your thoughts and yourself.
You plucked out reasons already in you,
refusing
to let the whisper reach you.

1

Kranti was looking at Maya's slippers, amused at the way she had taken them off. She would push her feet back, sliding them off the slippers, and walk ahead. They often resembled her last step, like a reminiscence of walking before she stopped, neither aligned nor together. Maya could sense that Kranti was stealing glances at her. She, in fact, waited for his attention. His validation defined her worth, to some extent. She was putting power over herself into the hands of someone else, yet again.

They were on the riverbank, at Maya's insistence.

They were sitting on a slightly elevated ground, a few metres away from the river. Looking from afar, they shared their admiration for it. Their ways, however, were not as natural as they used to be. They worried about insects, brushing them off the mat every now and then. They wiped their hands with wet tissue instead of going a step further and feeling the clear water in front.

City-bitten now, they were spoiled by concrete.

They lay on the mat and looked at the blue sky. The comfort that the river gave Maya brought out a clamour like never before. She spoke relentlessly to an attentive Kranti, and soon enough, she quashed the sound of the river with her words.

'Life wasn't this way,' she told him. Harry Potter watched at twenty. Outings allowed only to the district library. Sneaking out in the afternoons; first kiss witnessed by wild boars. School picnics allowed only once. Limited friends, never introduced to family. Boat ride to the island; swimming in the clear water. Collection of pebbles, forcibly thrown. Attending birthday parties, lost in language; songs played, never understood. The experience that continued even later, at meetings in offices or while boarding a bus; a silence filled with words. A faded presence. She lurked everywhere, and was received nowhere. Kranti agreed. He told her how he had experienced all this too, sitting clueless, feeling disconnected, with no one to share his childhood with. Such a small aspect, but an integral part of existing. 'Anchal has all her friends in Delhi,' he told her, finally an outlet to share his resentment.

Eventually, they decided to walk near the river. Kranti saw a finely shaped log, smoothened by years of the river's effort. He immediately picked it up. Handing it over to Maya, he told her about his father's fondness for these pieces, who often transformed them into functional pieces of furniture. Never to keep in his home, but to present them to those he knew. Searching for another piece, he went further into the shallow waters.

'This water. It's good, feels nice, but no one should be like it,' Kranti said as they walked on pebbles with clear water running over their feet.

'Meaning?'

'It doesn't have any shape or colour. No fixed identity. There is no resistance at all. It will just fall into a glass. If I freeze, it just turns into ice. No revolt, nothing. And if I boil, it will vanish. Not a trace would be left of its existence.'

'But we all know that we need it to live,' said Maya while looking at her feet and feeling the river bed.

'See yaar, how much importance do we give it? Not much. It's not like we revere water and cherish it. It has a granted presence in our lives. That's it.'

'Not always. It has different *avatars*. Sometimes we love it and sometimes we are scared of it. I mean, think of the ocean.

Especially the sea during a storm, like a tsunami. It's scary, but at the same time, we try to reduce our fear of ocean water with a glass of water to drink. That's its beauty, da.'

'Not beauty. It's chaos na. We polluted the sea. We take that glass of water for granted. And water, if you see, is either in submission or mindless rage.'

'You know, my mother is like water,' he said, as though wanting to end the discussion and bring it to a point of reason.

'Mine too.' *Not a glass of water, but an ocean*, Maya thought, aware how this search had transformed Ma for her. Her mother, a sea, with so much mystery and depth that no one but she knew. No matter how deep Maya dived, she got only what her mother chose to show. Maya knew it back then too. She accepted it now.

'You know... my mother isn't so educated like yours. Her parents were daily wage labourers,' Kranti said. A moment later, he couldn't understand why he did. Whether it was a final acceptance of having a mother from a class considered lower than his, or an effort to see the might of that shapeless water, he didn't know.

As they walked back, Maya handed back the log, a one-winged bird, and asked if he wanted to give this to his father. 'I don't know,' he replied.

'I feel your experiences are so much more intense. Especially with so many cities and all,' he told her as they reached home.

'Hmm, a wandering home is not ideal after all.'

'People write about all this kind of stuff, yaar. You have the material for a complete book!'

'Achcha? I should write a book then!'

'Why not?'

'*An Aying in the Adi land?* A good book should offend everyone,' she said and laughed at his raised eyebrows.

2

The sky didn't give her stars, so she decided to get along with the bulbs. A flicker of light was what she was going to live with, under a sky denuded of stars.

As soon as Maya woke up, she felt overwhelmed for leaving her stars too soon, for being content with whatever came to her. Guilt unmasked her short-lived happiness. Happiness was like the snow. Innocent and inviting, soft and fresh, but its touch froze her. Its apparent calmness numbed her.

At first, Kranti baffled Maya—yet, she was pulled towards him. A habitual occurrence, especially with men who wouldn't commit themselves to her entirely. They came with the idea of freedom and a threat of abandonment. They felt like home, similar to her past experiences.

Still in bed, wrapped inside a mosquito net, its edges tucked under the mattress on all sides, Maya wanted to cry out loud, throw things down, and tear everything into pieces. An unbearable pain made her immobile, as if she were stabbed. She looked at her bandaged finger, the cut she'd incurred last night. *The pain must be because of it,* she reasoned. She could feel the rhythmic throb of her bruise under the Band-Aid. She could hear her heart too, a separate beating at the centre. Different beats—one brought pain, another life to bear the same pain.

Getting out of the bed felt impossible, although she did want to get out of bed, run away, lock herself, and avoid speaking to anyone. So, she slept some more to delay facing Kranti who made her hopeful—even happy, last night.

Last few weeks gave them a routine, specific to a married couple. And the closeness and comfort erupting out of it felt imminent. So last night, when Kranti, who until then was sleeping on the adjacent cot, her father's, came on to hers, it felt like a natural progression. Maya had anticipated this moment for many days now, but wasn't sure yet.

She now lay thinking about the previous night. She could still hear his slow breathing, feel his heaving chest next to hers. His half-clad body, the brush of his leg against hers, and the weight of his hand on her waist. The proximity of his snores on her neck. Darkness helped them cover their awkwardness, allowing them convenient ways. Maya was eager too, but restrained herself. It was the situation that made her. Or maybe it was the tag that Kranti came with—'married'. She wasn't sure. Was she trying to hit the moral ground, or was she trying to buy some time? Time for appropriateness of the action, where her parents' shadows wouldn't judge her. Whichever it was, she turned her back. The hint was enough for Kranti to go back to his bed. Still, last night did bring out the questions of feelings and intent. And morning came, reproaching her for that.

Maya thought about her parents. She was still calling every helpline number. It had been more than a month, yet there was no information about them. Camps had been vacated. Injuries had been attended to; many were already buried. Even the searches were half-hearted now. Despite all that, Maya waited eagerly, hoping she would hear it soon, not about them, but from them. Today, she was worried about why *they* hadn't reached out to her. *Did destiny choose one over another? Did she pick Kranti over them? Were they to not return ever, because he had arrived?* Guilt crushed her again.

To push the guilt away, Maya decided to try the helpline numbers once again. Trying to connect to the mobile signal, she stepped out when she saw Kranti on the phone. They often went out to make calls. They still had a few inhibitions intact. Kranti was rapidly pacing on the ground in front. A distant sound reached her. *A probable fight with Anchal,* she hoped.

Her hopes soon came crashing down when he told her that it was his father who had called, for the first time in years, happiness apparent in his voice.

Later, as they settled in their usual way on the veranda, Maya asked, 'Do you ever feel guilty?'

'Guilty? About what?'

'Generally, in life. Do you ever regret your actions?'

'Don't know. I guess no. Never thought about it. No point in overthinking.'

He got up and marched inside. He had undone his relationship with two women in one single night, both awaiting his next step—one unaware, one unsure.

'Once,' he said as he returned and sat on the stairs again, this time facing her.

Straightening his back, he took a deep breath and told her about his friend. Of the time when she lay asleep in his hostel room. Slipping his hand inside her kurta, running his fingers from her stomach to the bra, he had eventually pulled the cups down. His friend, unaware of this breach, remained deep in her fever-induced sleep. He wouldn't have done it even in his dream. *He wasn't—isn't—a bad guy; it was an attraction that was at play,* he told Maya now. Finding reasons for him and her to accept it. Crying, he went on to detail about what had happened later. Accusations on him, repeated apologies, and rejection of his apologies.

'But I did marry her. After some years,' he told her, implying that the friend was Anchal.

Maya, though shocked, pitied Kranti. So she looked at him, but couldn't smile. She wanted to. She cried too. Just tears down her cheeks, nothing more. Kranti thought it was for him. An indication of her understanding him. He hoped to have undone his actions by informing her. He wanted her to believe in his repentance.

Maya did cry, but out of disgust that she felt towards him, for the helplessness she felt for letting him enter her life. She cried hearing his reasoning—the righteousness that was evident in his plea for forgiveness. She cried knowing it would never be the same again, though she might do nothing about it. She knew that she'd also played a role. Not then, but now. That she wasn't very different from Kranti after all, if Anchal were to decide. Should she?

She cried for the loss she was soon to face. For the addition to the people she was going to move away from.

She feared that if she didn't act soon, she would learn to ignore it and believe in his guilt and trust his transformation into a man who wouldn't do what he had done. She cried out of the fear that she might live with that fabricated belief. She, along with him, might create realities to make the truth suit them.

3

'What are you doing here?' Maya asked Kevin, shocked to see him in her bedroom. *How did he enter?*

Getting no answer, she asked again, 'Why are you here?'

'Uh … because I live here!'

'No, you don't!'

'Baby, what happened?'

He walked up to her and pulled her into his arms.

'Kevin!' she snapped, pushing him away.

'What? Who is Kevin?'

She looked puzzled. How could he not know himself? She frowned. But he spoke again, 'I am Kranti, jaan. What's the matter with you?'

'You are not Kranti. You don't look like Kranti. You are Kevin!' she shouted.

'Don't you remember dear? I am the real Kranti. He was in my place. I am the real one. You see, Kranti is leaving.'

She saw him walking out of the house. Smiling, with a bag for grocery. A kerosene stove was attached to his back. She called out his name. But he didn't turn back.

'No, you go away. I want Kranti back. He is the real one,' she said as she recalled the wave of his hair, his intense gaze whenever he looked at her, his smile, and his athletic body.

'I am the real one, honey. Only my body has changed. But I am still your Kranti.'

Maya looked at him. He was smiling. He sat the way Kranti would. Then he got up, went to his drawer, and took out a pack of cigarettes.

'Kranti quit smoking,' she said, delighted with her discovery. She now knew that the man standing in front of her, claiming to be her Kranti, was lying.

'I was not going to smoke. I was just about to throw it away,' he smiled and put the cigarette packet back.

'I am your husband. We live here. Don't you remember anything?' he continued. 'Come here, darling.' He pulled her to him again.

This time, she didn't resist. She went and sat next to him, holding his hand, searching his face. She thought, 'No, he is lying. He is not Kranti. I don't like this guy. I don't like his face. I don't like Kranti either.'

'I don't want you.' She pulled the man out of the bed, took him in her arms, and threw him out of her window, hitting the old Kranti walking on the road.

What a weird dream, Maya thought, waking up. Brushing it aside, she went to freshen up, all the while looking for signs of Kranti.

4

For the last two days they had been avoiding each other, although not much was possible in a house of one room, especially when they slept in the same room and crossed each other's paths throughout the day. Finally, Maya decided to embrace the exposure.

Kranti was in the front garden. So she went to the veranda. Her hair was still wet from the shower. She flipped them to one side, drying them with her towel, as she had seen in the movies. Somewhere deep down, she wished Kranti to notice and admire it. She, the damsel in long tresses; he, the rugged hero, working with the soil.

The water tap was not working in the garden. Kranti kept a mug of water before tending to the plants. He was using the *Dao*. An unusual use of a traditional dagger, but good enough for Kranti to dig soil and hack branches. Ma had bought this Dao, once her father's absence had become permanent.

When he was done, Kranti squatted near the mug and slanted it with his right arm, dropping water into his left palm. A slight tilt, pouring just enough water to fill his palm. He then straightened the mug, sprinkled water on the soap, and lathered it. Then he poured some more water to clean the lather. Once his left palm was clean, he lifted the mug and cleaned his right hand.

Maya noticed his meticulous process to not touch the bucket or the mug with soiled hands. A bucket was placed under the eaves to collect the rainwater. The rain that broke and blocked water pipes also provided for their necessities. A handful of soil, leftover from a recent pot mix, lay in the corner, next to the dried water tap. As the wind became strong, it jittered. It moved in circles first, and then back and forth. It appeared to dance with the wind.

'This is exactly how my father used to wash his hands,' she told him.

He smiled and handed over his raincoat for her to hang. Then they sat on the veranda, looking at the drizzle, relaxed and light. It was the kind of morning that had enough silence for the sound of the river to reach them. They could, in fact, hear it swirling up and down. There was an unsettling calmness that morning. Maya liked it, nevertheless. Looking at the faint green outline of a mountain blurred by the morning fog, she felt relieved.

Who are we? she thought. Nothing but a lyrical composition of experiences and expectations. And maybe emotions. *Who will we be?* The thought quailed her.

His words 'I didn't do anything wrong' echoed in her mind. It made her uncomfortable. She wasn't able to forget it. She got up and went inside. The calmness of the morning brought out the chaos within her.

SECTION 11

THE DILEMMA OF WAITING

Waves—I feel bad for them,
she told him.

The struggle they go through.
The pain of
being stuck between the moon and the sand

Between the fight
of their gravities.

One tries to pull them up,
Another pulls down.
While the Ocean waits to witness their fate.

Waves,
they try hard, she said again.
Neither do they fly away,
Nor do they sink in.

Instead,
they dance
on the ocean of struggles.

1

A darkening dusk. With no one around, Maya sat on the back porch, alone. She needed a break. *Break from what?* She wasn't sure yet.

She felt compelled to have Kranti around, almost as though against her wish. As though two distinct voices were directing her. The vulnerability she was in added to the voices within.

Kranti's arrival felt fated and she hoped for an emotional interlink that would be just theirs, not shared with anyone. In those moments, she would forget the marriage that Kranti wore on his finger and the revelation that he'd shared just a few days ago.

Tonight, she wanted to reassess both—her determination, and hopefully her transformation. Was she the ice thrown into a fire? Was she to evaporate? Whether this change was self-drawn or forced, she didn't know. What she knew was that the moment demanded action. It was the moment of her answer, a decision to leave doubts behind.

She had stepped out to think, understand, and soothe herself. Inside the house, a radio broadcasted news. The faint voice of a news presenter reached her. Kranti was listening to a tribute to A.P.J. Abdul Kalam, the president of hearts. The news of his sudden passing felt like a premonition to Maya, hinting at the loss she might have to face too.

The night was still, so much so that Maya could hear herself breathe—something which she never had the time to acknowledge. That constant mark of life within. Tonight, she could hear her inhalation and exhalation, nothing special, just the way it had been since the first day. She could hear the crickets too, and the *whoosh* of wind crossing by.

Above her, the moon shone. It was a full moon, taking a walk of glory, in and out of the clouds. *Is it the moon that goes ahead, or are the clouds moving away?* she mused. They both were changing their places from one moment to another. The movement, although true, fluctuated between the two. Their wavering left Maya dubious of their intent and action. Whose action was it, the moon's or the clouds'?

They reminded her of Kranti. Could a man be separated from his actions? Sometimes, no reason could justify the act, no matter who the man was. Sometimes, actions were just extensions of his personality. Maybe there were no reasons or thoughts behind it. Nothing more, nothing less. These thoughts unsettled her, so she looked ahead.

In front of her, the trees stood aloof, separated from each other by a few steps. Their green leaves holding a drop of white. They glinted in the milky moonlight—something they couldn't do in the daytime. Sunlight didn't comfort them like the moon; it often compelled the leaves to change their colour, tired and burnt.

Maya couldn't pay attention to the trees for long. She was searching for something else, deep in the darkness, with lights twinkling around.

I miss fireflies the most, she had told Kranti, and now she was searching for them. She had taken their presence for granted when they used to hover around every night outside the veranda; some would even fly inside. 'There was no surprise. Their presence was an everyday occurrence. We would just look at them for a second or two. That's it.'

Now, it had been years since she had seen a firefly. She had begun to doubt her memories, until her last Ooty trip. Once an everyday occurrence, it'd become a rarity in her life. Tonight, she wished to reverse it. She wanted to feel the warmth of light around her.

2

It was an eternal wait that she knew would not end. Not anytime soon. Yet, Maya had been waiting. She was used to it. Waiting, every minute, every single day.

The Maajorghat train derailment had turned into a stale topic now; there were other pressing matters that needed attention. Yet, she would still read the news and search for any new information that might have come up. By now she knew that coach B2, in which her parents were travelling, had suffered the maximum damage. Another coach had fallen on it, further mutilating it and those inside. However, they couldn't confirm her parents' death.

It was now a routine for her. Her mornings started with hopes and nights ended in dismay. Yet, Maya continued to slip into the groove of waiting. Why? Because she had chosen to.

Their return was no longer the catalyst of her actions. Her wait had reached a point where even they ceased to impact her. Their presence or absence, whichever that might be, was no longer the focal point of her actions. She now waited to wait. Nothing more. It wasn't a compulsion; she was merely expecting them to come and meet her, because Ma had told her, in her ever-hopeful voice, that she would be returning soon.

She longed for the promises to turn true—even those that had already failed. For the love to be showered on her, to be given priority and treated special, not held accountable for what she did or didn't, to be understood not only by them but by Kranti too, for she was to go beyond him as well.

Waiting had not been easy. There were days when it pushed her into immobility, crushing her under its weight. Especially in the mornings, when she would prepare herself for another day with it. It jeered at her. Aware of its presence and scared of it too, Maya would sit alone and wonder. Sometimes, she would cry out loud. Helplessness did lead to it, but her inclination for him, and the guilt that followed, made it unbearable.

Now, at a time when Ma's presence dwindled and her return was at best debatable, her life became clearer to Maya, an honest unsparing preview. This wait showed Maya something else too. How she had waited constantly for Ma's support, when she too needed a shoulder to lean on.

She now wanted to bring her mother back and give her what she couldn't have. Companionship, support, and a freedom to speak her heart out. Maya longed to see Ma smile, to ease her, and their relationship too. She wanted to confess, show her, and tell her that it was all right. That she needn't worry about everything anymore. It was fine if things didn't go as they wanted. That it was okay that father left us, and that he wanted to return now. It wasn't your fault, neither mine.

By accepting its presence and granting mercy, she, and her wait—both were altering.

3

'Hey … uh … I have been thinking. I think I should hold a gathering.'

'A memorial?'

'No, no. Just a get-together, for all of their friends. We all can meet and talk about them.'

'Hmm … sorry. Tell me what you want. I'll arrange.'

'Ah … no, no. I mean … I will do it.'

She stood opposite to Kranti, running her thumbs over her fingernails, mapping their shape and size repeatedly while simultaneously speaking to Kranti. Yet, she was unsure about what exactly she wanted to do.

'Isn't that what memorials are?'

'What?' She stopped mapping. Pushing her hands in her pocket, she stood silent for a while before speaking again. This time, accusing Kranti of insensitivity, of being the reason for her pain, of enjoying her parents' absence.

'It is nothing else. It is *just* a get-together,' she repeated it several times.

Later that night, as they both were tying the mosquito net, he again expressed his wish to stay, to be there for her, but she insisted him to return to Guwahati. Delhi she wouldn't utter. Neither did she ever speak about Anchal's existence. She was waiting for Kranti to acknowledge it.

Kranti, on the other hand, felt wronged. He was being asked

to leave, when he'd dreamt of waiting with her. He planned to show support through his actions. He was hoping to feel the indispensability of their relationship, but instead was shown the consistency of change.

She knew what he wanted. But his presence, no matter how intense it was, had to be pushed away. A distance from him to give herself entirely for the wait and its answers.

Looking at him entering the mosquito net meekly, such an innocent gesture of a well-built man, almost giving him a humble touch, she thought about it all.

Could she ever love a man when she hated his actions? Could there be respect, when the very thought of his doings disgusted her? Maya knew this. Kranti, like everyone else, was indeed a sum of his actions. Circumstances had long stopped playing an active role. It was he who was acting under the guise of circumstances. Maya, who had learnt to see herself, wasn't able to ignore him too.

Sitting on her bed, she spoke, 'You know, many years back, I read an article on forbidden places to visit in the world.'

Kranti looked at her, confused. This wasn't where their conversation was supposed to be going. A monologue on places she couldn't visit was not what he was expecting her to say. A teary explanation on why she wanted to be alone would also have been enough for him.

Maya had never been good at farewells. It wasn't her inability to speak; sometimes she would say thousands of words just to mean one—goodbye. In her mind, she confessed the conflict she felt for him. But now, she struggled to utter words of parting, even though she knew it was inescapable. Its inevitability, a creation of hers.

So, she spoke about the places where only a few could enter, like ghost towns and the secret archives of Vatican City. Those few who were allowed had to provide a lot of documentation and valid reasons. She used to dream of going somewhere like that—where she would have to prove her worth to enter. Once inside, her very presence would defy their exclusivity. But tonight, Maya didn't feel the urge to challenge those places and rules, the very reason why she shared it with Kranti.

'I feel I have lost that interest to explore. But there is one place I still want to see. There is a temple in Japan called Ise Grand Shrine. They build it every twenty years, and then break and build it again!'

Twenty years wasn't a long time, not even half of a human being's lifespan in general. Maya found the Shino tradition of death and revival relatable. To be aware of its death even before its creation, but still going ahead and putting efforts in beautifying its intricate structure seemed appropriate to her.

She too was ready to break the old structure of thirty years and create anew for the next thirty.

4

Mridula was sipping tea, light with a hint of freshness, brewed from the tea leaves that she had bought on her way back to Dibrugarh.

While crossing the tea estate, they got down. Rimi wanted to explore, eager to roam within its constricted lanes, occasionally stopping to touch and circle the trees that were strategically spread all over the estate. It was past five in the evening, yet women were still harvesting, plucking out the tender leaves and transferring them into their *tukuris,* the bamboo basket. A few of them had plastic bags hung on their backs. Under their straps, they either had a folded gamocha, or a cloth on their head. Surrounded by tea plants, they were rhythmically plucking and transferring tea leaves to their baskets, which also had umbrellas. Their heads were slightly bowed to balance them. They all were in sync—an exhausting synchronization.

It was the time of harvesting the second flush tea leaves, the kind that Priyom would have loved, full-bodied and malty. He didn't appreciate the subtlety of flavours that Mridula used to prefer. So, they often bought second flush for occasional drinks, never from the auctions where they were sold for thousands of rupees, but at a marginally decreased price from the tea estates. This time, sighting a packet from first flush, she bought it.

Sipping her tea, Mridula sat silently, listening to the chatter outside. Rimi was giving a detailed account of her stay at her cousins' and her adventures at Guwahati Zoo that they had taken her to. She was making paper boats with her friends. Many deep puddles had formed around the house, big enough to reach up to Rimi's knee, deep enough for them to float even bigger paper boats. Although the rest of the town was either under water or fearing a water surge, their area had only faced stagnation.

In front of her lay the empty tin trunk and a scatter of things. Mridula, a proficient day dreamer, was trying hard to not get lost in memories that each item brought out. The huge trunk that Mridula and Priyom had bought together. They had gone to the main market, which had a variety of storage options, from wooden vintage to cloth suitcases. After haggling for a discount at various shops, Priyom had finalized a tin trunk and got it for a thousand rupees. He hadn't consulted Mridula, who wanted to buy the one which was painted blue, adorned with floral patterns and small white flowers around a curvy pink stem. She'd later bought a wooden earring box, which Priyom deemed to be a waste of money.

She now picked each item, turning and twisting it under the yellow light of a bulb, allowing a thought or two for a second, before deciding its fate. The chore, which till now she was performing with utmost dexterity, halted when she chanced upon a framed picture.

A picture of Priyom and her from their first boat ride on the Brahmaputra, during their visit to her mother's home. His hand was on the railing and she was leaning towards him, both looking at the camera consciously. He seemed to be coming out of the picture. His smile reached out, as if it was meant only for her. In those moments, she felt the love he once had for her, nothing of which was left now.

Now tucked under the quilt, Mridula was sitting on the bed with Rimi sleeping sideways, her back turned towards her. *Just like her father,* Mridula couldn't help the thought.

Perturbed by the changes she had brought to her home, with his things nowhere to be seen, she was sceptical of the course her life would take now.

Do we stop existing when we change? What happens to our previous form? Does it die? Does it age and hover at the back? Mridula pondered, like every other night.

5

'Hey, come here, let's take a selfie.'

'Uh … wait … no. I mean, let's just remember this moment. Maybe we should let our memory work this time.'

'Hmm … but yaar, next time you can't stop me!'

Maya nodded while handing him the log they had collected at the river.

'For your Deuta,' she told him.

Kranti walked out. In the back stood the Chang Ghar, from where he had packed a bottle of freshly-made Apong (rice liquor). Behind him, Maya leaned on the wooden gate, mapping the compass engraved on the steel box, now deprived of cigarettes. Smiling, she waved to him, unaware that the hand waving back at the crossroad had no ring on it. The one that Kranti had pulled out a while back—the same ring with two diamonds. One for him, one for Anchal, as he had told his soon-to-be ex-wife at their engagement.

Kranti left with a hope to see her soon. While she stood there, watching him leave, allowing herself one last look. He was leaving like a rough sketch. A rough sketch, without the stagnation of finality, without the surety of end. A prelude to a masterpiece, or may be a work in progress. Whether to paint it further or leave it untouched depended on Maya. And she was ready. She was ready to close all the chapters of her life.

None would she carry forward—neither old, nor new; neither her's, nor others'. She, too, had become like the river, ready to change her course.

Home Transitioned

The train was about to reach Maajorghat. They were now sitting idly, looking at the view, wanting the train to move faster.

They had already had their morning tea with a packet of Marie biscuits that they both dipped occasionally in their sugar-free tea. It was too early for the hawkers to start their morning routine. So, he, leaving his walking stick on the side, had gone to the pantry to get two cups of tea again and come back with an update on the journey too. The train would reach Maajorghat in an hour, he had informed her. So, they pulled out their luggage and placed them on a seat. At Maajorghat, they were to take a bus to Itanagar, where they would be joined by the Baruas after a day.

'Look at that river, we will go over it,' he had told her, pointing his wrinkled finger in the direction the train was moving in. A stainless steel watch hung loose on his wrist, a thin plastic cover still attached to its white dial. In a beige formal shirt and brown pants, one of the few pairs that he'd bought for the tour, he sat with his other hand on his knees.

'Only ten or fifteen minutes more after we cross the bridge,' he explained to her further, while she sat near the window, looking at the distant blur of a river, her head resting on the window glass. A huge red bindi adorned her forehead. Her hair was parted in the middle, which was left uncoloured. White strands festooned one side of her head. She was in her thirties when she'd stopped wearing this mark of marriage. It wasn't because her husband shifted when his transfer paved the way for him to stay away from the family life he'd never wanted. It was a voluntary decision, born from the lack of interest in smearing her parting red. It was also because she had liked herself without it. The bindi she continued wearing, for she was fond of it. It was neither a symbol of married life nor a life without it. It suited her face and personality, she knew that.

The train was crossing a grassland, sprinkled with several small ponds, while mountains loomed in the background. As the view revealed itself, it hypnotized everyone. Most of the passengers, awake now, were looking outside when they heard a sudden sound. The train was moving with uneven jerks, as though it was tired of running overnight and could finish covering the remaining distance only through forceful pushes. She still sat near the window and gazed out. The bridge that the train just entered was trembling too, when the train increased its speed.

And then it happened.

For a second, she couldn't believe what she was seeing. They were falling. Their coach was about to perish, and with it they too. The thought scared her, ushering in more worries. *How would she contact Maya? Who would tell her? She wasn't even married. If she were to get hurt and remain handicapped, Maya might never leave her. She would not even think of marriage. But if she were to die, Maya would be left alone. This was not how she wanted to die. She wanted to see her child once, to see her daughter settling down in her life, leading a life she couldn't have.*

She wanted to die with her family around, even if that meant just one. She wanted to be home. She didn't want to die next to the person who had killed every desire of hers. She wanted to be away, to be on her own, maybe to smile again, maybe to laugh a lot before she died.

She didn't want to die, not in this way. She felt angry and helpless. A cry reached her throat but wouldn't come out. She was choking. She wanted to scream. She felt an urge to tell him that even this journey with him, after so many years, brought nothing but tragedy. Yet, she didn't react and continued to stare outside.

After less than a second, the window glass cracked. It was then that she felt a hand pulling her back. He was holding the iron stairs at the end of the berths with one hand and her with the other. She was pushed forcefully towards him, making her fall on his shoulders, while he tried to sit still, withstanding the coach's constant shaking. She looked at him, and for the first time she saw that he was trying to protect her—and possibly the last time too. His eyes were focused on her when he said, 'Don't worry.'

She was unable to believe that he was the same man who had left her unattended for all these years, who had not thought twice before moving away. Today, amid all the chaos, she saw that the time had changed him, and that this old, ailing man was trying with all his remaining might to save her. She held his hands tighter, giving him half a smile, finding comfort in him—something she had lost hope for.

And then, the coach jerked even more, making a deafening sound. The bridge too was disintegrating slowly, each part falling after the other. The coach in front was almost slipping away, while theirs still hung desperately. But it would soon give up too. Another forceful jerk pushed her out of the seat, and she knelt down. Her legs bled. He too had fallen down. His hands were still holding her.

Coaches staggered and those inside also gyrated with each movement. Crushed and crying, they too were unable to keep still. Some screamed for help to arrive and stop this train from falling, while some wished for a safe place. Some prayed for it to be a nightmare they hoped would soon be over. But even when they tried with all their strength, they couldn't come out of this dream. It didn't seem to end.

She tried to turn back and see him, but someone pushed her further down and she collapsed flat on the floor. Her hand pulled backwards, her fingers still intertwined with his. She could feel something warm falling on her back. He wasn't saying 'Don't worry' any more. She couldn't hear him. She wanted to turn once, to scream his name, but there were loud screams from every side, leaving no scope for hers to reach him.

Circumstances didn't allow her the time to ask if he was fine, or to tell him that she wanted him to be fine, that maybe they could go back and try to live together again. Maybe they could grow old in each other's company, with their lives intermingled, the way their fingers were.

Yet, she couldn't say anything. She had fallen down, and blood was filling her mouth. She wasn't even able to spit it out. The intensity of the pain was leaving her numb. With the flowing filth she could feel around her, she realized she was moving away.

The same anger that had controlled her life was now giving her the freedom and comfort her heart secretly craved for. It was then that she felt like a bird that was ready to fly—to take the plunge she always wanted to.

Acknowledgements

All I can say is thank you.

To write a book is to grow with it. I, too, have lived with its characters. I waited for months to understand them—their intent, actions, and responses. Yet, there was a time when life happened with all its might, and I distanced myself from this book.

Prachi, my guardian angel and second mother, came to my rescue during those moments of doubt. Prachi, if not for you, this book wouldn't have happened.

It's not only her; I have an army behind me, supporting my every decision and making it their aim to make my dreams come true! With all my heart, I thank my family, who have been my strongest support system.

Thank you, Papa, for always being there for me.

How can I go further without thanking my sister, Charu? Thanks for your confidence in my writing and, of course, for your detailed notes on the first draft. To my brother, Mohit, thanks for your faith in everything I do. Special thanks to my brothers Brijesh and Nilesh for making me understand the nuances of the Assamese language. Your trust in my abilities has been a driving force. Thank you, Pratibha Bhabhi, for your support.

I thank my husband, Priyadarshi. You showed me how to live for one's dream and achieve it.

I want to thank Shaheba Memon and Bhanita Haloi for providing me with information on Assamese culture, households, and cuisine. Thank you, Tsering Chemi Yeaton. It's because of you that I have the name Sigo Dolung for the town in Arunachal Pradesh.

First drafts, as they say, are almost unreadable. So, my special thanks to Vinesh and Apurva, who not only read but also helped me with their feedback. Madhulika Gautama, I want to thank you as well for your reviews and suggestions on the initial draft.

It is impossible not to acknowledge Aparna Rayaprol's generosity. Thank you, Ma'am, for your detailed review of the fifth draft. Amrutha, your review and generous doses of praise came at a time when I needed them the most. You know how much I value your opinions.

I would also like to thank everyone in the Editorial and Design team. I am glad that my book found its home with Nu Voice Press.

About the Author

Richa Sharma is an Indian writer and poet. She was born and brought up in Arunachal Pradesh. She has also lived in various cities across India for her education and career. Having lived a life of constant movement, she has drawn upon her experience of displacement. Her innumerable train journeys and first-hand experience of monsoon-led floods instigated her to write *Finding Home Again*. She is currently working on her next fiction and poetry collection.